Queer and Trans Fashion Brands

Queer and Trans Fashion Brands

Resistance and Revolution in the Twenty-First Century

Kelly L. Reddy-Best

BLOOMSBURY VISUAL ARTS
LONDON • NEW YORK • OXFORD • NEW DELHI • SYDNEY

BLOOMSBURY VISUAL ARTS
Bloomsbury Publishing Plc, 50 Bedford Square, London, WC1B 3DP, UK
Bloomsbury Publishing Inc, 1385 Broadway, New York, NY 10018, USA
Bloomsbury Publishing Ireland, 29 Earlsfort Terrace, Dublin 2, D02 AY28, Ireland

BLOOMSBURY, BLOOMSBURY VISUAL ARTS and the Diana logo are
trademarks of Bloomsbury Publishing Plc

First published by Bloomsbury Visual Arts, an imprint of
Bloomsbury Publishing Plc

© Kelly L. Reddy-Best, 2025

Kelly L. Reddy-Best has asserted her right under the Copyright,
Designs and Patents Act, 1988, to be identified as author of this work.

Cover design: Catherine Wood
Cover image model: C'est Kevvie, photographer: Colectivo Multipolar,
clothing: Rebirth Garments.

All rights reserved. No part of this publication may be: i) reproduced or transmitted in any form, electronic or mechanical, including photocopying, recording or by means of any information storage or retrieval system without prior permission in writing from the publishers; or ii) used or reproduced in any way for the training, development or operation of artificial intelligence (AI) technologies, including generative AI technologies. The rights holders expressly reserve this publication from the text and data mining exception as per Article 4(3) of the Digital Single Market Directive (EU) 2019/790.

Bloomsbury Publishing Plc does not have any control over, or responsibility for, any third-party websites referred to or in this book. All internet addresses given in this book were correct at the time of going to press. The author and publisher regret any inconvenience caused if addresses have changed or sites have ceased to exist, but can accept no responsibility for any such changes.

No responsibility for loss caused to any individual or organization acting on or refraining from action as a result of the material in this publication can be accepted by Bloomsbury or the author.

A catalogue record for this book is available from the British Library.

Library of Congress Cataloging-in-Publication Data
Names: Reddy-Best, Kelly L., author.
Title: Queer and trans fashion brands : resistance, revolution and commodity activism in the 21st century / Kelly L. Reddy-Best.
Description: London, UK : Bloomsbury Visual Arts, an imprint of Bloomsbury Publishing Plc, 2025. | Includes bibliographical references. | Summary: "Queer and Trans Fashion Brands highlights the resilience, creativity, and cultural contributions of 25 fashion entrepreneurs, showing how they serve as agents of change, actively challenging heteronormative norms prevalent in the fashion industry. Kelly L. Reddy-Best draws upon an intersectional feminist framework to offer a nuanced examination of the production, distribution, regulation, and consumption of the products and media associated with these queer- and trans-focused fashion brands and their collective impact on the fashion industry"– Provided by publisher.
Identifiers: LCCN 2024029177 (print) | LCCN 2024029178 (ebook) |
ISBN 9781350465879 (paperback) | ISBN 9781350465886 (hardback) |
ISBN 9781350465893 (pdf) | ISBN 9781350465909 (ebook)
Subjects: LCSH: Clothing trade–Social aspects. | Sexual minorities–Clothing. | Fashion–Social aspects.
Classification: LCC HD9940.A2 R4398 2025 (print) | LCC HD9940.A2 (ebook) | DDC 391–dc23/eng/20241016
LC record available at https://lccn.loc.gov/2024029177
LC ebook record available at https://lccn.loc.gov/2024029178

ISBN:	HB:	978-1-3504-6588-6
	PB:	978-1-3504-6587-9
	ePDF:	978-1-3504-6589-3
	eBook:	978-1-3504-6590-9

Typeset by Integra Software Services Pvt. Ltd.
Printed and bound in India

For product safety related questions contact: productsafety@bloomsbury.com

To find out more about our authors and books visit www.bloomsbury.com.
Here you will find extracts, author interviews, details of forthcoming events and
the option to sign up for our newsletters.

*For all the queer and trans folks out in the world
who embody every kind of existence.*

Contents

List of Figures   x
Foreword by Sonny Oram   xii
Acknowledgments   xvi

Introduction   1
  Saint Harridan and Tomboy Tailors   1
  The Current Project: Questions, Perspectives, and Why it Matters   3
  Chapter Overview   5

Part 1   Situating the Context   9

1   Identities, Style-Fashion-Dress, and Dressed Bodies   11
  Queer and Trans Identities and Intersectional Subject Positions   11
  Styling-Fashioning-Dressing, Identity (K)nots, and Situated Bodily Practices   16
  Ambiguity, Ambivalence, and the Dressed Body in the Fashion System   17
  Fashioning Queer and Trans Identities in a Western Context: A Selection of
    Nuances Spanning the Nineteenth Century to the Present   19

2   Political Landscapes and So-Called Heteronormative Ideals   27
  The Revolution of the Queer and Trans Landscape in the United States:
    A Brief Overview   27
  The Dominant, So-Called Heteronormative Western Fashion System:
    A Selective History   30

3   Gay Window Advertising and Capitalist Entanglements   35
  Gay Window Advertising: Vodka, Cars, and Fashion   35
  Entanglements in Commodity Activism, Corporate Pride,
    and Neoliberal Capitalism   36

4   Marketplace Influences: Politics and Technology   43
  Same-Sex Marriage, Consumerism, and Creating Space for Authentic
    Negotiations   43
  Social Media and Crowdfunding as Entry Points into the System   47

Part 2 The Brands   51

5 Queer and Trans Fashion Brand Entrepreneurial Beginnings: Before and After the 2010s Surge   53

Overtly Serving Their Queer and Trans Communities in the Twenty-first Century   54
Case Study 1: All Is Fair in Love and Wear and gc2b   59
Case Study 2: FLAVNT Streetwear and Queer Supply   62
Case Study 3: Bluestockings Boutique, FtM Essentials, and Transguy Supply   64
Case Study 4: Beefcake Swimwear and Outplay Swimwear   67
Case Study 5: Play Out Apparel and TomboyX   70
Case Study 6: Dapper Boi, Kirrin Finch, NiK Kacy Footwear, and Strapping Sacramento   72
Case Study 7: Kipper Clothiers and THÙY Custom Clothier   78
Case Study 8: Audio Helkuik and Rebirth Garments   80
Case Study 9: Show and Tell Concept Shop, Stuzo, and WE ARE MORTALS   83
Case Study 10: Greyscale Goods   88

Part 3 Positioning Consumer Products   91

6 Vehicles for Queer and Trans Sensibilities   93

The Custom Suit Experience as an Identity Journey   93
The Button-Up Shirt: Masculine for Folks Assigned Female at Birth   95
Jeans: Mixing and Matching Gender Details   97
Unbifurcated Queerness   98
Femme and Masc Shoes in Every Size   99
Unisex Swimwear Styles/Supporting or Compressing the Chest   103
Boxer Briefs and Underwear for the Femmes, Too!   106
Trans-Supportive Gear: Functional, Fleshy Body-Shifting Fashions   110
Genderfuck Styles: Fucking with Gendered Fashion or a Big Fuck You to Gender Styles   117
Subtle and In-Your-Face Pride   119
Queer Styling Services   123
Queer Makers and Queering Product Copy   124
Are My Socks Then Queer Fashion Socks? And Who Decides?   126

Part 4 Production, Pricing, and Media Considerations   131

7   An Ethical Balancing Act: Production and Pricing   133
   Producing Here or There?   134
   Pricing Tensions: Social Good in Capitalism   138

8   Queer and Trans Media: For Us and Them, Too   140
   Representation Matters and Doesn't   140
   When Representation Works and Doesn't at the Same Time   142

9   DapperQ, Qwear, and Contemporary Queer Fashion Shows Emerged on the Scene   148
   Qwear   149
   DapperQ   156
   Fashion Events as Queer and Trans Community Making   160

Conclusion   161
  There Will Always Be Haters … and Lovers!   161
  Closing Thoughts and Opening Questions   165
  Queer and Trans Fashion Brands' Collective Contributions to the Fashion System: Fashion Disrupters and Fashion Disrupting   166
  Entangling and Disentangling the Ever-Fluid Queer and Trans Fashion Brands: Meanings and Moments   168
  Where Do We Go from Here or There?   169

Appendix   172
  The Method   172
  Limitations of the Research   174
  My Positionalities   175

References   178
Index   197

List of Figures

I.1	Zel Anders in front of the Tomboy Tailors storefront in San Francisco	2
I.2	Saint Harridan advertisement photographed by Miki Vargas	3
1.1	Black and white photographic postcard of the singer and musician Gladys Bentley dressed in a men's white tuxedo and white top hat, holding a cane at her side tucked under her arm, c. 1927–45	21
1.2	Cyndi fixing furniture in the garage, 1997	22
1.3	Cyndi before going to work wearing a masculine-leaning style, c. 2017	23
3.1	United Colors of Benetton Fall/Winter 1990s advertisement	36
4.1	Two clients wearing THÚY Custom Clothier suits	46
5.1a and 5.1b	Trucker hat and camo tank-top by Dykes in the City	54
5.2	Timeline of brand founding	55
5.3	Pretty Boy T-shirt by FLAVNT Streetwear	63
5.4	NiK Kacy sitting behind shoes from their various lines	75
5.5	Alyah Baker, founder of Show and Tell Concept Shop	84
5.6	Love in front of their storefront in Los Angeles, California	86
5.7	Example of styling service ensembles that reflect a masculine-leaning aesthetic	89
6.1	Nguyen's social media post highlighting the numerous suit detail options	94
6.2	Kirrin Finch product copy, highlighting the structured collars on their button-up shirt	96
6.3	Dapper Boi button-up shirt featuring snaps on the placket interior	98
6.4	Dapper Boi product copy for its button-up shirt	99
6.5	Dapper Boi model wearing button-up shirt with sunglass slit feature	100
6.6	Dapper Boi jeans with coin pocket large enough to fit a cell phone	101

6.7	Fluidity Dress by WE ARE MORTALS	102
6.8	Gender-equal Chelsea Brogue Boots	103
6.9	Gender-equal high heels titled The Borga. Shoe on the left features the red embroidered equal sign	104
6.10	Swimsuits designed by Beefcake Swimwear	105
6.11	TomboyX period underwear with a floating gusset that can fit a pad with wings	107
6.12	Play Out Apparel underwear, featuring Low Rise Flat Front Boxer Brief in Anthem Stripe Print	108
6.13	Play Out Apparel underwear, featuring Pouch Front Bikini in Anthem Stripe Print	109
6.14	AFLW binder prototype	112
6.15	Ensemble created by Sky Cubacub with chain mail packer inserted in the packing shorts	115
6.16	Chain mail packer created by Sky Cubacub	116
6.17	Audio Helkuik queer scouts collection	118
6.18	Pins from the Queer Scouts collection by Audio Helkuik	119
6.19	Cubacub design that reveals the midsection and emphasizes stretch marks on the body	120
6.20	"Yup, Still Gay" T-shirt by Stuzo	122
8.1	Packer sold by FtM Essentials	146
9.1	Sonny Oram, founder of Qwear	150
9.2	Pages from *Radical Fashion* magazine that Sonny Oram created in childhood	152
9.3	Ru adjusting model's top backstage at Qwear's 2015 "Dismantle Me" fashion show. The model's top is one of Ru's original designs that features a tie as the drawstring for the hoodie	154
9.4	Model who participated in Qwear's 2016 fashion installation at the Institute of Contemporary Art, Boston	155
9.5	"(un)Heeled: A Fashion Show for the Unconventionally Masculine" at the Brooklyn Museum in 2014. Events producer Anita Dolce Vita and models from Sharpe Suiting at the end of the show with the "hands up" sign	157

Foreword

Growing up outside Boston in the 1990s and 2000s, I did not see myself represented in fashion. Wearing my brother's hand-me-downs as a young kid was affirming to me, and with my bowl haircut I look like a boy in many old photos, despite my birth certificate, and everyone around me, saying otherwise. I asserted that I wanted to be a boy when I grew up in preschool, and teachers told me that was impossible. On nice occasions I was expected to embrace a level of femininity that I just didn't possess. Wearing dresses and all clothing deemed feminine made me cringe. When I was about five or six, my mom and grandma determined that I needed a new dress. They took me to the mall and had me try on a dozen dresses I hated. We left the mall with nothing. I felt like there was something wrong with me.

Cis people observing me around age ten, wearing baggy T-shirts to hide my developing chest and baseball caps, might think I was a tomboy who hated fashion. But it was just the opposite. I loved fashion, but I hadn't yet figured out how to use it as a tool to express myself. From ages ten to thirteen, my friend and I cut up her mom's old *Vogue* magazines and made our own fashion magazines—we called it *Radical Fashion*. You will be graced with images from these magazines later in the book. Through cutting and pasting and writing my own articles I could play with gender—cutting out men's heads and putting them on women's bodies. Looking at those old pages really illuminates how disjointed I felt from the person I knew I was and the person everyone expected me to be.

In the white world I grew up in, men were thought to be boxy. Everyone said men's clothes would not fit me because they were too big for me, and I had curves. My Trinidadian/Scottish partner, Ru, later pointed out that Black people assigned male at birth often have curves like mine and there's nothing inherently feminine about curves, which helped me embrace my hips and feel less dysphoric. If only I'd known Ru back then!

There were so few role models for me of people assigned female at birth who dressed in ways society deems masculine. Missy Elliot was the best dresser of the time, and I wish I'd had the confidence to dress more like her. Ellen DeGeneres's style left much to be desired when she first came out on her sitcom in 1997—it seemed her stylists hadn't yet learned how to dress a non-femme woman. *The L Word*, in 2004, introduced one non-femme character—Shane—whose greasy hair, androgynous look, and baggy clothes were liberating for many but her style did not offer much for my clean-cut aesthetic.

After graduating college, I returned home depressed and aimless. One day I decided to go on a walk and wander around Boston. In the Downtown Crossing T (subway) station, I came across some doors that led into the department store Macy's. Curious, I opened the doors and discovered the boy's department. It donned on me that with my small frame, boys' clothes might fit me better than men's. The floor was devoid of people, leaving me safer to shop without stares or getting redirected into the "right" department. My heart pounding, I looked through the clothes, terrified someone would see me and think I didn't belong. I picked out some preppy T-shirts and sweaters. When I put them on and looked in the mirror, everything made sense. I finally knew who I was. The cut of the garments emphasized my shoulders, making my chest appear flatter. I could stand up taller and smile at myself. I didn't know what word to ascribe to my gender, but I knew that I was meant to wear boys' clothes and to have a flat chest, and that was all the information I needed at the time to move toward a more authentic version of myself. That was the gift fashion gave me.

Shortly after I started wearing boys' clothes, my friend told me she was starting a fashion blog. New to the concept, I looked up fashion blogs and saw all these straight, cisgender women modeling clothing. I saw a need for more queer representation. So, on June 6, 2011, I created a tumblr account, took some photos of myself in one of my new outfits, and published the photos. First dubbed Dyke Duds, the platform grew into its current name Qwear, and is now an internationally recognized incubator where LGBTQ+ people around the world can explore their style.

Embarking on this new journey of queer fashion discovery, I researched queer-owned fashion brands and came across only a handful. Around 2012, with gay marriage passing in more states, people saw economic opportunity in queer fashion. The suit start-up Saint Harridan launched their first Kickstarter and raised an impressive $137,562 to launch their business. As gay marriage continued to be legalized in more states, other companies cropped up including THÚY Custom Clothier, Kipper Clothiers, NiK Kacy Footwear, and Bindle & Keep. Bindle & Keep was different from the other brands in that it started out as a mainstream, custom-suit brand, and then butch fashion icon Rae Tutera approached them to ask if they wanted to expand to the queer community. The brand was featured in the documentary *Suited* in 2016 by Lena Dunham and Jenni Konner, showcasing participants crying with joy when they tried on their first properly fitting suit. This demonstrated to mainstream viewers how powerful fashion can be to the queer consumer.

After formal brands established the need for queer fashion, other brands popped up catering to a wider range of styles, adding swimwear and underwear, such as WE ARE MORTALS, Rebirth Garments, and Outplay. Now there are too many brands to count. It was a wild ride witnessing this explosion of queer fashion brands. I felt that I was seeing history in the making.

As a movement operating within a capitalist structure, there were downsides. Like many aspects of society, the queer fashion industry mainly profited white, masculine people of means, while femmes, Black, Indigenous, People of Color (BIPOC), and low-income people were left to their own devices. The queer fashion industry favored masculine aesthetics, and this further marginalized trans women and femmes, contributing to femme erasure in queer spaces. Many of my femme friends have entered queer spaces only to be assumed straight. I would enter those same spaces and be immediately greeted and assumed to be part of the group. A lack of femme representation in queer fashion brands exacerbates the alienation of femmes in queer spaces.

Another issue is cost. Producing clothing is not cheap when done ethically, and producing in smaller batches makes it that much more expensive. It's understandable for people to get frustrated that a poplin dress shirt from Kirrin Finch costs $150, more than twice the cost of a $60 poplin shirt at GAP. With much of the queer population experiencing a lower socioeconomic status, many queer community members cannot access this merchandise. This is not the fault of queer fashion brands but of an imbalanced society where necessities are made inaccessible to those who need them most.

Finally, another major issue is sizeism. Sizeism affects the entire fashion industry, and queer-owned brands are no different. I've spoken to many queer brand owners who lament that they can't carry as many sizes as they wish due to costs, availability, or factory limitations. This further ostracizes people of size within the queer community, as not being seen as worthy of the fashion that thin people enjoy. This is a society-wide problem that the queer community can't solve on our own.

To show that queer fashion should be for everyone, I tried to make queer fashion as accessible as possible through Qwear by providing inspiration for people of all sizes, presentations, and income brackets. People on Qwear obtain clothing through all kinds of methods—clothing swaps, thrift stores, and making things themselves, in addition to buying things new. I met my partner Ru in 2014 and brought them on as our Fashion Director. They prioritized BIPOC voices, using almost exclusively BIPOC models for our fashion shows to disrupt the white queer norm. In 2019, we became co-owners.

While the term "queer fashion" now has multiple meanings, a few aspects of queer fashion haven't yet reached the public discourse. First, there is the health component. Fashion helped me discover that I am trans, and the way I chose to have my clothing fit taught me that my chest is meant to be flat. Fashion was my early healthcare before I could access top surgery in 2014. People have told me that Qwear saved their life. The medical community understands this to some extent. Health plans have historically forced trans people to follow rigid steps to be considered for hormones or surgery. The first step is called "social transition" and is defined as "the process of expressing one's gender identity through actions such as changing one's name, pronouns, appearance, or behavior." While these rules are discriminatory, as everyone transitions differently, they did highlight the necessity clothing has for many of us in the process to self-actualization. The right to choose one's own clothing and expression is essential for everyone to lead healthy lives—especially for people in the LGBTQ+ community. Wouldn't it be great if every doctor had a rack of donated clothes for people to try on?

While social transitioning is often considered a trans-specific experience, I do not think one needs to be trans to desire a social transition into the gender expression that best suits them. Many LGBTQ+ people go through a period of social transition, whether consciously or not. We use clothing to communicate who we are to the world as queer people, and whether our clothing deviates from the cishet norm or not, our expression sends a message. It's impossible to escape this reality—and only people with privilege can claim that fashion is a frivolous interest. Force them to wear something they hate, and they will quickly realize that fashion is an essential element of their identity.

Queer fashion has another purpose beyond health, and that's safety. For trans people, passing keeps us safe when navigating the cis world, and we use fashion as a tool to demonstrate our gender. For femme-presenting people, clothing can be used to discourage street harassment and/or attacks. Many of us queer people make difficult decisions every day about what we wear. I had a hat with a pom pom on it that I thought was cute, but everyone gendered me using "she" while wearing it. So, Ru ceremoniously cut off the pom pom, thus solving my problem. It is amazing how one simple cue can throw my entire gender off balance. Many people who share outfits on Qwear love to play with other people's perceptions of their gender through fashion as a form of visual activism.

Queer and Trans Fashion Brands: Resistance and Revolution in the Twenty-First Century is the first scholarly work on queer fashion brands: an important work centering the queer liberation movement. Though the brands in *Queer and Trans Fashion Brands* are not accessible to all, they demonstrate that it is possible to design clothing for the queer population, and they have paved the way for more designers to consider queer bodies in their designs. My hope is that queer fashion brands can educate the cis fashion world about creating clothing for queer bodies so that queer fashion can be integrated into the mass market and become affordable to more people.

Someday I hope we will all be safe to dress however we please, and no kid has to feel like something is wrong with them because of how they wish to express themselves. *Queer and Trans Fashion Brands* marks a significant step toward that reality.

—Sonny Oram, Founding Editor & Co-Owner, *Qwear Fashion*

Acknowledgments

I thank all of my mentors, both formal and informal. They have been instrumental in helping me develop how I think and write, ultimately leading to this book. Suzanne Baldaia, my professor at Johnson and Wales University, was largely the first scholar who inspired me. I took many classes from her, but one that stands out was her fashion history course. Each session, she'd lecture and pull out the slide machine, and I felt so immersed in what she was saying. She told me she wrote a book chapter, and I remember how cool I thought that was and how I wanted to do the same one day. It never crossed my mind that I could write a whole book, but here I am. Professor Baldaia told me about a Textiles, Fashion Merchandising and Design program at the University of Rhode Island, and I wanted to do that next. After finishing my undergraduate degree, I met Margaret Ordoñez and Linda Welters at University of Rhode Island, where I took lots of classes from both of them and began to really think like a scholar and to even really understand what a scholar is. They taught me to ask questions, read literature, and understand the world around me in a different way. Margaret has become my lasting, life-changing mentor, and I thank her so much for teaching me. She was my major professor during my MS degree and did not settle for subpar work. She pushed me in productive ways, and I attribute much of my success to this.

After working with Margaret, I began my PhD at Oregon State University working with Elaine Pedersen and Leslie Burns. Elaine served as my major professor and taught me much about theory and writing. I took her theory course my first semester, having never taken a class like that before. I hated it at the time, but it became instrumental in how I engage with theoretical works. Elaine was meticulous and constantly challenged my ideas. These women helped shape the scholar I am today, and I am so thankful for the effort, time, and commitment they made to all of their students. I don't think I would be at this stage in my career without these highly dedicated professors.

I have also learned so much from different scholars and working with them in different ways. For instance, Jennifer Paff has been a research partner since I began working at Iowa State University. We have done numerous projects together, and on each I have learned so much about theory, writing, methods, and literature. Watching her lead teams has been so influential in how I take and give feedback and shift and change ideas. Susan Kaiser has also influenced me tremendously, in not only her scholarship but also her support. She and my dear friend Denise Green have both been very kind collaborators. Both Susan and Denise have been so important to how

I think, continually challenging my ideas, and have become lifelong friends who are not afraid to tell me what they really think about my work.

I am also thankful for other scholars whose work has inspired me or made me think in new ways. Reading and engaging with their scholarship has been important for my growth as a scholar. I can give only a very incomplete list of these folks: Ben Barry, Annette Becker, Anne Bissonnette, Missy Bye, Laura Camerlengo, Kelly Cobb, Marilyn DeLong, Karen DePauw, Rachel Eike, Tanisha Ford, Melissa Gamble, Joseph Hancock, Susan Hannel, Isabelle Held, Ally Howell Adobo, Susan Jerome, Laura Kane, Elena Karpova, Abby Lillethun, Rachel Lomonoco-Benzing, Kristen Morris, Belinda Orzada, Jaleesa Reed, Jessica Ridgway-Clayton, Nancy Rudd, Eulanda Sanders, Arti Sandhu, Clare Sauro, Sarah Scaturro, Anneke Smelik, Dina Smith-Glaviana, Casey Stannard, Annamari Vänskä, Elizabeth Way, and Lynda Xepoleas. I am also so thankful to other scholars writing about queer studies and fashion: Nicola Brajato, Chloe Chapin, Shaun Cole, Vicki Karaminas, Zara Korutz, Michael Mamp, Peter McNeil, Frank New, Andy Reilly, Valerie Steele, and Elizabeth Wilson.

I am also grateful to my past and current students, who certainly keep me on my feet when thinking in new ways: Shanti Amalanathan, Eunji Choi, Honor Edmonds, Zahra Falsafi, Juliana Guglielmi, Dyese Matthews, Blake Mudd, Amanda Ortiz-Pellot, Joshua Simon, Ginger Stanciel, and Kyra Streck. Dyese Matthews, in particular, has been my writing partner throughout this book project—listening to my ideas, challenging them, and simply being a badass person keeping me grounded. She often refers to me as a mentor, and in many ways I feel the same about her! Of course, the late Dana Goodin, who was my PhD student and tragically passed away during the pandemic in 2020, will forever be an inspiration, as will her work on Indigenous ways of knowing and thinking. May she rest in power, always.

I give a special shout out to Kyra Streck who helped me with some of the data collection and data analysis on this project. She also helped me interact with many fashion brand owners. Of course, her critical perspective always kept me alert.

Many thanks also go to my friends helping me to create the very important work–life balance: Shannon, Tony, and Will Kooima; Chris and Karina Butler; Steph and A. J. Hutt; Courtney Martin and her kiddos, Braxton and Teagan; Taylor Ward; and Allya Yourish. I am also thankful for my friends on all my softball and volleyball rec leagues here in Ames and the folks from my online art activities group. My therapist, Amanda, also deserves a shout out. During our biweekly sessions, she helps me keep perspective on what is important in life. I am also thankful to my immediate family members, Siobhan, Maureen, Doug, and Kroy. I joined their family in 2009 when I married Maureen and Doug's son, Brendan. Their support and love is essential to who I am.

Brendan Reddy-Best, my husband, partner, friend, deserves so much thanks. He has been there for this entire academic journey. We met the summer of 2008, when I was just starting my master's degree. His emotional and intellectual support have been by far the most influential in my life. He's been there during the everyday highs and lows, struggles and successes. I am so thankful to him and that our relationship continues to thrive in its ups and downs.

As a self-identified queer, feminine-presenting, heterosexual-appearing person, I am thankful to all the queer and trans folks who created space and visibility for the spectrum of people in the queer and trans communities. Without their representation and hearing their stories, I most likely would not have understood, accepted, and embraced my identities, and may not have ventured on this path critically thinking about queer and trans identities and fashion in my research. Folks like Anita Dolce Vita and Sonny Oram, who work extensively on queer and trans fashion media representation, are champions. They make people feel seen, heard, and represented—myself included.

Of course, this book would literally not be possible without the help and trust from each brand owner whom I interviewed for this project. They trusted me to hear and write their stories. Thank you to Alyah Baker, Anji Becker, Erin Berg, Sky Cubacub, Searah Deysach, Christian Dominique, Fran Dunaway, Marialexandra Garcia, Naomi Gonzalez, Audio Helkuik, Peregrine Honig, NiK Kacy, Jeanna Kadlec, Kit, Lindsay Krakauer, Liz Leifer, Stoney Michelli Love, Sara Medd, Laura and Kelly Moffat, Thúy Nguyen, Vicky Pasche, Chris and Courtney Rhodes, Sade, Scout Rose, Abby Sugar, Susan Stewart, Marli Washington, and Mel Brittner Wells. To them, I am forever thankful.

Declaring Interests and Funding

As the author of this book, I must mention that while I have strong relationships with the queer and trans fashion brands featured herein, they did not provide any financial backing or nonmonetary incentives. As I compiled their oral histories, I did ask the brand owners if they were interested in donating products to the ISU Textiles and Clothing Museum, as I wanted to build the collection with these pioneering fashion brands. TomboyX, Play Out Apparel, and FtM Essentials each donated a few items that are now in the permanent collection and available for study and use in classes.

I also received a $10,000 grant from Iowa State University's provost office, which partially funded this book. The grant was meant to support faculty in building diversity-focused courses. I wanted to develop a course on queer fashion, yet there was little published literature on queer fashion brands. Thus, the grant enabled me to pay the interviewees $95 apiece for their time in completing their oral history. I used the remaining funds for a course buyout so that I could teach one class instead of two for one semester and thus begin working on the oral history project. I also used part of my start-up research funds provided by Iowa State's Fashion Design and Merchandising program to travel to some of the interviewees.

The reason I actually started my brand was because of my experience. My whole life, since I was a kid, I couldn't find shoes that fit, I guess, my inside? My outside and my inside never matched, you know, being born in the wrong body and knowing that I was in the wrong body, but never really being able to pinpoint what it was exactly, because I didn't understand. But I knew that whenever I saw guys' shoes I would be like "Oh, that's what I want to wear." That's why I started my company.

—NiK Kacy, NiK Kacy Footwear

Introduction

What makes a queer fashion brand? What makes a trans fashion brand? Is it that they say they are? Is it that they make products for queer people? Is it that the people who work for the brand are queer? Is it that they overtly or subtly market their products to queer and trans people? What if only heterosexual people bought the products? Do the products have to be worn on queer bodies? What about socks? Will there be queer socks and non-queer socks? Certainly, the same questions can be asked of any identity category (menswear, womenswear, etc.). I ask these questions not assuming they have concrete answers but more to help think through the complexities of how the brands in this research position themselves and what it means to embody identities through fashion. This research began by first encountering two pioneering fashion brands in the twenty-first century: Saint Harridan and Tomboy Tailors.

Saint Harridan and Tomboy Tailors

Saint Harridan, a queer fashion brand catering to masculine of center women and transmen, began its Kickstarter in 2012, and it was all over social media. At this time, I was working on my dissertation at Oregon State University, focusing on queer women, fashion, shopping, and styling. When I asked the participants in my study where they liked to shop and why, many of them mentioned these new fashion brands focused on queer and trans people. They said things like "There is this new brand, and their pop-up is coming to my town" or "I saw advertisements for brands with advertisements that looked like me." Fast forward to 2013: I moved to Oakland, California, in August to start my first tenure-track job at San Francisco State University. I was riding around Oakland on my bicycle getting to know the area and I stumbled on Saint Harridan's pop-up shop in the pedestrian mall at Clay and Thirteenth Street in downtown Oakland. I went inside on that hot, late summer day and saw suit samples, accessories, and lots of folks engaging with these products. Additionally, customers were looking through swatch books, ordering custom suits in the fabrics they desired. Mary Going, Saint Harridan founder, was there, and as I tried on a sample suit jacket, I asked Going what made the suits unique. Going replied, "They are engineered to fit curves of a body but give you a masculine look."

After this experience, I began looking more into these fashion brands that were around the Bay Area and discovered Zel Anders, founder of Tomboy Tailors, a fashion brand which, like Saint Harridan, focused on designing men's suits for women's bodies. I met Anders, who was wearing a suit and bowtie, in her downtown San Francisco storefront in the Crocker Galleria, a three-floor, indoor shopping square with numerous boutiques and restaurants (Figure I.1). Like Saint Harridan's pop-up shop, Tomboy Tailors had a showroom environment with numerous suit samples. There were sample fabric books, illustration books with numerous garment details to choose from (e.g., collars, lapels, pockets, etc.), and numerous framed paintings on the walls, including a copy of Romaine Brooks's 1924 oil painting *Una, Lady Troubridge*, depicting an early iconic lesbian dressed in a masculine style, similar to the aesthetic of Anders' showroom. The store's environment reflected a classy, sophisticated, and dapper style. I informally asked Anders about the business and saw how the customers went through the process of purchasing the products by looking at samples and line drawings after getting body measurements completed.

After these interactions, I started my first research project related to these fashion brands: "The Politicization of Fashion in Virtual Queer Spaces: A Case Study of Saint Harridan and Tomboy Tailors" (Reddy-Best 2015, 2020a). I focused on the two brands, specifically their digital spaces and how they challenged heteronormative assumptions deeply entrenched in the fashion system. After this initial research, I was introduced to Miki Vargas, a queer fashion photographer who worked with Mary Going, and I published another research paper focused on Vargas and her contributions to queer fashion imagery and photography (Reddy-Best 2017) (Figure I.2). After completing these more focused papers, I aimed to uncover the larger story

Figure I.1 Zel Anders in front of the Tomboy Tailors storefront in San Francisco. Photo courtesy of Steven Kasapi.

Figure I.2 Saint Harridan advertisement photographed by Miki Vargas. Photo courtesy of Miki Vargas.

about these fashion brands as they emerged on the market. I had also begun other research projects centering queer women and again asked them about where they shopped and looked for style ideas, and they provided many similar responses about seeing these new brands catering to them, which continued to confirm a need for exploration of these revolutionary fashion brands catering to queer and trans identities (e.g., Reddy-Best 2018a, 2018b).

The Current Project: Questions, Perspectives, and Why it Matters

All of these experiences led me to this current project, in which I examine the narratives of fashion entrepreneurs who created queer- and trans-focused fashion brands, illuminating their journeys of self-expression, identity formation, and resistance within the fashion industry. Through these personal accounts, I highlight the resilience, creativity, and cultural contributions of these fashion entrepreneurs. That is, I argue they are agents of change, actively challenging heteronormative ideas prevalent in the fashion industry. To comprehensively analyze the subject matter, I draw on an intersectional feminist framework, which allows for a nuanced examination of various aspects of the production, distribution, regulation, and consumption of the products and media associated with these queer- and trans-focused fashion brands and their collective impact on the fashion industry. These questions informed my work:

1. Why, when, and where did the brands emerge?
2. How do the founder's identity and personal experiences set a context for the fashion brand's positioning?
3. How do the brands and their products reflect, embody, and serve as vehicles for queer and trans sensibilities? How do they actively resist, subvert, and uphold traditional notions of gender and sexuality through their branding, designs, and marketing?
4. What do these brands collectively contribute to the fashion system? That is, how do they position themselves in the context of the broader fashion system?
5. What are the challenges and opportunities faced by queer- and trans-focused fashion brands in terms of intersectional justice such as accessibility, affordability, and size inclusivity? How do they address these challenges and strive for justice-oriented practices while immersed in the capitalist marketplace?

Answering these questions and writing this book holds immense importance for society and business by promoting inclusivity, social change, economic opportunities, business innovation, and cultural understanding. This work helps create a more equitable and inclusive fashion industry while inspiring readers to challenge norms, celebrate diversity, and strive for positive social impact in their own endeavors.

The book contributes to increasing representation and visibility of queer and trans individuals within the fashion industry. By highlighting their journeys and experiences, it challenges the historically dominant heteronormative narratives in fashion. This representation is crucial for fostering a more inclusive society and empowering marginalized communities. Fashion also has the potential to be a powerful vehicle for social change. By documenting the stories of entrepreneurs who challenge heteronormativity, the book amplifies their activism and showcases the transformative power of fashion as a means of challenging societal norms and advocating for marginalized communities. It encourages readers to question existing systems and promotes social change.

My work also sheds light on the economic potential of queer- and trans-focused fashion brands. It demonstrates the viability and success of businesses that cater to underserved markets and niche communities. By showcasing the creativity, resilience, and cultural contributions of these fashion entrepreneurs, my research encourages the recognition and support of such brands, leading to economic opportunities, and the growth of a more diverse and inclusive fashion industry. The narratives in the book can inspire and stimulate innovation within the broader business community. They encourage aspiring entrepreneurs to think outside the conventions of the fashion industry and develop unique socially conscious business models. This can lead to new ideas, approaches, and strategies that challenge the status quo, foster creativity, and promote sustainable and inclusive business practices.

Lastly, the book promotes cultural appreciation and understanding by providing insights into the experiences and perspectives of queer and trans communities. It helps bridge gaps in knowledge and empathy, fostering dialogue and reducing prejudice and discrimination. By engaging with these narratives, readers gain a deeper understanding of the intersectionality of identities and the importance of diverse representation in shaping a more compassionate society.

Chapter Overview

In the first chapter, "Identities, Style-Fashion-Dress, and Dressed Bodies," I explore the relationship between identities, style, fashion, and dressed bodies, particularly within the context of queer and trans experiences. Exploring the intersectional subject positions within the realm of styling, fashioning, and dressing, I unravel the knots of identity while highlighting the situated bodily practices involved while drawing upon various literature, theories, and conceptual ideas. The concepts of ambiguity and ambivalence are explained through the complexities of the dressed body within the fashion system. The chapter concludes with an overview of historical nuances spanning the nineteenth to the early twenty-first centuries, illuminating the processes of fashioning queer and trans identities within a Western context, offering an insight into the evolution of self-expression through attire.

In Chapter 2, "Political Landscapes and So-Called Heteronormative Ideals," to situate the surge of queer and trans fashion brands in the 2010s that overtly targeted queer and trans folks, I first highlight the political landscape for queer and trans folks in the United States, followed by a selective history of various milestones, trends, and practices that have contributed to the so-called heteronormative nature of the fashion industry, with a focus on its adherence to heteronormative ideals and norms and the ways queer designers intersect with the fashion system.

In Chapter 3, "Gay Window Advertising and Capitalist Entanglements," I outline how numerous fashion companies subtly targeted queer people; that is, since the 1980s, mainstream brands noticed the queer and trans communities as a potential profit-driven market segment. Some engaged in gay window advertising, trying to ensure that their conservative, anti-LGBTQ+ consumers would not reject or boycott the brand due to its alignment with liberal ideologies. Although seemingly a progressive step, gay window advertising also reveals important entanglements with commodity activism and corporate pride, illuminating the complex interplay between consumer choices and corporate strategies. I explore how corporations have increasingly capitalized on the visibility and marketability of queer identities, using rainbow-colored products and marketing campaigns to align themselves with the LGBTQ+ community during Pride Month. I also unpack the numerous tensions and contradictions that arise from these entanglements and how the commodification of LGBTQ+ identities and activism has become intertwined with neoliberal capitalist structures.

In Chapter 4, "Marketplace Influences: Politics and Technology," I explore the significance of the legalization of same-sex marriage as a catalyst for the rise of these queer and trans brands, reflecting societal progress and shifting attitudes.

Furthermore, I discuss the roles of crowdfunding and social media as powerful tools that have enabled the entry and growth of queer and trans fashion brands in an industry traditionally dominated by established players.

In Chapter 5, "Queer and Trans Fashion Brand Entrepreneurial Beginnings: Before and After the 2010s Surge," I trace the entrepreneurial beginnings of the queer and trans fashion brands in this research, showcasing their resilience and innovation. I first highlight the existence of pioneering brands such as Dykes in the City, which helped pave the way for the twenty-first-century surge of queer and trans fashion brands. Within this chapter, I also provide short case studies examining the featured brands of this research. By examining the entrepreneurs behind these brands, we gain insight into their motivations, visions, and contributions to the fashion system. Moreover, I emphasize how queer and trans identities serve as a crucial context for the positioning and messaging of these fashion brands. That is, these brands wanted to create a space where folks in the queer and trans communities could feel seen and heard through embodied practices.

In Chapter 6, "Vehicles for Queer and Trans Sensibilities," I examine the diverse range of consumer products offered by the queer and trans fashion brands. From suits and suit accessories to the iconic button-down shirt and gender neutral footwear, each fashion item challenges traditional notions of gender and style. These brands also prioritize the representation of queer and trans identities, with Pride-related merchandise, swimwear, undergarments, trans gear, and gender-fluid styles playing significant roles. I also delve into the emergence of queer styling services, whose fashion professionals cater specifically to queer and trans individuals, helping them navigate and express their unique identities. I also raise questions about the nature of queer socks and the authority responsible for defining them, further emphasizing the nuanced exploration of identity in the realm of fashion.

In Chapter 7, "An Ethical Balancing Act: Production and Pricing," I explore ethical challenges in queer and trans fashion brands, focusing on production and pricing dilemmas. The chapter delves into the complexities of choosing production locations, balancing support for local communities with global supply-chain considerations. Sustainability emerges as a key concern, acknowledging the intricate decision-making processes involved. Brand owners express a commitment to environmental justice, navigating the influence of socioeconomic status on choices. Pricing strategies are examined with sensitivity to accessibility for queer and trans individuals across income levels. The intersectionality of socioeconomic factors prompts a reevaluation of traditional business models, highlighting brand owners' dedication to balancing financial viability with social responsibility. Sustaining businesses is portrayed as a delicate equilibrium between profit and ensuring product accessibility for marginalized communities, challenging conventional notions of success.

In Chapter 8, "Queer and Trans Media: For Us and Them, Too," I explore media's influence on shaping the representation of queer and trans fashion. I first highlight the importance of representation and its profound impact on the visibility and experiences of queer and trans individuals. I also acknowledge instances in which representation falls short or fails to capture the diversity and complexity of queer and trans experiences. By analyzing both successes and failures in representation, a deeper understanding is gained of the transformative power of media. I examine how these queer and trans fashion brands produced their products. Many of them thought critically about representation and media: whether in print or via live fashion shows, these brands recognized media's power as a tool for reshaping societal perceptions and promoting inclusivity. By considering representation, they aimed to challenge norms and foster a more diverse and accepting narrative that goes beyond the actual products. In essence, the power of media became another catalyst for dismantling stereotypes. In Chapter 9, I continue the examination of the emergence of queer fashion media, specifically DapperQ and Qwear, as platforms that celebrate and showcase queer and trans fashion, including the brands in this research, providing a space for designers and models from these communities to shine and be recognized.

In the conclusion, I highlight how the brands' ups and downs, challenges and successes are acknowledged. I highlight how the brands have had significant positive impact on people's lives, based on consumer feedback in various spaces. That is, the consumers feel better about themselves, more authentically themselves, and seen and represented; they used the products to learn about their identities; they feel more confident wearing the products, they are able to leave their houses now that they have these products; they feel prouder wearing the products, their life is changed for the better; they feel more comfortable with themselves; and the products saved their lives or helped them feel safer. I draw on rich interviews with representatives from each brand, highlighting how, despite the sometimes emotional rollercoaster of dealing with the haters, the brands create moments of pure, emotion-filled joy and love.

In the conclusion, I also reflect on the transformative role played by queer and trans fashion brands in challenging the heteronormative fashion landscape. These brands embody various forms of fashion disruption, contributing to inclusivity and acceptance. I suggest that navigating the dynamic nature of fashion involves considering its tangible, social, economic, political, and embodied dimensions. Exploring entangled meanings and moments within the fashion system helps unravel these complexities. I contemplate the future trajectory of queer and trans fashion brands, anticipating continued growth and impact. Last, I pose open-ended questions, encouraging exploration of the movement's evolution and its ongoing influence on the fashion sphere. My practical queries for fashion entrepreneurs invite further dialogue on shaping the future of this transformative movement.

Part 1 Situating the Context

1 Identities, Style-Fashion-Dress, and Dressed Bodies

To situate the work, I will first introduce an overview of the complexity and nuance of identities, specifically queer and trans identities. Next, I will unpack foundational concepts related to fashion and identity and how our identities are intricately related to our bodies and dress.

Queer and Trans Identities and Intersectional Subject Positions

Identity, or subject position, is a multifaceted concept that encompasses the characteristics, traits, beliefs, and experiences that help define an individual or a group. It is how we perceive ourselves and how others perceive us. Identity is not static; it is fluid and changes over time due to various factors such as personal experiences, cultural influences, and social interactions. At its core, identity is a complex interplay between individual attributes and the broader social, cultural, and historical contexts in which we exist.

Scholars have extensively explored the topic of identity as early as the late nineteenth century, spanning into the twentieth and twenty-first centuries. Earlier researchers, such as Cooley (1902) and James (1890), have delved into this complex concept, revealing its multifaceted nature. More contemporary scholars like Lennon, Johnson, and Rudd (2017) and Schwartz, Luyckz, and Vignoles (2011) have also highlighted the diverse ways identity can be understood.

In social science and cultural studies, the term *identity* is used in various ways, both in theory and practice. Early theorists like William James, Charles Horton Cooley, and George Herbert Mead laid some of the groundwork for identity theory. James proposed that individuals' thoughts and feelings influence their behavior and that people possess multiple internal selves based on their interactions with others. Cooley distinguished between biological and social identities, introducing the concept of the looking-glass self, in which individuals shape their self-awareness through others' reactions. Mead explored the objective *me* and subjective *I* selves within the social context.

Erik Erikson (1968) contributed by introducing the concept of ego identity, providing individuals with a consistent sense of self amidst change. Scholars like Stryker (1968) empirically tested Mead's framework, defining identity as internalized role expectations associated with social roles. Each social group or society shapes an individual's behavior, reinforcing their identity (Burke 1980; Burke and Tully 1977). Burke and Reitzes (1981) emphasized the connection between identities and behavior, highlighting a mutual reinforcement process. Identity is also often categorized into individual, relational, and collective levels, with a focus on both content and processes (Schwartz, Luyckz, and Vignoles 2011).

The complexity of identity can be explained through the concepts of being and becoming. That is, as humans, we are ever evolving (Kaiser and Green 2021). As we move into different spaces and places, we react and respond in different ways. Thus, we are experiencing new ways to view ourselves, how that is materialized in and around the body, and how we understand ourselves in relation to others. While we often describe ourselves in more static terms, "I am queer," mostly for ease in everyday communication, this language does not necessarily reflect how in each new moment we realize, even slightly, new ways to think about who we were or are in the past, present, and future.

Understanding subject positions is crucial in analyzing how individuals are situated within various social structures. It allows us to explore how power operates in society and how certain identities (race, ethnicity, sex, gender, sexuality, religion, body size, etc.) are marginalized and privileged in different contexts, time periods, and spaces. People's subject positions affect how they are perceived, treated, and represented. For instance, a person's racial or ethnic identity can influence how they are treated by law enforcement, employers, or institutions (e.g., Carbado 2017; Hall, Hall, and Perry 2016; Matthews and Reddy-Best 2022). Similarly, gender identity can affect access to opportunities, healthcare, and education (e.g., James et al. 2016).

The complexity and nuance of identities, particularly queer and trans identities, is important to explore, as they are entangled with and central to the fashion brands in this research. It is imperative to recognize the intricate layers that constitute these identities, understanding that they span a vast spectrum of experiences, expressions, and intersections that differ across cultures, geographic locations, and time periods. Gender, one of the numerous intersecting subject positions, is multifaceted and goes much beyond the traditional Western binary of man and woman and is one of the central identities entangled in this research. Gender encompasses multiple possibilities, experiences, expressions, and understandings. For instance, prior to white settlers, many Indigenous communities on Turtle Island (what settlers now refer to as North America) had their own language to describe gender-variant individuals. While pan-Indian terms like *Two-Spirit* are frequently adopted, many of the 500 or more surviving Indigenous cultures have diverse ways of thinking about and interpreting sex and gender (Indian Health Services n.d.: para. 3).

In a Western context, gender is so often tied to one's assigned sex at birth, yet an entire spectrum of gender possibilities are experienced and expressed, and the language surrounding these identities is ever shifting and changing. For instance, individuals assigned one sex and gender at birth may experience varying and contrasting connections with those assigned identities. Terms such as *trans*, *transgender*, *transmasculine*, *transfeminine*, *trans nonbinary*, *nonbinary*, and *genderqueer* have been adopted to embody these experiences. Terms that some still use but have largely fallen out of favor include *transexual*, *tranny*, and *transvestite*. Additionally, though, across the globe, folks embody different gender systems, such as *kathoeys* in Thailand or the *köceks* in the Ottoman empire. Overall, regardless of the language used to self-identify, these diverse gender experiences are varied and nuanced (Kaiser and Green 2021; Reddy-Best 2020b; UC Davis LGBTQIA Resource Center 2023).

Some individuals within the transgender community express desires to transition and present themselves with a gender different from the one assigned to them at birth (Factor and Rothblum 2008). Conversely, others reject the traditional binary gender system, embracing a gender-neutral identity and preferring they/them pronouns (Tate, Ledbetter, and Youssef 2013). Some individuals navigate among different gender identities, embracing a gender-fluid identity (Factor and Rothblum 2008; Tate, Ledbetter, and Youssef 2013). These diverse identities, sometimes referred to as the "messy middle," defy consistent categorization, leading to shifting self-narratives throughout one's life (Garrison 2018: 619). Moreover, some transgender individuals frequently modify the language they use to describe themselves, influenced by cultural, geographic, and socioeconomic factors (Simmons and White 2018).

Factor and Rothblum (2008) studied individuals who identify as MTF, FTM, and genderqueer and found "tremendous variation among trans individuals in gender experience and gender expression" (251). Contemporary community resources also highlight the nuances of diverse gender experiences. For instance, the National Center for Transgender Equality offers multiple ways to understand nonbinary people. The center explains that most transgender people do not necessarily align with nonbinary or related concepts (National Center for Transgender Equality 2023b). Similarly, they describe how some transgender people may connect more with nonbinary, genderqueer identities where they do not feel connection to being a man or a woman, but perhaps a combination or something outside of this binary completely (National Center for Transgender Equality 2023a).

In much of my scholarship (e.g., Ogle et al. 2023; Reddy-Best 2018a, 2018b; Reddy-Best and Goodin 2020; Reddy-Best and Olson 2020), I have centered trans and nonbinary folks and their relationship to the consumption, distribution, regulation, and production of fashion products and fashion media. In all the interviews I conducted for these projects, I asked the participants to describe their gender identity. Some of the responses from participants in a research project I coauthored with a colleague highlight significant nuances in gender identity:

- "I do identify as transgender, at this point I don't identify as gender nonconforming anymore, because my appearance usually lines up with what others would see as more gender binary presentation."

- "[I identify as] transgender. And I say that only now because it's out there, it's so public, and that is the term that is used. But I personally always felt like I was a boy and I just really feel like as I transitioned medically, um, it was just me, finally hitting the right puberty, you know. So it's like me finally growing up, didn't really feel like I turned into a man. I just finally hit manhood."

- "In Black spaces, I feel like I'm a woman—because that's just, the struggle is a lot different. But I also am a queer woman in Black spaces. And to get to the point of being intersectional is hard. And so, it's not like, oh, like, 'I'm a woman.' It's like I don't identify as a woman or a man. Right now it's [gender identity] floating in the stratosphere. I identify as just neutral, who is fem-presenting. I've always been fem-presenting. Because that's what I like to do. So that kind of makes sense. I mean, right now I'm kind of [in] gender struggles, I might be a demi-girl [demi-sexual] … it's very confusing."
- "I don't fall on the [gender] scale at all. The scale just isn't me. I'm just not on it, I'm like somewhere to the left of the scale. The scale is two-dimensional, and I feel like my gender is like three- or four-dimensional so I don't really, I just don't relate to it. I feel like I'm in another galaxy so they/them/theirs is like the closest coherent word that some people can understand to what I feel like I experience in terms of gender without limiting my experience to like the perception of other people, which is like the antithesis of what I want for myself."

Sexuality is another identity central to this research. Sexual identity, orientation, expression, and behavior are integral aspects of human nature, encompassing a wide range of experiences, feelings, and actions. *Sexual identity* refers to how individuals perceive themselves in terms of sexual orientation, and it is much intertwined with gender identity. *Sexual orientation* reflects one's emotional, romantic, and sexual attractions. *Sexual expression* encompasses the various ways individuals communicate and manifest their sexualities. This can include verbal communication, body language, and nonverbal cues that convey interest, desire, consent, and boundaries. *Sexual behavior* refers to the actions and activities individuals engage in based on their sexual desires and preferences. These behaviors can range from romantic gestures and emotional intimacy to sexual intercourse and other forms of sexual activities. There is not necessarily always alignment among these concepts; that is, an individual may identify one way and express that identity or behave in other ways.

Individuals adopt and embody diverse sexual identities, and the language shifts and changes. For instance, lesbian, gay, bisexual, queer, questioning, asexual, two-spirit, and pansexual identities represent a spectrum of sexual orientations and gender expressions. A *lesbian* may be a woman who is romantically, sexually, or emotionally attracted to other women. *Gay* often refers to men who are attracted to other men, while *bisexual* individuals are often attracted to two or more genders. *Queer* is often an umbrella term that encompasses a wide range of diverse sexual orientations, as well as gender nonconforming and nonbinary individuals. *Questioning* may be used by folks who are inquiring about how they identify, whereas *asexual* typically refers to folks who experience little to no sexual attraction. Other phrases that may be less common include *same-gender loving* or *queer platonic relationships*. These identities are nuanced and ever-changing, evolving with our understanding of gender and sexuality. These sexuality terms, like gender, are not rigid categories, and they exist on a continuum, meaning different things to different people, often dependent on context, space, and place. Certainly, there are numerous terms and phrases not included here, and, depending on when and where you read this text, some of these terms may be considered offensive, derogatory, or wrong (The Center 2023; UC Davis LGBTQIA Resource Center 2023).

While I discussed gender and sexuality separately, the interconnectedness of identities and the unique experiences of individuals at the intersections of multiple marginalized identities is an intricate aspect of human existence. Crenshaw's (1989, 1991) groundbreaking concept of intersectionality has been instrumental in shedding light on this complexity. Intersectionality emphasizes the idea that social categorizations such as race, gender, class, sexuality, and other forms of identity are interconnected and cannot be examined in isolation. Instead, these categories intersect and overlap, shaping the experiences of individuals in multifaceted ways. This framework challenges traditional approaches to social justice by highlighting the intersecting systems of oppression and privilege that influence people's lives.

In the realm of intersectionality, individuals with multiple marginalized identities face compounded and distinct challenges. For instance, a person who belongs to both racially marginalized and queer communities may encounter discrimination qualitatively different from that faced by individuals belonging to either group independently. This is highlighted in the Black person who explained to me: "In Black spaces I feel like I'm a woman—because that's just, the struggle is a lot different. But I also am a queer woman in Black spaces. And to get to the point of being intersectional is hard." The interplay of these identities can lead to nuanced experiences of marginalization, as well as resilience and resistance strategies that emerge from navigating complex social terrains.

Understanding intersectionality is crucial for creating inclusive and equitable societies. It enables us to recognize the diverse needs and experiences of individuals, moving beyond one-size-fits-all approaches to social policies and activism. Acknowledging the interconnected nature of identities makes it possible to address the complexity of social injustices and work toward dismantling intersecting systems of oppression. Moreover, intersectionality highlights the importance of amplifying the voices of individuals who are often overlooked or silenced. Their experiences offer valuable insights into the intricacies of discrimination and privilege, prompting necessary conversations about social change and policy reform. In essence, the concept of intersectionality challenges us to move beyond simplistic and static notions of identity, encouraging a more nuanced understanding of diverse and interconnected lived experiences.

In this book, I use the descriptors *queer* and *trans* in relation to the fashion brands. In many ways this is reductive as the fashion brands cater to so many different identities, bodies, and personal experiences that expand far beyond the two terms. I recognize the problematic nature of settling on this language. The words *queer* and *trans*, although valuable in highlighting the inclusivity efforts of certain fashion brands, risk overlooking the intricate tapestry of human experiences that these brands cater to. People's identities and expressions are complex, fluid, and multifaceted, defying easy categorization within the confines of a few words. By employing these terms, I do not intend to negate the richness of the myriad identities and narratives.

Styling-Fashioning-Dressing, Identity (K)nots, and Situated Bodily Practices

One way we communicate and negotiate our varying identities, including gender and sexuality, is through dress (Davis 1992; Kaiser 1997, 2012; Lennon, Johnson, and Rudd 2017). *Dress* refers to "an assemblage of modifications of the body and/or supplements to the body" (Roach-Higgins and Eicher 1992: 1). The term *dress* encompasses not just clothing or accessories but also body modifications and supplements. *Modifications* refers to changes to hair, skin, or nails, whereas *supplements* can refer to enclosures, attachments to the body, attachments to enclosures, or hand-held objects. While the terms *appearance*, *adornment*, *apparel*, *clothing*, *costume*, and/or *fashion* may be used interchangeably, they all fall under the comprehensive, umbrella *dress* as defined in Roach-Higgins and Eicher's (1992) foundational paper in the fashion studies discipline.

In a 2010 article, fashion theorist Carol Tulloch delves into the intricate connections within the realms of style, fashion, and dress. She elucidates these concepts as an interconnected system, using hyphens to signify comprehensive relationships. Tulloch emphasizes the significance of each term, asserting that their meanings, when clearly defined, contribute cohesively to the broader study. She defines *style* as a form of personal agency, a means through which individuals construct their identities by curating garments, accessories, and beauty routines, whether or not these choices align with current fashion trends. Tulloch extends the idea by describing style as a method of self-expression, a way for individuals to narrate aspects of their life stories through their clothing selections, a concept she terms *style narratives*.

The broader concept of *style-fashion-dress* places style within the framework of fashion, a social phenomenon in which style narratives evolve over time. That is, fashion, as a social process, encompasses more than clothing style: it extends to food, furniture preferences, popular culture, language, technology, science, and various other aspects of culture and everyday life. However, fashion's significance becomes particularly striking when one considers its relation to the human body's appearance, as it is intimately personal and experienced in daily life. Fashion holds importance in everyday existence and is expressed and lived through individuals' bodies.

Dress, much like style and in connection with fashion, starts with the human body. This concept encompasses the ways people modify or adorn their bodies, following Roach-Higgins and Eicher's definition (1992). Fashion sociologist Joanne Entwistle (2023) has pointed out that understanding dress necessitates considering the body, as the body has always been dressed in various ways across different cultures and times. Entwistle (2000) argues the importance of the body in context with the development of the concept the "situated bodily practice"; she proposed that "it is through our bodies that we come to see and be seen in the world" and that "the body forms the envelope of our being in the world, and our selfhood comes from this location in body and our experience of this" (334). The physical body on which the dress is enacted is an important aspect of understanding dress and identity negotiations. The living, fleshy body and the physical actions it engages with interacts constantly with the materiality of the dress and the meanings constructed through the dress, all occurring in a way that cannot be disentangled (Entwistle 2000).

Through the mediums of style, fashion, and dress, individuals find avenues to visually, materially, and physically express aspects of themselves that might be difficult to put into words. That is, in everyday conversations, when people describe who they are, they often do so by saying what they are not, as expressing their true identity verbally proves a much more challenging task, as noted by Freitas et al. (1997). During Freitas and colleagues' interviews, individuals tended to strongly emphasize what they are not or the specific looks they wanted to avoid, as they did not embody the individuals' identities.

Who I am versus who I am not certainly puts identity in a binary framework. Kaiser and McCullough (2010) theorized the metaphor of *entanglement* to complicate rigid binary distinctions and dress and identity. They explained that even in the absence of clear patterns, entanglement suggests that various elements are complexly intertwined. By expanding our imagination beyond rigid binaries, we can explore more intricate and nuanced perspectives on subjectivity and the interactions between individuals. When we shift our perspectives and view differences (who I am versus who I am not) not as separate from our own identities but as intertwined elements, a new understanding can emerge. That is, embracing this entangled perspective fosters a greater openness to differences and allows for the discovery of unexpected commonalities that may be exposed and hidden at different times. Then, the concept of *not* becomes intricately woven into a complex *(k)not*, where these entanglements act as substitutes for opposition (Kaiser and McCullough 2010: 363). Theorizing via a knot in the context of fashion enables us to contemplate how truths can be temporarily obscured, only to be unveiled as a knot is loosened and is perhaps retied (e.g., from a trucker's hitch to a bowline). Consequently, truths about dress and who we are can be seen as partial and conditional, influenced by numerous factors such as time, space, place, and, importantly, power dynamics. Visualizing a knot's three-dimensional surface and using the same rope to form different knots highlights temporary prominence while concealing portions of the material beneath. Using the knot metaphor, one can begin to unpack relationships between the self and others as entangled and to move beyond the simplistic binary distinctions so frequent in everyday conversations.

Ambiguity, Ambivalence, and the Dressed Body in the Fashion System

Next, I summarize and make connections between literature discussing the concepts *ambivalence* and *ambiguity* as related to the dressed body and highlight the ways queer and trans folks fashion their bodies. As individuals curate their everyday appearances, style-fashion-dress, and situated embodied practice, they navigate complex power dynamics, giving rise to a pervasive sense of ambiguity. The term *ambiguity* encompasses various nuances: it can involve mixed metaphors, layered messages, and elusive, hard-to-express concepts, like emerging fashion trends (Razinsky 2016). It also includes contradictory messages that hover between different possibilities, blurring distinctions and causing overlaps between different types of ambiguity. Ambiguity is prevalent in verbal communication; in visual mediums like fashion, it proliferates, whether intentionally on the wearer's part, perceived by the observer, or both.

This ambiguity often leads to ironic and thought-provoking expressions, bringing underlying contradictions to the forefront. For instance, sociologist Gregory Stone (1969) argued that ambiguous appearances often carry profound meanings, requiring observers' thoughtful interpretation. Perceivers weigh alternative meanings, navigate the fuzziness, and explore the ambiguous spaces between conflicting interpretations. Ambiguity, in essence, prompts questioning and deliberation, fostering interactions and sparking new negotiations of meaning and understanding between wearer and observer, and wearer and the self. Additionally, Davis has noted, fashion "'merely suggests' more than it can (or intends to) state precisely" (1992: 3), again reinforcing its interconnection with ambiguity. New styles, no matter where they come from—for instance, via Instagram influencers or local communities—inherently possess ambiguity, or this fuzziness. Then, ambiguity can amplify when individuals incorporate popular styles into their own embodiments, often in ways not envisioned by those responsible for the initial creation (e.g., turning a glove into an evening purse). Kaiser, Nagasawa, and Hutton (1995) argue that as a social phenomenon, fashion relies on ambiguity to inspire fresh styles and reshape perceptions of what is considered fashionable.

Fashioning the body is a domain that is also ripe with ambivalence, that is, having mixed feelings or contradictory attitudes toward a particular person, object, situation, or idea. Ambivalence is a state of uncertainty or fluctuation, in which an individual experiences conflicting emotions, opinions, or beliefs. In the context of ambivalence, a person might simultaneously feel positive and negative emotions, making it difficult for them to make a clear decision or form a definite opinion. This internal conflict often arises when someone is faced with a complex or emotionally charged situation and find it challenging to reconcile their conflicting thoughts and feelings. Ambivalence can create a sense of inner tension and indecision, leading individuals to feel torn between different options.

Fashion can offer a canvas for self-expression, enabling individuals to explore diverse styles, experiment with fabrics, and embrace creativity. This allows people to construct unique identities and celebrate their individuality, fostering a sense of empowerment and pride. However, this creative freedom can be at odds with societal expectations and the pressure to conform to conventional fashion standards. Conflicting interests can emerge, where individuals seek to express their authentic selves through clothing while navigating the desire to fit in and meet societal approval that may be strict (corporate dress code) or loose (general accepted workplace styles). This conflict can give rise to ambivalence, as people grapple with the tension between embracing their distinctive fashion choices and adhering to prevailing social norms.

Ambivalence and ambiguity are captured in the fashion system via a visual Kaiser and Green (2021) developed titled "structures of feeling in the circuit of style-fashion-dress," which they modified from Kaiser's (2012) circuit of style-fashion-dress and the circuit of culture by du Gay et al. (1997). The circuit is meant to illustrate and interpret the tangible, social, economic, and embodied aspects of styling-fashioning-dressing. The fundamental idea behind the model is that fashion and the related processes (production, consumption, distribution, regulation, and subject formation) are in constant flux. They employed a circuit with double-headed arrows rather than a straight line to suggest perpetual motion and multiple locations, interconnected by pathways that might deviate, twist, and turn. The routes depicted in the circuit are not linear; instead, movements can occur in various, potentially spontaneous, directions and are influenced by diverse factors (and reciprocally influence these factors). Each element within the circuit represents a process, yet these processes are not static and are entangled, knotty. Inside the circuit are meanings and feelings (anxiety, materiality, creativity, power, ambiguity, ambivalence, and agency), which demonstrate that during the processes (production, consumption, distribution, regulation, and subject formation), multiple meanings and emotions emerge and are entangled, in no particular order. This circuit is useful in interpreting how the fashion brands in this research emerged and continue to create products for the queer and trans communities to negotiate their identities via dress.

Fashioning Queer and Trans Identities in a Western Context: A Selection of Nuances spanning the Nineteenth Century to the Present[1]

Mainstream media perpetuates so many stereotypes as to how queer and trans folks negotiate their identities via dress, such as the butch lesbian who wears Birkenstocks or the lipstick lesbian who dresses in a high femme style. In a study of popular press articles in the United States spanning from the 1960s to the 2010s, my colleague and I observed that these publications predominantly portrayed lesbian aesthetics and styles as white, slender, and feminine (Reddy-Best and Jones 2020). This representation lacked the complexity and diversity of styles that actual lesbian-identifying women have adopted throughout history. Notably, these mainstream depictions were lacking in the intricacies, conflicts, and the wide array of styles embraced by lesbian communities. However, much scholarship exists to debunk these stereotypes.

For instance, historical evidence of Western women embracing unique styles within same-gender relationships can be traced back to the eighteenth century. Wilson (2013) notes that Eleanor Butler and Sarah Ponsonby, Anglo-Irish aristocrats

---

[1] In this section, I primarily focus on fashioning women, people assigned female at birth, trans, and nonbinary folks. Of note is that there is significant literature on gay men's fashion (e.g., Cole 2000, 2023), which is important, yet I do not engage with it deeply due to the scope of this research.

believed to be romantically involved, defied societal norms by regularly wearing masculine riding habits. In her diaries, Anne Lister, a late nineteenth-century wealthy woman from Yorkshire, UK, documented her desires and relationships with "mannish women," embracing an unconventional masculine fashion. In the 1928 novel *The Well of Loneliness*, Radclyffe Hall portrayed a lesbian identity through a white masculine aesthetic. Rolley (1990) documented how Radclyffe Hall and her lover Una Troubridge, both born in the late nineteenth century into white upper-class families, challenged traditional gender norms in their dress. Their wealth, Rolley described, contributed to their ability to "disregard public opinion and appear together in clothes which announced, to an informed viewer, their respective roles within a lesbian relationship" (55). Additionally, photographs from the 1920s captured women at Le Monocle, a lesbian club in Paris, showcasing white-appearing women adopting the fashionable *garçonne* look, characterized by short hair and absence of feminine curves, as well as those embracing highly feminine styles with bias-cut dresses, makeup, and longer hair (Wilson 2013). Around the same time, Gladys Bentley, a musician, pioneering drag king performer, openly lesbian in the early years of her life, and Black woman, often dressed in masculine aesthetics including her iconic look with a top hat and tuxedo (Figure 1.1) (National Museum of African American History & Culture n.d.). The concept of distinct lesbian dress aesthetics, often referred to as *butch* and *femme*, gained prominence in 1940s American bar culture, as explored by Faderman (1991). Leslie Feinberg's historical fiction novel, *Stone Butch Blues* (1993), based on the author's own experiences, vividly described the mid-twentieth-century identities of butches and femmes, including bar culture, when the main character, Jess, shares experiences seeing burly women dating feminine women in high heels.

Rothblum (1994) has highlighted that lesbian communities developed distinct styles and aesthetics that set them apart from mainstream society. One notable manifestation of this divergence is the adoption and negotiation of the masculine, butch aesthetic. This masculine-lesbian style, recognizable within and outside the lesbian community, includes elements like comfortable shoes, minimal or no makeup, tattoos, piercings, unconventional hairstyles or colors, and clothing and accessories with masculine leanings (Clarke and Turner 2007; Esterberg 1996; Reddy-Best and Pedersen 2014, 2015; Rothblum 1994, 2010).

Despite the tendency to view various lesbian styles, including the butch aesthetic, as uniform, women adopt masculine styles in nuanced and diverse ways (Levitt and Hiestand 2004; McLean 2008). For instance, Reddy-Best and Goodin's (2020) research highlighted Cyndi, a white lesbian woman from Iowa, who identified as soft butch despite her masculine-leaning appearance (Figure 1.2 and Figure 1.3). Blake (2019) explored androgynous Black lesbians in North Carolina, refraining from essentializing their style as "Black lesbian" but instead conceptualizing it as "BlaQueer Style" (11). This approach acknowledges the nuanced racial and class politics inherent in this attire. Lane-Steele (2011) delves into the world of studs, Black lesbians embracing masculinity, and noted their sartorial choices mirroring those of their Black male counterparts—characterized by baggy clothing, hats, high-top shoes, Timberland

Figure 1.1 Black and white photographic postcard of the singer and musician Gladys Bentley dressed in a men's white tuxedo and white top hat, holding a cane at her side tucked under her arm, *c.* 1927–45. Collection of the Smithsonian National Museum of African American History and Culture. Photo is in the public domain.

Figure 1.2 Cyndi fixing furniture in the garage, 1997. Photo courtesy of Cyndi.

boots, and flashy jewelry. Lane-Steele draws parallels between these women's styles and "protest masculinity," a concept Connell and Messerschmidt (2009) have defined as a form of masculinity emerging in local working-class contexts. This manifestation, lacking the economic resources and institutional authority of mainstream masculinities, often takes shape through hypermasculine aesthetics, as observed in the fashion choices of these Black lesbian women.

Furthermore, extensive research has focused on feminine-leaning aesthetics, often categorized as femme, high-femme, or lipstick lesbian styles or identities. Women adopting these feminine-leaning lesbian styles may opt for long hair, makeup, and clothing such as dresses or high heels (Hemmings 1999; Levitt, Gerrish, and Hiestand 2003; Levitt and Hiestand 2004; Levitt and Horne 2002; Maltry and Tucker 2002). Due to the enduring connection between femininity and heterosexuality, feminine-leaning lesbians are frequently misidentified as heterosexual (Huxley, Clarke, and Halliwell 2014; Levitt, Gerrish, and Hiestand 2003), leading to challenges within the LGBTQ+ community where people sometimes face accusations of not being "queer enough" (Reddy-Best and Goodin 2020). Some of these individuals conceal their lesbian identities until they are physically present with a masculine-leaning partner (Rossiter 2016).

While many individuals embrace these stereotypical aesthetics, others have substantially critiqued and rejected these styles. As social movements gained momentum in the latter part of the twentieth century, criticism arose against both feminine- and masculine-leaning aesthetics for perpetuating heteronormative

Figure 1.3 Cyndi before going to work wearing a masculine-leaning style, *c.* 2017. Photo courtesy of Cyndi.

performances (Walker 1993). In Freitas, Kaiser, and Hammidi's 1996 study, participants expressed their reluctance to confine themselves to a single style. Hammidi and Kaiser (1999) proposed that there is no singular definition of beauty for lesbian women, emphasizing that these negotiations are intertwined with ambivalence and tensions in everyday life. This sentiment was highlighted in a recent *New*

York Times article, "Lesbians Invented Hipsters," in which the author lamented, "You're all lesbians now, America ... I'm sorry. But mostly for myself. Because it's hard to tell who's queer now" (Burton 2016, paras. 23 and 25), underscoring the evolving complexity of queer identities in contemporary society.

Several scholars have delved into the unique ways individuals identifying as bisexual negotiate their identity through their choice of clothing. Taub (2003) surveyed predominantly white, bisexual women, revealing a diverse range of strategies they employed to navigate societal gender norms and stereotypical lesbian appearance ideals. While some rejected mainstream norms and developed their own empowering beauty practices, others felt compelled to adhere to lesbian norms, such as the soft butch aesthetic (21).

In Hartman's (2013) interviews with mostly white, bisexual women, participants expressed a strong desire to be visibly bisexual in public, combating what they perceived as societal invisibility, often termed *bi-erasure*. These individuals used terms like *attitude* and *androgyny* and a blend of heterosexual and homosexual aesthetics to describe a bisexual identity, emphasizing the significance of style in negotiating gender. They utilized overt pride symbols, such as pins or slogan T-shirts in bi-pride colors (pink, blue, and purple), to assert their identities. Although these participants used specific aesthetics to highlight their bisexuality, they also acknowledged the complexity of encapsulating such descriptions (Hartman 2013). Similarly, various researchers noted a lack of distinct dress aesthetics for bisexual individuals (Clarke and Spence 2013; Clarke and Turner 2007; Hayfield 2011; Hayfield et al. 2013; Holliday 1999; Huxley, Clarke, and Halliwell 2014).

Hartman-Linck (2014) emphasized the importance of bisexual signifiers in intimate spaces like among close friends or family. Participants used, for example, home aesthetics, such as magnets or artwork featuring lesbian symbols, to signify their identities. While these items aren't traditional "hand-held objects" (Roach-Higgins & Eicher 1992: 1), they can be considered extensions of the body within these private spheres, thus certainly related to dress.

A study by Daly, King, and Yeadon-Lee (2018) further explored the appearance and dress choices of bisexual women. Similar to findings in previous research, the markers of appearance among bisexual participants often aligned with stereotypical lesbian aesthetics (or masculine-leaning styles), or they adopted mainstream gender norms by incorporating feminine elements. The gender of the participants' partners frequently influenced their style choices; for instance, some women in same-gender relationships embraced feminine aesthetics to avoid being assumed lesbians. This underscores the intricate interplay between bisexuality, gender expression, and societal perceptions.

The attire of trans and nonbinary (TNB) individuals is often a complex interplay between conforming to cisgender stereotypes, aiming to pass, or challenge traditional notions of femininity and masculinity to present a visible TNB identity. Expressions that defy binary gender constructs by blending or negating feminine and masculine aesthetics are often interchangeably labeled as genderqueer, genderfuck, genderless, nonbinary, or unisex (Beemyn 2015). TNB individuals have diverse motivations; some strive for a more cisgender appearance ("passing"), while others emphasize their TNB identity (Allen 2010). Additionally, TNB individuals consistently navigate their gender presentation, engaging in shape-shifting, altering their appearance based on the context (McGuire et al. 2016). Numerous factors influence these choices. Some may prefer cisgender appearance for correct gender recognition and/or to avoid potentially unsafe situations (Schrock, Boyd, and Leaf 2009; Snorton 2009). Conversely, appearing visibly TNB allows individuals to challenge cultural assumptions about gender and promote visibility. Clothing choices serve multiple purposes, such as camouflaging body parts incongruent with one's gender identity or accentuating parts aligning with it, with various motivations to reveal and/or conceal body parts—such as safety, comfort, and feeling authentic to the self (McGuire et al. 2016; Reddy-Best et al. 2023b; Reilly, Catalpa, and McGuire 2019).

Researchers McGuire and Reilly (2022) developed an "aesthetic identity" framework, incorporating aesthetic, gender, and human development theories to study TNB clothing choices. This model encompasses performativity and safety aspects; sensory, cognitive, and emotional aspects of clothing; exploration and commitment; scaffolding and feedback; and role-making and role-taking. As individuals mature in their gender identities, their aesthetic identities consolidate, shaping their placement within gender roles assigning meaning to those roles for themselves and others.

Rahilly (2015) pointed out that TNB individuals often face discomfort when wearing clothing due to physical or psychological reasons. While this observation mainly involved white participants, the sentiment may resonate across various racial and cultural backgrounds. Ready-to-wear clothing designed for cisgender bodies often fails to meet TNB individuals' functional and aesthetic needs. Reilly, Catalpa, and McGuire (2019) identified three common themes associated with TNB individuals' clothing preferences: issues with fit, cut, and sizing in mainstream ready-to-wear clothing; the desire to conceal body parts revealing TNB identities; and the desire to showcase body parts, either to celebrate their forms or mark bodily changes post-gender confirmation treatment. These themes were consistent among diverse racial and ethnic groups.

Dress choices hold significant meaning for TNB individuals. According to Catalpa and McGuire (2020), clothing plays a pivotal role in Serano's (2007) "mirror epiphany," representing the first conscious connection between how trans individuals imagine themselves and the physical reality of their presence. Additionally, tattoos can serve as a form of self-acceptance, a means to connect with their bodies, mark their identity, or celebrate physical changes (McGuire et al. 2016; McGuire and Chrisler 2016). These diverse forms of self-expression underscore the intricate relationships among identity, appearance, and clothing in TNB individuals.

In addition to the various identity intersections influencing dress, clothing has also played a crucial role in LGBTQ+ activism in North America from the mid-twentieth century to the present day. Many styles that LGBTQ+ individuals adopt can be viewed as forms of activism, challenging societal norms and expressing unique identities. For instance, in the 1950s, the butch style subverted the expectation that women had to be gentle and feminine (Stein 1998). The femme/butch dynamic, prominent since the late nineteenth century, declined in the 1970s as some feminists criticized it for mirroring heterosexual dynamics (Blackman and Perry 1990). During this period, lesbian revolutionary feminists rejected traditional fashion, associating makeup, high heels, and formfitting dresses with heteropatriarchal femininity and capitalism, distancing themselves from these symbols both visually and ideologically (Clark 1995; Stein 1998). A more ascetic style became popular among white lesbian feminists, while lesbian feminists of color incorporated racial or ethnic dress from their cultures as statements of activism. Despite the dominance of ascetic aesthetics, butch and femme presentations persisted. Femmes, in particular, faced criticism for passing, yet many used their femininity strategically for safety and to infiltrate traditionally heterosexual spaces (Blackman and Perry 1990). Following the decline of women's liberation, lesbian feminists diversified their styles, embracing punk, roots, and sadism/masochism.

The 1980s and 1990s saw a new trend in LGBTQ+ activist dress triggered by the AIDS crisis. ACT UP, for example, used slogan T-shirts as powerful visual tools to attract media attention for HIV/AIDS issues. Slogan T-shirts, often featuring upside-down triangles, became emblematic of LGBTQ+ activism, representing solidarity. The pink triangle, a symbol of oppression during the Nazi regime, was reclaimed by the LGBTQ+ community and incorporated into activism, including graduation stoles for lavender graduation ceremonies, ceremonies specifically for LGBTQ+ graduating students (Katz 2013; Lautmann 1981; Reddy-Best and Goodin 2020).

In the twenty-first century, queer and trans activist dress is heavily influenced by the oppression generated by neoliberalism and the new Right in the United States. Activist fashion is approached through a "hacking" lens, allowing individuals, particularly those with multiple marginalized identities, to express their identities through garments. For instance, queer and trans high school students have participated in workshops where they refashioned garments to reclaim derogatory terms and assert their identities (Barry and Drak 2019). Moreover, the rise of online platforms has allowed LGBTQ+ activists to sell clothing and accessories, fostering a sense of community and solidarity among diverse identities.

The literature described in this subsection highlights the varied and nuanced ways that folks in the queer and trans communities fashion their bodies. It emphasizes the need that some queer and trans fashion brand owners noticed in the market and built their companies around. It also highlights some of the complexities of considering building a fashion brand for queer and trans consumers. Additionally, all the research focuses mostly on consumption and regulation (formal and informal influences on what people wear and why they wear it) and, thus, I sought to view these dress perspectives from other parts of the fashion system (e.g., production, distribution via fashion brands).

2 Political Landscapes and So-Called Heteronormative Ideals

To contextualize the surge of queer and trans fashion brands in the 2010s, I focus on the twentieth- and twenty-first-century political landscape in the United States. I highlight various milestones, trends, and practices contributing to the industry's heteronormative nature, alongside how queer designers intersect with the fashion system.

The Revolution of the Queer and Trans Landscape in the United States: A Brief Overview

From colonization until the early 1970s, queer and trans rights in the United States were virtually nonexistent, even though many queer people lived their lives and often signaled their queer identities via dressing and appearing (Chauncey 1994). In the late nineteenth century, as urban centers became increasingly populated, many Americans became concerned about upholding morals in these new frontiers. Several cities adopted penal codes criminalizing behaviors associated with so-called sexual deviance (Eskridge 2007). Some of these included sodomy laws, which made oral and anal penetration illegal. By the 1960s, every state had some form of sodomy law. Unequal enforcement typically discriminated against men who had sex with men, and some states only criminalized sodomy between gay couples (McHugh 2014). Some states had arrested folks for wearing clothes outside their gender norms. For instance, in San Francisco in the nineteenth century, police arrested folks such as John Roberts for cross-dressing or wearing "female attire" (Sears 2015: 1). In response to these and many other social injustices, activists in Los Angeles in the 1950s formed the Mattachine Society, a part of the broader homophile movement; these activists sought to change the public perception of gays and lesbians. At the same time, Christine Jorgensen became one of the early publicly visible trans people in the United States. Jorgensen and the homophile movement sparred, each believing that they threatened one another's respectability and momentum (Schilt 2009). Although it unified gays and lesbians, by the mid-1960s, the movement had crumbled, due to warring ideologies.

In 1969, the Stonewall Riots broke out at the eponymous gay bar in New York City's Greenwich Village, igniting a new wave of activism. In the mid-twentieth century, police commonly raided mafia-run gay bars, fined them for something trivial, and arrested patrons, usually targeting transgender individuals, drag queens, and people of color. On June 27, 1969, patrons fought back against police in an effort led by two trans women of color, triggering three days of violent rioting (Coke 2020). Scholars credit the Stonewall Riots with sparking the lesbian, gay, bisexual, and transgender (LGBT) rights movement in the United States and the Gay Liberation Front (GLF) formed in its wake. GLF activists fought along with leaders of other social movements for equality; however, tensions rose between movements (Mirola 2007). For example, one of the women's liberation movement leaders, Betty Friedan, regarded lesbians as the "lavender menace" that would discourage her own movement's momentum (Brown 1998).

The 1970s showed significant improvement for queer and trans rights. Then, in 1981, medical professionals documented the first case of HIV/AIDS, sparking an epidemic that eventually killed millions of people in the queer and trans communities. HIV/AIDS spread quickly, and fear and miscommunication about the disease led to stigmatization of people living with HIV/AIDS. Lack of understanding and the modes of transmission fueled discrimination and prejudice against queer and trans individuals. The US government slowed response to the AIDS crisis once scientists discovered the disease often was spread through sexual transmission (Brier 2004). Activists sought to end the AIDS epidemic and formed ACT UP (AIDS Coalition to Unleash Power), which used direct-action tactics to spread public awareness and place pressure on the government to make changes (Greenberg 1992). Activists pressured pharmaceutical companies to make lifesaving medications more accessible. Eventually, medical research transformed HIV/AIDS from a death sentence to a manageable chronic condition, for those with access to treatment. The AIDS crisis had a profound impact on the queer and trans communities. It took the lives of many LGBTQ+ individuals, including prominent figures in the arts and in activism. Entire social circles were decimated, leaving deep emotional scars. The crisis also galvanized the LGBTQ+ community to fight for their rights and access to healthcare. Yet, it strengthened the sense of community and solidarity among queer people, leading to significant social and political change (Carter 2004).

In the late twentieth and early twenty-first centuries, activists achieved major advances for queer and trans rights, providing much visibility for these communities. For example, in 1993, President Clinton approved a bill commonly known as "Don't Ask, Don't Tell" (DADT), which lifted the ban on queer people serving in the military, as long as they did not disclose their sexuality; however, legal scholars argued DADT was a First Amendment violation (Wolff 1997). By 2008, more than twelve thousand service members had been discharged as a result of DADT; in 2011, President Obama repealed the bill. During the Obama administration, trans people also gained the right to serve in the military; however, in 2017, President Trump announced he was reversing this law (Jackson and Kube 2019). In 2020, the House of Representatives voted to overturn Trump's bill (Artavia 2020). After Joe Biden took office in 2021, he signed an executive order preventing discrimination based upon gender or sexual identity (Sadeghi 2021).

There has also been much legislation surrounding same-sex marriage. For instance, in 1996, Hawai'i became the first state to legalize same-sex marriage. In response, conservative politicians across the country advocated against this legislation. The United States passed the Defense of Marriage Act (DOMA) that same year, legally defining marriage as a union between a man and a woman, which allowed states to reject same-sex marriage (Barrow and Allen 2014); in 2013, the US Supreme Court overturned DOMA (Peralta 2013). A pivotal moment came in 2015, when the Supreme Court's ruling in *Obergefell v. Hodges* legalized same-sex marriage across the nation, granting LGBTQ+ couples the right to marry in all fifty states. This historic decision marked a watershed moment in the fight for marriage equality. However, progress has been uneven across states since this ruling. While many states have implemented comprehensive antidiscrimination laws that protect LGBTQ+ individuals, others still lack these vital safeguards. Several states, notably California, New York, and Illinois, have passed inclusive laws that prohibit discrimination based on sexual orientation and gender identity in employment, housing, and public accommodations. In contrast, states like Mississippi and North Carolina faced controversies and legal battles over laws that were perceived as discriminatory, such as North Carolina's bathroom bill, which required transgender individuals to use public restrooms corresponding to the sex on their birth certificates (Miller 2017).

On the healthcare front, strides have been made in transgender rights. States like Oregon and California have expanded Medicaid coverage to include gender-affirming procedures, ensuring that essential healthcare services are accessible to transgender individuals. Furthermore, efforts to ban conversion therapy have gained traction, with states like New York and Illinois enacting laws to protect minors from this harmful practice (Gold 2019; Gomez et al. 2022).

In education, progress has been visible in several states. Schools in states such as Massachusetts have implemented comprehensive anti-bullying programs that specifically address LGBTQ+ students' needs, creating safer environments (Massachusetts Commission on LGBTQ Youth 2023). Moreover, LGBTQ+ representation in politics has increased, with openly LGBTQ+ individuals holding public offices in states like Wisconsin, contributing to more diverse and inclusive policymaking (LGBTQ+ Victory Fund 2023). However, setbacks persist. Some states have introduced legislation undermining transgender rights, particularly concerning participation in school sports (Barnes 2023). The federal landscape has also been challenging, with ongoing debates over the rights of LGBTQ+ individuals in areas like healthcare, adoption, and military service.

While there have been significant achievements, the fight for LGBTQ+ rights in the United States remains multifaceted and varies greatly by state. Prioritizing LGBTQ+ folks and their needs are still urgent given their heightened suicide rates (King et al. 2008; The Williams Institute 2021a, 2023) and in particular, the heightened violence, rape, and assault experienced by trans folks (The Williams Institute 2021b). Additionally, Dinno (2017) reported that in the United States between 2010 and 2014, transfeminine Black and Latina folks were "almost certainly more likely to be murdered than were their cisfeminine comparators" (1446). The US pro-queer and trans legislation has improved mostly the lives of young, white gay men in positions of privilege (Johnson 2019). For example, the various movements typically neglect priorities for elderly people, such as social isolation and ageing-related healthcare needs (Knauer 2019). Activists also have largely ignored the needs of queer and trans people of color; for example, Black queer men have the highest rates of HIV/AIDS diagnoses in the United States and are routinely discriminated against in gay establishments (Johnson 2019; Wolitski 2018). Overall, the longstanding context of oppression from which these queer and trans fashion brands and retailers in this research emerged is of great importance in demonstrating their revolutionary status and business practices arguably rooted in activist ideologies.

The Dominant, So-Called Heteronormative Western Fashion System: A Selective History

The queer and trans fashion brands in this research are also entrenched in the dominant fashion system. The history of the North American fashion system largely, and arguably almost entirely, demonstrates adherence to so-called heteronormative ideals and norms mirroring the discrimination in the broader society, despite the significant presence of LGBTQ+ designers, models, journalists, photographers, and stylists (Brown 2019; Steele 2013). That is, evidence suggests that since at least the eighteenth century, the man-milliner, or the "men in the fashion trades, who made, decorated, and/or sold dresses, hats, and other fashionable items of women's clothing," laid the foundation for the stereotypical fashion designer across the globe as a gay man (Steele 2013: 15). Fast forward to 2013: walking into a clothing store, you are most certainly going to find binary gender categories for apparel, shoes, and accessories in separate sections of the store, despite the LGBTQ+ community's continued influence on the fashion industry. This binary rigidity has been present in much of the production and distribution of fashion throughout nineteenth-century Western history to the present, with, of course, numerous exceptions. Again, here the focus is on the Western context, and these gender norms vary widely throughout the globe (Anawalt 2007).

The history of sizing systems illuminates the heavy emphasis on binary clothing categories (men and women, girls and boys, etc.). In the nineteenth century, most clothing for women was made by women either at home or by seamstresses, whereas tailors, who were men, produced much of men's clothing. Due to the growth of the textile industry and the invention of the sewing machine in the mid-1800s, the concept of ready-to-wear gained traction as the production of standardized sizes and patterns became more feasible, allowing for the mass production of garments (Tortora and Marcketti 2021). Documented evidence suggests garment makers developed patterns as early as the fifteenth century, yet they contained minimal information beyond basic pattern shapes; for instance, they lacked pattern labels, instructional text, and sometimes whole patterns pieces necessary to create the garment (Moore 2020). In the United States, patterns with sizing were available as early as the 1860s (Kidwell 1979). However, these systems were not based on body measurements or anthropometric data (Schofield and LaBat 2005). Documented nineteenth-century evidence related to childrenswear also illuminates how twenty-first-century concepts of gender and color differ, as, for instance young boys often wore pink and dresses (Paoletti 2012; Reddy-Best 2020a).

The Civil War generated much demand for standardized uniforms, as the North and South needed over a million uniforms a year for the men on active duty. To help the mass production of these uniforms, the military collected body measurement statistics on male bodies, which influenced development of the ready-to-wear industry. In 1941, the US Department of Agriculture sponsored the nation's first anthropometric survey of women. Statistical averages based on ten thousand women in sixty different locations were used to create standard size specifications for women's patterns and apparel. This standardization in part sped up production and the amount of products available to purchase, thus more consumer spending (Mullet et al. 2009). Certainly, there are differences in the bodies of people assigned female and male at birth, and these differences are reflected in these early anthropometric surveys and thus the patterns used to create ready-to-wear clothing. These early categorizations reflect then-prominent notions of the binary gender, despite evidence of gender-pushing boundaries being adopted by gender nonconforming individuals (e.g., Oscar Wilde, male aesthetes, and Armande Braizer) (Steele 2013).

In the late nineteenth century, department stores, such as Macy's and Marshall Field's, emerged and revolutionized the retail experience; they offered a wide variety of goods under one roof, including gendered ready-to-wear clothing, making shopping more convenient for consumers (Tortora and Marcketti 2015). The early twentieth century also saw the rise of companies selling via mail-order catalogs, such as the national Sears, Roebuck & Co., which offered a wide range of ready-to-wear clothing options, with separate sections for men and women. Development of the assembly line further streamlined production processes, making ready-to-wear garments more affordable and accessible to people at varying socioeconomic statuses.

Specialty clothing stores catering to specific demographics or fashion niches began to emerge in the early twentieth century. The Great Depression of the 1930s had a significant impact on consumer spending, leading to the rise of discount stores and thrift shops where people could find affordable clothing. In the mid- to late 1940s, the American economy experienced a post-Second World War boom, leading to increased consumer spending and, in part, the rise of indoor shopping malls. Malls became popular one-stop-shops, social destinations for suburban consumers, housing a variety of clothing stores and other retail outlets with numerous ready-to-wear options. These ready-to-wear options proliferated due to many technological developments, including patternmaking and sizing systems (Moore 2020; Tortora and Marcketti 2015). At this time, most American fashion designers worked for ready-to-wear manufacturers and produced lines for each season (fall, winter, spring, summer). Local stores sent buyers to New York to place orders, which were then sent to production and shipped out for consumers to buy off the rack (Tortora and Marcketti 2015).

In this first half of the twentieth century, numerous high-profile men in the fashion industry identified as gay or bisexual, yet they rarely disclosed these identities. For instance, designers such as Christian Dior, Cristóbal Balenciaga, and Charles James were known to identify as gay, yet James was the only one who openly discussed his homosexuality (Steele 2013). These designers, though, worked in the French couture system, creating the highest quality garments sold to private, often wealthy, consumers and other fashion industry segments who could then copy the designs. Gay couturiers like these, along with their clothing, had a profound impact on the elite, and their influence extended significantly throughout the international fashion scene (Tortora and Marcketti 2015).

The 1960s and 1970s saw the emergence of youth-oriented fashion stores, reflecting the changing cultural and social norms of the time. That is, streetstyle flourished as young people began identifying with counterculture movements (Polhemus 1994; Tortora and Marcketti 2015). Different fashion market segments proliferated as more options were available on the market. Until this point, most American designers remained anonymous, with exceptions—for example, Claire McCardell and Norman Norell—yet now consumers sought specific designer names. With the significant social changes, some well-known fashion designers, such as Rudi Gernreich, introduced unisex fashions including the monokini (Paoletti 2015). The monokini had a bikini bottom with two thin straps, exposing the chest of any gender that wore the swimsuit. Gernreich identified as gay and cofounded the Mattachine Society; however, due to fear of discrimination against LGBTQ+ communities, he resigned from the organization in 1953 and did not come out publicly about his sexuality until just before his death (Steele 2013). Additionally, the peacock revolution of the 1960s marked a turning point in menswear from somber to bright and colorful, which many gay men contributed to. Boutiques such as Vince Man's Shop in lower Manhattan emerged and embraced homoerotic advertisements and fashion promotions (Steele 2013). Luis Estévez, a Cuban American designer who experienced great success from the 1950s to the 1990s, like James was open about identifying as bisexual, and one of only a select few who did so at the time (Simon and Reddy-Best 2024).

In the 1980s, catalog companies and malls thrived, boosting sales for large department stores and specialty chains (Farrell-Beck and Parsons 2007). The late twentieth century witnessed the rapid expansion of national retail chains such as Walmart, Target, and The Gap. These stores offered affordable and fashionable clothing to a wide range of consumers, leading to the decline of many small independent retailers. Computer technology revolutionized much of the world including aspects of the fashion industry. Developers invented the internet in 1977, which would significantly change the future clothing and accessory retail landscape (Tarnoff 2016). Online clothing stores which became increasingly popular, allowed consumers to shop from the comfort of their homes. Ecommerce quickly became a large part of retail sales (Singh 2019). Part of ecommerce's appeal is that it facilitates "communicating electronically, getting collaborated with a third party and discovering information to develop its own business" (Singh 2019: 30). Customers could now purchase on demand, and more brands were selling direct-to-consumer, omitting the need for brick-and-mortar stores or wholesale-buyer pitches (Worsley 2011). In the mid-1990s, Land's End was one of the initial retailers to enter the ecommerce business model (Tortora and Marcketti 2015).

During the 1980s and 1990s, the AIDS epidemic, sometimes referred to as the "gay plague" devastated the fashion industry. Major designers—such as Perry Ellis and Willie Smith—died from the disease (Steele 2013). Investors looking to back fashion businesses frequently desired that male designers be screened for AIDS. They viewed male designers as significantly risky; thus, many bankers sought "safer" options, or firms headed by women (Tortora and Marcketti 2015).

In the 1990s, home-shopping television channels and e-tailing flourished, prompting many department stores to remain competitive by offering new channels (Farrell-Beck and Parsons 2007). Additionally, the late twentieth century and early twenty-first century saw the globalization of fashion, largely due to increased communication from the internet, and the proliferation of fast-fashion retailers. Fast-fashion brands rapidly produce inexpensive, trendy clothing, catering to ever-changing consumer tastes and desires for more products. Certainly, much of fashion catered to binary genders, yet a few emerging designers began challenging this rigidity. For example, Martin Margiela, among other Belgian designers, produced avant-garde aesthetics rooted in challenging heteronormative silhouettes (Brajato 2020, 2023; Reddy-Best and Burns 2013). Similarly, high-profile designers from Japan, including Rei Kawakubo and Yohji Yamamoto, challenged binary gender oppositions (Mears 2008).

At the beginning of the twenty-first century, niche fashion brands such as Hot Topic and Abercrombie & Fitch proliferated (Farrell-Beck and Parsons 2007). After the 2008 financial crisis, though, many nascent or struggling brands turned to crowdfunding (Best and Neiss 2014) Entrepreneurs launched the crowdfunding platform Kickstarter in 2009, allowing anyone to contribute money toward small businesses' goals. Simultaneously, social media became a part of Americans' everyday lives with the introduction and spread of Facebook starting in 2004, followed by numerous other platforms, such as Instagram and Twitter (now X), allowing the public easy access to Kickstarter campaigns (Best and Neiss 2014; Curtin 2018). Betabrand, a San Francisco-based clothing company, was an early adopter of crowdsourcing and flourished by using it as a central component of its business model. Instead of the traditional product-development process, where designers produce lines that are then sold to the consumer through targeted marketing, Betabrand started with the consumer to co-create products, with consumers voting on potential products and financially contributing to their creation (Dishman 2020). In the 2010s and into the

2020s, the United States boasted a diverse and dynamic retail industry, with a wide array of clothing stores catering to different tastes, styles, and budgets.

Despite the fashion industry's long history, however, and how interwoven LGBTQ+ community members were and are in the system, so much, not all of course, of the industry remains rooted in heteronormative practices.

3 Gay Window Advertising and Capitalist Entanglements

Next, I explore the intersections of gay window advertising, capitalism, and LGBTQ+ identities. From Absolut vodka's daring campaigns featuring artists like Keith Haring to Subaru's subtle nods to queer culture, I delve into how mainstream brands strategically incorporate queer imagery to appeal to both queer and heterosexual consumers. Through case studies and analyses, I shed light on the evolving landscape of consumer culture and its entanglements with commodity activism and neoliberal capitalism.

Gay Window Advertising: Vodka, Cars, and Fashion

Since the late twentieth century, some mainstream brands have subtly embraced queer and trans communities through strategic advertising known as gay window advertising, employing homoerotic imagery to appeal to queer and trans consumers while remaining innocuous to heterosexual consumers (Brownski 1984; Kaiser 2021). This tactic emerged in the 1980s during heightened LGBTQ+ visibility and activism, aiming to tap into identified queer and trans markets for capitalist gain (Sender 1999). Notably, these early ad campaigns coincided with significant political turmoil for the LGBTQ+ community, such as the DADT and DOMA legislation, preceding major television visibility like Ellen DeGeneres' coming out in 1997 (Rothman 2022).

In the 1980s, Absolut vodka targeted the queer community with full-page ads in queer-focused publications and featured the work of gay artist Keith Haring in mainstream ads (D'Auklaire 2020). Similarly, United Colors of Benetton challenged societal norms with provocative ads in the 1990s, including one depicting an interracial lesbian family, avoiding overt sexualization or fetishization common in earlier media attempts at queer representation (Figure 3.1) (Duffy 2017).

Subaru subtly incorporated LGBTQ+ messaging into its marketing, gaining a strong following within the LGBTQ+ community, particularly among lesbians, through coded messages in advertisements. For instance, in the 1990s, it included subtle coded messages on the license plates of the cars in its advertisements, such as "P-TOWN" for Provincetown, a popular queer destination on Cape Cod, Massachusetts, and "XENA LVR" referring to the popular television show *Xena: Warrior Princess* which many lesbians loved (Cummings 2016). Kmart also utilized queer-coded imagery in a 1996 ad featuring Rosie O'Donnell, sparking ambiguity about the nature of relationships. Mainstream brands like Calvin Klein and Abercrombie &

Figure 3.1 United Colors of Benetton Fall/Winter 1990s advertisement. Photo courtesy of Oliviero Toscani Studio.

Fitch targeted young, white, gay men with erotic male imagery in the 1990s, despite denying homoerotic intentions, resonating with many gay consumers (Givhan 1998; Varangis et al. 2012).

These examples shed light on the complex relationship between consumer culture, branding, and queer identities. They emphasize how certain brands and products can become associated with queer identity and community, highlighting the significance of consumption practices as a form of self-expression and cultural identification within the LGBTQ+ community. That is, queer individuals engage with these mainstream consumer goods and brands, finding meaning, affirmation, and connection in unexpected places within the consumer landscape. These negotiations became more complex as numerous brands began openly "embracing" the LGBTQ+ via questionable marketing practices.

Entanglements in Commodity Activism, Corporate Pride, and Neoliberal Capitalism

Although seemingly a progressive step, gay window advertising also reveals important entanglements with commodity activism (Mukherjee and Banet-Weiser 2012) and corporate pride illuminating the complex interplay between consumer choices and corporate strategies. As society grapples with these complexities, fostering genuine social change necessitates a collective effort from consumers, corporations, and policymakers. That is, corporations have increasingly capitalized on the visibility and marketability of queer identities, using rainbow-colored products and marketing campaigns to align themselves with the LGBTQ+ community during Pride Month (e.g., Abad-Santos 2018; Riedel 2022). Yet, numerous tensions and contradictions arise from these entanglements (e.g., Lodewick 2022). Overall, the commodification of LGBTQ+ identities and activism has become intertwined with neoliberal capitalist structures.

Neoliberal capitalism, often referred to simply as neoliberalism, is an economic and political ideology that emerged in the mid-twentieth century and gained prominence in the following decades (Cahill and Konings 2017). At its core, neoliberalism advocates for minimal government intervention in the economy and emphasizes the importance of free markets, private enterprise, and individual entrepreneurship. Proponents of neoliberal capitalism believe that unrestricted competition and the pursuit of self-interest lead to economic efficiency, innovation, and overall prosperity. This ideology promotes policies such as deregulation, privatization, and reductions in government spending and taxation. Neoliberalism also emphasizes the significance of globalization, encouraging the free flow of goods, services, and capital across borders.

Critics argue that neoliberal policies often exacerbate income inequality, undermine workers' rights, and prioritize corporate interests over social welfare. The debate around neoliberal capitalism continues to shape economic policies and discussions on a global scale. The multifaceted criticisms of neoliberal capitalism have been articulated by numerous scholars, economists, and social activists. Neoliberal policies, by emphasizing minimal state intervention, often lead to deregulation and tax cuts for the wealthy and corporations, contributing to a growing wealth gap between the rich and the poor. Critics argue that this exacerbates social tensions and reduces social mobility, making it harder for individuals from disadvantaged backgrounds to improve their economic situations.

Labor exploitation is another significant critique. By prioritizing market efficiency, neoliberalism can lead to the erosion of workers' rights and protections. Labor unions are often weakened, and, in pursuit of cost-cutting measures, corporations may outsource jobs to countries with lower labor costs and weaker labor regulations, leading to job losses and precarious working conditions for many.

Furthermore, neoliberal policies have been blamed for financial instability. Deregulation in the financial sector, a hallmark of neoliberalism, can lead to speculative bubbles and risky financial behavior, as was evident in the 2008 global financial crisis. Critics argue that the pursuit of short-term profits can compromise the stability of the entire economic system, causing widespread suffering when crises occur. Social services and public welfare are also often negatively affected under neoliberal regimes. Privatization of essential services such as healthcare, education, and utilities can make access to these services contingent on one's ability to pay for them, leaving marginalized communities at a disadvantage. Critics contend that this approach prioritizes profit over citizens' wellbeing, leading to disparities in access to basic necessities. Additionally, neoliberalism has been accused of undermining democratic processes. The influence of powerful corporate interests, often through lobbying and campaign financing, can distort democratic decision-making, leading to policies that favor the wealthy elite at the expense of the broader population. Overall, scholars critique neoliberal capitalism for exacerbating income inequality, fostering labor exploitation, causing financial instability, undermining social services, and potentially eroding democratic values. These concerns have sparked extensive debate about the merits of neoliberal policies and their long-term impact on society and the global economy.

Within the framework of neoliberal capitalism, commodity activism thrives as corporations strategically incorporate social and political causes into their marketing strategies. Commodity activism, epitomized by the incorporation of LGBTQ+ symbols and slogans into products and advertisements, capitalizes on the visibility of these initiatives to attract socially conscious consumers. Within commodity activism, "individual consumers act politically by purchasing particular brands over others in a competitive marketplace" (Mukherjee and Banet-Weiser 2012: 40). Neoliberalism, with its emphasis on minimal state intervention and market-driven solutions, provides an environment where social causes are commodified. This commodification simplifies intricate social issues into marketable symbols, making them easily consumable. Moreover, companies integrate these symbols under the guise of corporate social responsibility, fostering a positive brand image while fulfilling their societal obligations. The concept aligns with neoliberal ideals of individual choice, presenting consumers with options that seem to reflect their values. However, this curated selection prompts critical questions about the sincerity of these efforts, raising concerns about whether such initiatives genuinely contribute to meaningful social change or are merely strategic marketing ploys.

For instance, Gebhart and Reddy-Best (2023) examined slogan T-shirts from two organizations—Raygun and For Everyone Co.—and their approaches to slogan T-shirt activism, particularly in addressing racial injustices. Raygun pursues a profit-driven model, employing catchy slogans but lacking substantial impact, while For Everyone Co. focuses on prison abolition, emphasizing specific social causes and sharing profits with aligned organizations. Their analyses critique the empathic fallacy prevalent in activist fashion, highlighting the ineffectiveness of simply changing words without substantial action. They emphasize the need for consumers to be critical and demand genuine activism from businesses and encourage consumers to consider ethical supply chains and seek out organizations dedicated to specific activist pursuits. Despite its limitations, they argue that T-shirt activism holds some potential for critical social change, offering a source of hope for transformative progress in society (Glass 2014; Kvidal-Røvik 2018).

Within the realm of neoliberal capitalism, the incorporation of LGBTQ+ themes into products and marketing campaigns is often manifest through the vibrant spectrum of rainbow merchandise flooding the market particularly during Pride Month. These products, ranging from clothing to pencils, are emblazoned with the rainbow hues symbolizing LGBTQ+ pride and unity. In the capitalist landscape, these symbols, like those analyzed in Gebhart and Reddy-Best's (2023) work, not only resonate with some members of the LGBTQ+ community but also attract allies, thereby expanding the consumer base. Neoliberalism's emphasis on individuality and personal expression finds synergy with the diverse identities celebrated through these rainbow-themed items.

Moreover, companies driven by the neoliberal ethos of maximizing profit actively promote equality by featuring LGBTQ+ couples and families in their advertisements. By doing so, these businesses seek to normalize various sexual orientations and gender identities, aligning with neoliberal capitalism's superficially inclusive narrative. This approach, while appearing progressive, is often critiqued for its commodification of social movements, hence commodity activism (Mukherjee and Banet-Weiser 2012), reducing complex LGBTQ+ issues to marketable symbols.

In the neoliberal paradigm, businesses go a step further by launching campaigns that ostensibly champion LGBTQ+ causes. They pledge support, both financial and vocal, for LGBTQ+ rights—funding organizations and sometimes leveraging their influence to shape legislation. Concurrently, corporations exploit the ethos of inclusivity by creating product lines explicitly tailored for diverse gender identities, effectively challenging conventional norms. This seemingly progressive stance aligns with neoliberal capitalism's adaptability, catering to evolving societal values while simultaneously bolstering market share.

The Dove Campaign for Real Beauty serves as an illustration of marketing strategies focused on championing justice issues. One of its primary objectives was to enhance awareness of the unrealistic beauty standards prevalent in society (Dye 2009). To accomplish this, Dove adopted a more inclusive approach by featuring diverse models in its advertisements and using commercials to educate female consumers about these unrealistic standards. However, the campaign faced significant criticism for linking beauty and self-acceptance directly to the purchase of Dove products, which led to accusations of commodification (Johnston and Taylor 2008).

Lane Bryant's #PlusIsEqual campaign shared a similar motivation for positive change but approached it a little differently. This campaign incorporated the concept of voluntary behavioral change, a characteristic observed in other social marketing initiatives (Andreasen 2003). It actively encouraged consumers to promote body positivity, engage with the movement, express their viewpoints, spread the campaign message, and even participate in mock billboard displays. Additionally, the campaign openly urged mainstream media outlets to be more inclusive of diverse body types. Harmon and Reddy-Best (2020)'s analysis of consumer responses to the campaign revealed that the concept of embracing larger body sizes as beautiful received predominantly favorable responses. This underscores the positive impact experienced by individuals, potentially those who were fat, overweight, or plus-sized, when they engaged with the campaign and encountered these models and ideas. They argued that Lane Bryant aimed to challenge societal norms by advocating for fat acceptance. Throughout history, the fashion industry has often excluded plus-size women. Lane Bryant, driven certainly by financial interests, embarked on a mission informed by sociocultural theory. Its goal was to redefine conventional beauty standards and encourage fat acceptance. The company achieved this through large-scale social marketing initiatives, promoting voluntary changes in how fat women perceive themselves and how society perceives them. On social media platforms like Twitter (now X), the campaign received positive responses from users who expressed love and admiration. Many individuals embraced self-acceptance, rejecting prevailing stereotypes that label fat people as lazy or uninterested in fashion solely based on body size. But certainly the campaign cannot be without critical examination, as Lane Bryant is a for-profit, capitalist-driven company with motivations to sell fat fashion.

Neoliberal capitalism's reliance on influencers and online platforms has also paved the way for collaborations between businesses and LGBTQ+ activists and organizations. These collaborations, often seen as authentic alliances, lend credibility to corporate inclusivity efforts. Capitalizing on the neoliberal emphasis on personal branding, businesses co-opt the credibility of LGBTQ+ influencers, leveraging their reach to promote rainbow merchandise and other LGBTQ+-themed products. This strategic alliance reinforces the products' marketability, using the influence of LGBTQ+ figures to amplify their commercial success.

Additionally, neoliberal capitalism fuels corporate sponsorships of Pride parades, events, and LGBTQ+ organizations. These sponsorships, while ostensibly fostering awareness and acceptance, are met with skepticism. Critics argue that some businesses engage in these practices primarily for profit, questioning the authenticity of their commitment to LGBTQ+ rights. Within the neoliberal framework, where profit often takes precedence over genuine social change, it becomes crucial for consumers to critically evaluate a company's actions and motives. The discerning consumer must navigate this landscape, ensuring that their support translates into meaningful social progress rather than serving as a mere cog in the marketing machinery of neoliberal capitalism.

The intersection of neoliberal capitalism, social activism, and corporate branding becomes palpable when one analyzes Nike's collaboration with Colin Kaepernick (Cobb 2018). In choosing to partner with Nike, Kaepernick's agency serves as a fascinating example of how individuals navigate the complexities of corporate activism within the framework of neoliberal capitalism. Nike's decision to feature Kaepernick—the former NFL quarterback who knelt during the national anthem to protest racial injustice and police brutality—in its "Just Do It" campaign was a bold move. This collaboration was a strategic business decision rooted in the principles of neoliberal capitalism. Nike recognized the shifting societal landscape and saw an opportunity to align itself with Kaepernick's activism, appealing to the growing consumer demand for socially conscious products and narratives.

From a neoliberal perspective, Kaepernick's agency in this collaboration is essential. Kaepernick made a deliberate choice to partner with Nike, leveraging his status as a social activist and aligning his message with the brand's ethos. In this capitalist framework, individuals are not merely passive recipients of corporate agendas; they also possess agency and can negotiate their terms of engagement with corporations. Kaepernick's decision to work with Nike allowed him to amplify his message to a broader audience, utilizing the brand's global reach and marketing prowess to bring attention to issues of racial injustice and police violence.

However, this partnership was not without controversy. While some applauded Kaepernick for his agency and Nike for taking a stance on a divisive social issue, others viewed the collaboration cynically within the context of neoliberal capitalism. They argued that Nike's support for Kaepernick was a calculated business move, tapping into the market of socially conscious consumers to boost sales (Carrington and Boykoff 2018). This perspective questioned the authenticity of the brand's support for Kaepernick's cause, highlighting the tension between genuine social activism and corporate profit motives within the neoliberal framework.

In this complex interplay, the partnership showcased the nuanced dynamics of agency. Kaepernick exercised his agency by choosing to collaborate with a powerful corporate entity, utilizing its resources to advance his activism. Simultaneously, Nike exercised its agency by strategically aligning its brand with a socially relevant cause, catering to the demands of an evolving market. This collaboration, whether seen as a genuine alliance for social change or as a shrewd marketing tactic, exemplifies the intricate relationship between individuals, corporations, and the neoliberal capitalist landscape in the realm of modern activism.

The partnership between Target and TomboyX, an LGBTQ+ underwear brand, also exemplifies the intricate dance between social activism, corporate strategy, and public reception within the context of neoliberal capitalism. Target's collaboration with TomboyX, a brand known for its gender-neutral and body-inclusive designs, is a strategic move within the retail giant's inclusive marketing efforts (Oram, n.d.a.; Riedel 2022). In this neoliberal capitalist landscape, corporations like Target actively seek partnerships with socially progressive brands to cater to diverse consumer needs and sentiments. By teaming up with TomboyX, Target aimed to align itself with the LGBTQ+ community, showcasing its commitment to inclusivity and diversity. This partnership allowed Target to tap into a market segment that valued gender-neutral and body-positive products, thereby expanding its customer base and reinforcing its image as a socially conscious retailer.

However, this collaboration was not without controversy (Riedel 2023). The conservative segment of society, often resistant to LGBTQ+ visibility, voiced their discontent. It viewed Target's association with TomboyX as a deviation from traditional norms, sparking backlash and calls for boycotts. In the realm of neoliberal capitalism, where profit margins are paramount, such reactions posed a challenge to Target's bottom line. The conservative backlash highlighted the tension between corporate inclusivity efforts and the resistance faced in a society still grappling with acceptance of LGBTQ+ identities.

Simultaneously, even within the queer and trans communities, the collaboration sparked diverse reactions (Riedel 2022; Yates 2022). While some celebrated the partnership as a step forward in normalizing gender diversity and body positivity, others voiced concerns. Some individuals criticized Target for commodifying queer and trans identities, accusing the corporation of exploiting social issues for profit. This internal critique underscored the complexities of corporate activism within the neoliberal framework, where genuine social progress often intersects with profit motives.

In this complex interplay, Target exercised its agency by choosing to partner with TomboyX, aiming to be a leader in inclusive retail practices and diversify its offerings. TomboyX, too, used its agency by aligning with a major retailer, enabling its message of inclusivity to reach a wider audience, scale its business, and increase its profits. The public's varied responses, ranging from conservative resistance to internal community critiques, illuminated the challenges and nuances of corporate activism in a neoliberal capitalist society. This partnership between Target and TomboyX serves as a microcosm of the larger socioeconomic landscape, where corporations navigate the delicate balance between profit-driven motives, social responsibility, and public perception. It exemplifies how the convergence of corporate interests and social activism in the neoliberal era triggers complex debates and discussions, shaping the trajectory of both consumer culture and societal acceptance.

4 Marketplace Influences: Politics and Technology

The early twenty-first century presented a dynamic backdrop of shifting political landscapes, technological advancements, and evolving communication platforms. Against this backdrop, these fashion brand entrepreneurs seized the opportunity to not only express their personal narratives but also leverage the broader societal shifts. The increasing visibility and acceptance of the LGBTQ+ community, coupled with the rise of social media and online platforms, provided a unique avenue for these brands to connect with local and global audiences. In navigating this cultural context, these entrepreneurs adeptly utilized technology to amplify their messages, foster community engagement, and promote a sense of belonging, thereby contributing to the broader societal discourse surrounding diversity and inclusivity.

Same-Sex Marriage, Consumerism, and Creating Space for Authentic Negotiations

The introduction of same-sex marriage in the United States has had a profound impact on countless individuals and families, granting them legal recognition, rights, and protections that were previously denied. It symbolized a shift in societal attitudes toward LGBTQ+ rights and served as a catalyst for further advancements in LGBTQ+ equality in areas such as employment, housing, and healthcare. A 2017 study uncovered that within the United States, nearly 1.1 million individuals were married in the lesbian, gay, bi-sexual, and/or transgender (LGBT) community (Romero 2017). Additionally, the count of same-sex marriages witnessed a consistent rise annually subsequent to the *Obergefell* v. *Hodges* verdict (Jones 2017). As of 2020, it was approximated that the economic upswing, amounting to $3.2 billion in the United States following the *Obergefell* v. *Hodges* enactment, resulted from the direct expenditure on weddings by same-sex couples (Mallory and Sears 2020).

Throughout the twentieth century, economic and cultural factors consistently influenced perspectives on marriage and wedding ceremonies. While the percentage of US women entering marriage steadily decreased in the second half of the century (Zagorsky 2016), the average cost or outlay for weddings rose. This surge is in part linked to advertising, print publications, broadcast media, and the social media, as well as the development of the retail wedding industry, collaborating to endorse the concept of the "flawless wedding" (Gillis 1985; Howard 2000; Otnes and Pleck 2003). More precisely, by drawing from brand management discourse, wedding media advocates the idea that weddings should be meticulously and strategically orchestrated to create a unique and flawless occasion propelled by consumption and the spectacle of consumption (Winch and Webster 2012). Contemporary Western weddings frequently embody consumption rituals or events that couples invest in to symbolize or legitimize their union; the preference for such rituals is evident in the thriving wedding industry in both the United States and the United Kingdom (Carter and Duncan 2017; Otnes and Lowrey 1993), as well as in today's pervasive media impact.

In the context of Western weddings, participants partake in symbolic consumption, where the use of products and experiences is aimed at constructing and reinforcing identity (Boden 2003; Currie 1993; Pepin et al. 2008; Piacentini and Mailer 2004; Zukin and Maguire 2004). Heterosexual wedding ceremonies often showcase the bride's identity through "lavish displays of femininity" (Pepin et al. 2008: 331), emphasizing her role as the focal point or star of the event. The portrayal of the bride's identity as feminine, the idealization of the wedding day, and the framing of wedding planning as women's work are recurring themes in bridal magazines and various media outlets. All these aspects demand significant time, effort, and financial investment (Besel et al. 2009; Boden 2003; Currie 1993). Given the emphasis on traditional gender roles in wedding ceremonies, the bride usually takes on primary responsibility for planning and consumption. Consequently, the wedding preparations represent an uneven distribution of labor between the bride and groom (Besel et al. 2009; Boden 2003; Currie 1993; Pepin et al. 2008). Although research extensively covers brides' possessions and associated identities, grooms and their symbolic consumption activities receive less attention in the literature (Kols and Sobal 2013). Phrases like *absent groom* and *reluctant groom* suggest the groom's peripheral and marginalized role in the wedding consumption process (Howard 2000). While traditional wedding descriptions highlight the bride's white gown, the groom's attire often remains undiscussed (Carter and Duncan 2017). The groom's appearance, like other decisions, is likely influenced by media, popular culture, and fashion advertising (Barry and Phillips 2016; Kols and Sobal 2013) but lacks the symbolic significance of the wedding gown (Howard 2000). Examining customs outside the Western traditions would bring light to a plethora of other traditions and customs (e.g., Tawfiq and Marcketti 2017).

Previous research on wedding consumption primarily focuses on heterosexual couples, emphasizing adherence to gender norms tied to traditional wedding roles ("bride" and "groom"). This heteronormative perspective is reflected in wedding discourse across various media sources (Besel et al. 2009; Boden 2003). Limited research on commitment ceremonies or weddings of same-sex couples explores how these couples navigate the "personal versus political" aspects of their ceremonies (Hull 2006; Smart 2008). Lewin's (1998) study revealed varying attitudes among same-sex couples toward heteronormative wedding traditions; Smart (2008) found ambivalence among British same-sex couples. Clarke, Burgoyne, and Burns (2013) expanded the inquiry, exploring the personal and political meanings associated with relationship celebrations among same-sex British couples. Their findings highlighted the absence of scripts for same-sex ceremonies, ambivalence toward ceremonies, and the importance of familial and legal recognition. Kimport (2012) analyzed same-sex marriage in the United States, observing disruptions and reinforcements of heteronormativity in couples' appearance and dress choices. Fetner and Heath (2016) investigated the adoption or resistance of heteronormative wedding traditions, identifying categories of participants embracing, negotiating, resisting, or adopting a frugal approach.

Reddy-Best et al. (2022) explored the fashion choices of lesbian married couples and discovered a diverse range of approaches in navigating their attire on the wedding day. These discussions mirror the longstanding theme in which lesbian and queer women manage gender and its expression as a reflection of their sexuality in their clothing (Geczy and Karaminas 2013; Reddy-Best and Pedersen 2015; Wilson 2013). The negotiations around gender led to authentic self-expression, as the couples perceived it, fostering a sense of empowerment despite occasional feelings of ambivalence, labor, renegotiations, and/or experiences aligned with heteronormativity. Marketed products and cultural portrayals of queerness play roles in shaping these genuine expressions through attire. Despite the tension between perceived authenticity and cultural influences, the distinctive wedding attire worn by the couples carried political significance, serving as a means to reclaim and navigate the subtleties of their queer expressions during an official, publicly binding event that legally formalized their lifelong commitment. Consequently, the wedding space became a platform for political change, challenging established definitions of being a bride or someone entering marriage, regardless of how these expressions engaged with or defied cultural expectations.

Kipper Clothiers, Kirrin Finch, and THÚY Custom Clothier, which all produce suits and suit coordinates, cater for queer and trans folks getting married, specifically people who are masculine-leaning, masculine-of-center, and/or trans masculine (Figure 4.1). The emergence of such specialized brands not only signifies a response to a growing market demand but also represents a crucial aspect of the broader intersection between the fashion industry, activism, and capitalism. In targeting the LGBTQ+ community, these brands actively contribute to the ongoing narrative of inclusivity and equity, challenging traditional norms associated with wedding attire, specifically, the so-called absent groom. By offering a diverse range of options that cater to same-sex couples, these brands provide a platform for authentic negotiations of identity within the confines of a traditionally heteronormative wedding industry.

The engagement of fashion brands with same-sex couples adds a layer of complexity to the intersection of activism and capitalism. On the one hand, these brands play a pivotal role in breaking down gender norms and promoting a more inclusive representation of love and commitment. On the other hand, their existence within a capitalist framework raises questions about the motivations behind their inclusivity. Some may question whether these brands are genuinely committed to social progress or are simply capitalizing on a lucrative market segment. The delicate balance between activism and capitalism becomes evident as the fashion industry

Figure 4.1 Two clients wearing THÚY Custom Clothier suits. Photo courtesy of Thúy Custom Clothier.

navigates the fine line between fostering authentic representation and profiting from the commodification of identity.

In the realm of same-sex weddings, where authenticity and political expression are intertwined with fashion choices, the involvement of specialized brands becomes a nuanced form of activism. By recognizing and responding to the unique needs of the LGBTQ+ community, the fashion industry becomes a vehicle for social change.

However, the industry's inherent capitalist nature introduces a layer of complexity, which some argue challenges the sincerity of these efforts. As same-sex couples negotiate their authentic expressions through fashion, the fashion brands negotiate their own positions within the broader socioeconomic landscape.

The integration of same-sex couples into the wedding industry, particularly through specialized fashion brands, certainly marks a step toward inclusivity and representation. However, the intricate dance between activism and capitalism requires continuous scrutiny to ensure that the progress made in the realm of LGBTQ+ rights is not overpowered by commercial interests, despite examples of companies like Kipper Clothiers, Kirrin Finch, and THÚY Custom Clothier, whose owners have obvious personal connections with fashioning the masculine aesthetic. The fashion choices of same-sex couples, influenced by both personal authenticity and cultural influences, serve as a microcosm of the broader societal negotiation between genuine activism and the pervasive forces of capitalism. As the fashion industry continues to evolve in response to changing societal norms, it is the role in shaping and reflecting the narratives of love, commitment, and identity remain a crucial part of the ongoing struggle for equity and authentic representation.

Social Media and Crowdfunding as Entry Points into the System

Crowdfunding initiatives, launched within the same cultural moment as same-sex marriage primarily through Kickstarter, allowed many of the queer and trans fashion brand entrepreneurs to test the market for viability and at the same time raise capital funds.

Entrepreneurs launched the crowdfunding platform Kickstarter in 2009, giving everyone the chance to contribute money toward small-business goals. Simultaneously, social media became a part of Americans' everyday lives, with the introduction and spread of Facebook in 2004, followed by numerous other platforms, such as Instagram and Twitter (now X), allowing the public easy access to Kickstarter campaigns, thus helping them succeed (Best and Neiss 2014: para 29; Curtin 2018).

AFLW, Beefcake Swimwear, Dapper Boi, FLAVNT, Greyscale Goods, TomboyX, Kipper Clothiers, NiK Kacy Footwear, Play Out Apparel, and Rebirth Garments each used Kickstarter to raise of funds. It helped Abby Sugar (Play Out Apparel), gauge which products to focus on. She said,

> It's interesting and very exciting for me because when my ex and I first started the company, we originally started that out with three styles: a boxer brief, a bikini, and the thong, because I want it to be inclusive in that way, but actually when we did that first Kickstarter, the overwhelming response was towards the boxer brief and was towards the more masculine, so we saw that.

Kacy, of NiK Kacy Footwear, described community support for other queer and trans fashion brands. Another queer-owned and -operated business, Matriarch, was doing similar gender-neutral shoes:

> Matriarch actually ... reached out to me before they did their Kickstarter campaign. I don't know if they had talked to Kirrin Finch, but they talked to somebody that knew me. After my Kickstarter campaign, I tried to help pay it forward and, like, help a lot of other Kickstarter campaigns, especially in our queer community. It's all about being a community and teaching them and being like, "This is my experience, these are my learnings." So, they reached out to me and told me what they were doing and I was just like, "Oh my god this is fantastic," and, "How can I help you?" I spent a few hours talking to them and really giving them a lot of insight that I had. I tried to even offer like, "Hey, if you're making your shoes in Portugal and I'm making my shoes in Portugal maybe we can combine efforts and get one factory to do it for us because that actually gives us more leverage." They weren't into it, so I left it at that.

Cubacub (Rebirth Garments) also reported that Kickstarter centered community-building for their brand but said it also highlighted the emotional labor involved in running a queer-focused brand and responding to the LGBTQ+ hate, even, in their case, serious death threats:

> Then when I did my Kickstarter, I was having so many positive reactions I then wasn't expecting people to try to attack me in a very aggressive, violent-seeming way online. I mean, it makes sense because there's just horrible people everywhere, but yeah, I was having death threats by white supremacist folks. The most hatred that I've gotten is because I dress plus-size and fat folks. That is the most hatred and the most outright, unabashed, evil comments are from folks who are fatphobic. I wasn't expecting that. I thought that the most hatred would be for the queer-ness or the trans-ness.

Despite the challenges and hate that some entrepreneurs faced, crowdfunding initiatives not only provided a means of financial support but also served as a powerful tool for community-building within the queer and trans fashion communities. The collaborations and outreach efforts between entrepreneurs like Kacy and Matriarch exemplify the solidarity that emerged. The willingness to share experiences and insights and even propose collaborative ventures demonstrated a commitment to uplifting and strengthening the collective presence of queer- and trans-owned businesses.

Moreover, Kickstarter became more than a mere fundraising platform; it grew into a dynamic space where marginalized voices could resonate and find resonance. The experience of Sugar, from Play Out Apparel, underscores the platform's significance in shaping product direction based on genuine market feedback. This democratization of market research not only empowered entrepreneurs but also facilitated a more nuanced understanding of consumer preferences within the queer fashion landscape. The challenges Cubacub of Rebirth Garments faced highlight the harsh reality of existing in a world where bigotry and discrimination persist. However, their determination to navigate through hate and threats serves as a testament to entrepreneurial resilience. It raises crucial questions about the broader societal landscape and the ongoing struggle for acceptance and understanding.

While the journey for queer and trans entrepreneurs is undoubtedly fraught with adversity, the intersection of crowdfunding, social media, and a supportive community is a transformative force. It has not only enabled financial backing for innovative projects but also fostered a sense of belonging and unity among those striving to make their mark in the vibrant and diverse world of queer and trans fashion.

Part 2 The Brands

5 Queer and Trans Fashion Brand Entrepreneurial Beginnings: Before and After the 2010s Surge

While I extensively discuss the queer and trans fashion brands in this research that overtly claimed their positioning in queer and trans ideologies, which largely emerged in the 2000s, others certainly existed in various forms before the brands that are central to this research. That is, I am confident that queer and trans entrepreneurs produced and sold items in the twentieth century, particularly those with a DIY approach and/or in local communities. I am describing just one example here, but this is worthy of its own in-depth research project.

One such fashion brand that existed before the surge is Dykes in the City (DITC). Denise Green (2018, 2023) documented DITC via an informal interview that she later published on Cornell's Fashion + Textile Collection's blog. Green had also collected some of their objects for a 2006 exhibition she was curating (personal communication). Green explained that the fashion label DITC, although no longer in operation, had a significant impact. Founded in 2004 by Nicky Cutler, a former teacher, the brand aimed to reclaim the derogatory term *dyke* by empowering queer folks to express themselves through fashion and develop connections with one another. The brand had a distinctive graphic logo, featuring the acronym *DITC* with an upside-down triangle as the dot of the i. The triangle, which has significant meaning for the queer communities, dates to the Holocaust, when Nazis used triangles of various colors to identify different groups of people in concentration camps. Gay men were labeled with pink triangles, while lesbians were given black triangles. In recent years, the LGBTQ+ community has reclaimed the upside-down triangle as a symbol of pride and resistance. It is used to remember the persecution LGBTQ+ individuals faced during the Holocaust and to honor those who suffered and died. By embracing this symbol, queer people are asserting their identity and standing against oppression (Elman 1996). This logo, adorning a variety of items the brand produced, was recognizable within lesbian communities.

Green continued that DITC gained visibility through popular queer media outlets like *Curve* and *Velvetpark* magazines, as well as television shows such as *The L Word*. The tank top and trucker hat combination from the 2005–6 "Do Ask, Do Tell" collection is archived in Cornell's collection (Figures 5.1a and 5.1b). The front of the camouflage tank top features a pigtailed feminine silhouette holding a large, missile-style bomb dripping blood into a pool on the floor. The image is accompanied by the slogan "No to bombs, yes to bombshells," on the back, and the designer has creatively replaced the o in bombshells with the DITC logo. This design overtly

Figure 5.1a and 5.1b Trucker hat and camo tank-top by Dykes in the City. Photos courtesy of Cornell Fashion + Textile Collection.

draws on military aesthetics, for instance, the green camouflage used for military fatigues, and by subverting the language of the US military's "Don't Ask, Don't Tell" policy. Cutler began to identify as transmasculine, and their evolving identity led to the brand's closure in 2011. Cutler explained to Green, "I could no longer support the name of my own company because my own thoughts of myself had altered."

Overtly Serving Their Queer and Trans Communities in the Twenty-first Century

Each of the fashion brands in this research has a unique story. The entrepreneurs who started them came from various backgrounds, with different interests, to start their business operations, all of which were founded between 2010 and 2017 (Figure 5.2). Each founder had a vision for their niche fashion brand; serving the queer and trans communities and their personal stories, identities, and relationships within the LGBTQ+ communities help set the context for their beginnings. One similarity across the fashion brands is that they largely, not entirely of course, cater to individuals assigned female at birth and/or nonbinary folks who subvert gender norms.

Every brand spotlighted here had a close connection with the LGBTQ+ community, either through the founders' own identity journeys or their partners' and friends'

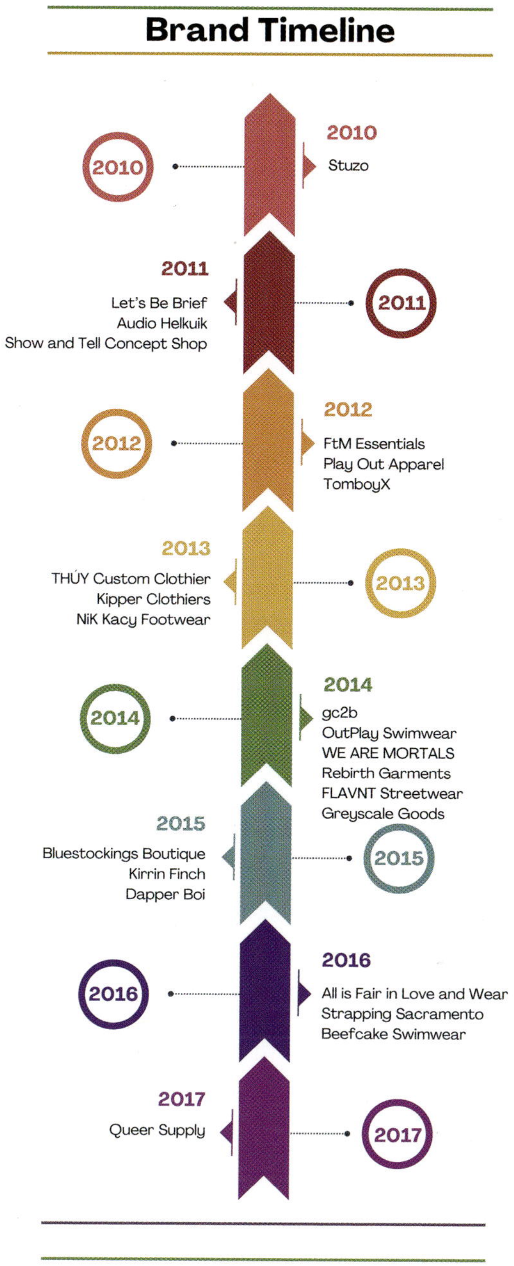

Brand Timeline

2010
Stuzo

2011
Let's Be Brief
Audio Helkuik
Show and Tell Concept Shop

2012
FtM Essentials
Play Out Apparel
TomboyX

2013
THÚY Custom Clothier
Kipper Clothiers
NiK Kacy Footwear

2014
gc2b
OutPlay Swimwear
WE ARE MORTALS
Rebirth Garments
FLAVNT Streetwear
Greyscale Goods

2015
Bluestockings Boutique
Kirrin Finch
Dapper Boi

2016
All is Fair in Love and Wear
Strapping Sacramento
Beefcake Swimwear

2017
Queer Supply

Figure 5.2 Timeline of brand founding. Graphic courtesy of Zahra Falsafi.

experiences. In nearly every case, these entrepreneurs had difficulty finding products in the market that helped them negotiate their identities through dress and found these shopping experiences were often negative. Thus, they wanted to create a space where folks in the queer and trans communities could feel seen and heard through embodied practices.

In the few instances when the entrepreneurs did not identify specifically with the communities they intended to serve, they experienced criticism or worked to not center their identities in the brand. For example, Peregrine Honig of AFLW understood her positionality as a cisgender woman aiming to develop, market, and sell binders to trans folks. Thus, she brought Dominique, a person who identifies in the trans community, on board. This deliberate inclusivity is in some ways a manifestation of commodity activism, whereby entrepreneurs conscientiously consider the social implications of their products. Honig's decision not to centralize her identity in the brand demonstrates a nuanced understanding of the complexities at play, emphasizing a commitment to ethical business practices without entirely forsaking capitalist goals. The collaboration with Dominique underscores the potential harmony between capitalism and commodity activism, as it can lead to a more authentic and respectful product but also exemplifies a proactive approach to social responsibility within a market-driven framework.

This interplay highlights the nuanced path entrepreneurs tread, recognizing the potential for positive impact on specific communities while navigating the imperatives of a capitalist market. However, the intersection of commodity activism and capitalism, as demonstrated by Honig's strategic decisions, is not without its potential for negative perception. Some critics argue that such initiatives may be seen as opportunistic, with entrepreneurs exploiting social issues to enhance their brand image or market share without genuinely addressing systemic problems. Detractors might question the authenticity of Honig's commitment, viewing the inclusion of Dominique as a calculated move to mitigate potential backlash rather than a sincere effort to center the transgender community. Moreover, there is a risk that these actions could be perceived as tokenistic, with the entrepreneur merely using the inclusion of an individual from the targeted community as a symbolic gesture without fundamentally reshaping power dynamics or addressing broader issues of representation. In this way, the delicate balance between commodity activism and capitalism can be fraught with skepticism, demanding a careful and transparent approach to navigate the complexities of socially conscious entrepreneurship, if that even is possible. Honig and Dominique discussed how they grappled with this tension:

> Honig: And sometimes doing the right thing is more important than doing what's right for me as a cis-white female from a middle-class family. To try and build a brand based on something that I know very little about—maybe it's not right, but I do believe, that I am doing the right thing and I know ... I started All Is Fair ... from place of empathy and compassion. And, and need. There was a need.
>
> Dominique: I have as much of a voice as I should have in the community.
>
> Honig: The other thing that I think about too, is that if I had laid it out on the table, like, "Oh, this is my plan of attack: I'm going to start this brand, and I'm going to gift it to the person that makes a better figurehead for this brand." I mean, like, I can't think of a more manipulative or horrible thing. I can't understand how people would see me that way, because it's so far from who I am, and it just

seems like an actual decision, not like a plan. It wasn't like I went out into the universe or into my city looking for someone who's trans and wants this business.

Dominique: Discussion has been difficult, and from my perspective in, within, the community—because I am all for criticism—I think that critique is the only way to move forward, but there are times where … you get into a polarizing conversation about "I'm either going to support you or not, and if you were a cis-white woman, I can't support you," and it's just like, "Wow, I can't do anything about that, for one, and we're at the point where we are right now because of that and two, there is no negating the importance that it had in getting us where we are now." I've made a lot of changes to All Is Fair in Love and Wear, and we've been focusing on refining our message, but it['s], by no means, [as] if I had been doing that refinement on my own. Refinement is a two-step process. You have to start somewhere, and work your way to something better.

A brand's name reflects its core identity. The ambivalence within the context of queer and trans identities—as reflected in the naming choices of brands like FtM Essentials and TransGuy Supply—highlights the dynamic nature of identity within these communities. The chosen names serve not only as labels but also as representations of personal and collective experiences. In the ever-evolving landscape of queer- and trans-identity language, there exists a constant negotiation between fixed definitions and the fluidity inherent in how individuals perceive and express their identities.

The use of names that are personal, fun, and direct suggests an intention to celebrate the diverse and multifaceted nature of queer and trans experiences. However, as the language surrounding identity continues to evolve, some brand owners engage in critical self-reflection about their initial naming choices. The acknowledgment that these names might not be chosen today reflects a broader awareness within the community about the increasing fluidity in how individuals identify. For example, the owner of FtM Essentials recognizes that the term *FtM* (female to male) does not fully encapsulate the spectrum of gender identities embraced by the community today (as of the writing of this book, the company is now Trans Essentials, and its owners are working to build brand awareness around the new name). Similarly, the owner of TransGuy Supply acknowledges that the landscape of trans identity has become more nuanced, with individuals embracing identities that may not fit neatly into traditional categories. This ambivalence underscores the importance of remaining open to the evolving language and understanding that accompanies the rich tapestry of queer and trans experiences.

As societal attitudes and language norms shift, individuals within the queer and trans communities navigate a complex interplay between historical connections and contemporary interpretations of identity. Many of the brand names can accommodate multiple and mixed interpretations, and those who were looking to be more direct, demonstrating overt commitments to queer and trans justice, are acknowledging that identity is a deeply personal journey that defies rigid categorization, highlighting the difficulties of choosing an everlasting brand name.

These brands emerged largely with significant influence from personal identities; coming out and self-discovery journeys; and a mission to create products, marketing, and shopping experiences with trust at the core with an emphasis on businesses being run for LGBTQ+ folks by LGBTQ+ folks. While their founders' and owners' stories influenced much of their entrepreneurial beginnings, the cultural context in the early twenty-first century related to politics, technology, and communication also played a pivotal role in shaping the trajectories of these brands.

For the remainder of this chapter, I provide a brief introduction to each fashion brand through case studies. I include how and when each brand started, what product categories they engage with and sell, and a short introduction to their business model. I also include other relevant details each brand owner mentioned that would be important to understand their context and existence.

Case Study 1 All Is Fair in Love and Wear and gc2b

All Is Fair in Love and Wear

All Is Fair in Love and Wear (AFLW) was part of the brick-and-mortar retail store Birdies Panties, in Kansas City, Missouri. At the time of writing this book, however, AFLW has since closed. Peregrine Honig (she/her), an artist who grew up in San Francisco's Castro District in the 1980s, founded Birdies, a lingerie store initially, as an art installation in 2003. Honig began thinking about All Is Fair in 2015, as one of her friends was going through transitioning processes. She explained that the marketplace did not have high-quality products for trans folks and that her friend was wearing sports compression garments to affirm their gender identity. Honig checked online for wholesale binders, but could not locate any well-made options. Thus, in 2016, Honig founded All Is Fair in Love and Wear, which sold mostly chest binders in addition to a few other products, such as T-shirts.

The name AFLW is based on a quotation from John Lyly's 1579 novel *Euphues: The Anatomy of Wit*: "All is fair in love and war." Honig explained, "It references the idea that when you are fighting for what you believe in, pioneering territory, protecting your love or someone you love, that rules are not applicable. And even if they are, you are going to break them to get what you need and get what you want." However, because Honig is a cisgender woman, the initial launch of AFLW had pushback from individuals in the queer and trans communities. Honig explained that she started AFLW with the assumption that her consumers would be trans men who were interested in purchasing higher quality binders with good fabric and a product that was easy to don and doff. She based her purchasing decisions on her sales history knowledge and experience from her lingerie business by ordering two smalls, two mediums, two larges, and an extra-large. However, she quickly realized that her sizing was incorrect, as many of her customers were mothers of trans boys, and she needed to stock child sizes.

Honig's business partner Christian Dominique (they/them) became involved when she discovered the sizing issue. Dominique and Honig had known each other since about 2013. Their business relationship emerged because Honig recognized the need for leadership change in the brand. Dominique, who identifies as antetrans, explained that a cisgender woman owning and directing the business had a response that was "mixed, to say the least," because "the LGBTQIA+ community is very protective of itself, especially the transgender community and rightfully so because they're one of the most marginalized, oppressed groups in the United States, if not the world." They explained that they created the term *antetrans* to reflect their gender identity:

> In seventeenth-century architecture, an antechamber is a room that leads into a larger room like the larger hall of the cathedral. At amusement parks, it's the place where guests are told about the ride, right before they step on the

rollercoaster. I'm approaching that larger part of my life, but where I am financially and how much time I can devote to that [transitioning] and the decisions that I still need to make regarding that are still being tailored and nuanced. That's how I consider myself. Definitely still with and in the larger spectrum of just trans, a trans-feminine person.

Dominique took over in January 2017 and began refining the marketing language to "accommodate more of the community through my own experiences," which led to more positive reactions to the brand. On April 22, 2017, AFLW posted on Instagram "We are back," indicating that the brand was moving forward after leadership change, which had many positive comments. However, @wickedation asked, "Are u owned/operated by trans folk?" where AFLW replied, "Well, that was a surprise for later, but unofficially yeah … fantastic question … more on that soon." Then another follower, @bethybijou, asked: "What does it mean to 'unofficially yeah' owned/operated by trans people?" AFLW responded: "We just haven't made an 'official' announcement. But we've been trans-owned/operated since late January 🙈. Our new owner/director will bring attention to that change in the near future." On June 7, 2017, AFLW officially announced it was "trans-directed," with a post featuring Dominique.

gc2b

Marli Washington (he/him), a trans man—who specifically says he is "not nonbinary. I'm not gender fluid"—founded gc2b, an ecommerce trans-gear company, in 2014. He grew up in suburban Prince George's County, Maryland, where the gc2b office is now located. At the University of Arts in Philadelphia, he initially studied photography, but after his foundational year he switched to industrial design. After he graduated, he also went to the University of Arts' Corzo Center, an incubator program, to gain some background knowledge in business. He explained that he had a "breakdown" in his senior year and had an extension over the summer to finish his senior thesis. So in this break period, he needed something to focus on—and that's when gc2b emerged: "I knew I needed this, so I made it. I knew that other people could use it too, so I did some prototypes and some user-testing with some people I met in Philadelphia, who were actually the first trans men that I've ever met. That's when it started to become clear for me." After he graduated in 2014, he began selling in October of that same year.

The name is an homage to his parents, who were clothing designers in the 1990s and 2000s. They had a junior clothing line, yet when the recession hit, their company suffered, even though they had significant industry knowledge, and manufacturing equipment, and fabric. So after surveying the market, they realized that exotic dancer apparel needs were still in demand. The name of their original company was GC2, or Gear Company. Washington added the *b,* making his company "part b" to his parents' original company. He explained he did not want to have an overtly queer company name but that his business's official name is gc2b transition apparel. While its main products are binders, it also sells items such as T-shirts, and at the time of the interview was looking to add packing shorts. The business sells mostly through Shopify but also vends at some in-person events such as conferences or Pride. Washington works directly with manufacturers and feels strongly about keeping the brand standards high:

> We've had a lot of people ask for wholesale prices, but I think that [the] nature of the product, with the knitting, custom sizing, and the high possibility of needing exchange, doesn't lend itself to wholesale. I feel that if I let other stores sell it then it will kind of take away from the brand. I don't want people having issues and not having our customer service handle it …. We have a 90–99.7 percent factory rating, so I don't want to tarnish that, or our reputation.

Case Study 2 FLAVNT Streetwear and Queer Supply

FLAVNT Streetwear

Chris (he/him) and Courtney (she/her) Rhodes founded FLAVNT Streetwear. Twins who were born and raised in San Antonio, Texas, Chris and Courtney studied graphic design at Texas State University. Following school, they moved to Brooklyn, New York, for a year and a half and then moved back to Austin, Texas in 2015. At the time of the interview, they both worked full-time graphic design jobs. Courtney explained she identifies as female and lesbian and Chris identifies as a trans guy. Even though he is binary presenting, he is "cool with being known as being trans." He also explained he is queer.

The idea for FLAVNT emerged in 2013 in preparation for Austin Pride. The siblings were making shirts for Pride, and Chris made one that said, "Pretty Boy," with a rainbow stencil (Figure 5.3). When he wore it at Pride numerous people, from every identity on the spectrum, asked where he got the shirt. Chris explained:

> We never thought about it [pretty boy] because it was just how I always identified. This was back before I transitioned and I was always identifying with some term that wasn't like, "a lesbian." I identified very much with like, "I'm a pretty boy" or "I'm a stud" and that sort of stuff. I realized, then, that it wasn't just me who identified that way. We just kind of both were like, "Well we should make that shirt," because our friends are like. "People would buy that." So that's how it was born.

They named the company FLAVNT because they were trying to convey something related to pride. Courtney explained:

> I had always joked that if Chris was an animal, he would be a peacock because he's like so pretty and in-your-face, and in the wild the boy peacocks are the pretty ones and the girls are like the brown ones. I have always said that about Chris. So we came up with ... this sort of, like, "peacock mascot" idea, and then the idea of like "flaunting" your pride and being really open and out about that. That's where the idea for FLAVNT came from and he ... thought of the word.

They decided to use a *V* instead of *U* in the word *FLAUNT* for the angular lines and because it would be easier to copyright. Thus, FLAVNT was official in Spring 2014, and it began printing the first run of T-shirts. The business is almost entirely ecommerce, but FLAVNT does occasional pop-up events. It started with the T-shirts, and then expanded to sweatshirts, accessories, hats, stickers, and, eventually, binders. Courtney saw Chris struggling to find something to wear, explaining that the binders on the market were not comfortable, so they began designing and selling binders.

Figure 5.3 Pretty Boy T-shirt by FLAVNT Streetwear. Image: author's own.

Queer Supply

Kit (they/them) and Sade (they/them) co-founded Queer Supply, an ecommerce store that sells graphic tees and other items such as buttons and magnets. Sade was born in California and has lived in Atlanta, Georgia and South Africa. They moved to Canada when they were eighteen years old. Kit grew up in Kitchener, Ontario and moved to Toronto, when in their late teens. Kit and Sade met as students at the University of Toronto. Kit also studied at the University of Waterloo for a short period of time. They both engaged in much self-taught education surrounding craft and art.

Queer Supply began from conversations with friends about gender, which culminated in a handmade, silkscreened shirt, which they sold to friends. Years later, they started Queer Supply with the intention of "making a statement in regards to gender identity and sexuality." They said there were not a lot of graphic tees to show queerness, and thus they began their company in 2015, with the official launch party at a queer bar in Toronto in 2017. They chose the company's name because it was direct and to the point. Currently, they both work other full-time jobs, and Queer Supply is a "mini second job."

Case Study 3 Bluestockings Boutique, FtM Essentials, and Transguy Supply

Bluestockings Boutique

Jeanna Kadlec (she/her), a native Midwesterner who grew up in rural, working-class Iowa and Wisconsin, founded Bluestockings Boutique, which has since closed. She has lived in Davenport, Waterloo, and Parkersburg, Iowa, and also Albany, Wisconsin. She attended Cornell College in Mount Vernon and tripled majored in English, politics, and women's studies. She continued on to a PhD program in English literature at Brandeis University, in Boston. She grew up in a very religious, fundamentalist evangelical church and, following her religious path, married her college boyfriend, both planning to be professors. However, at the start of the fourth year of her graduate program, she came out to herself, divorced her husband, left the church, quit her PhD program, and had to think of something new to do with her life. She decided to start a lingerie company catering to the LGBTQ+ community, though aside from working in retail had no experience outside of academia. One night in in 2014, Kadlec and a friend were talking, and when lingerie came up, Kadlec wondered why boutiques centered heteronormativity. The next morning, she began digging, using her academic research skills, and determined that no LGBTQ+ lingerie shops existed, so she would start one. She had many transferable skills, particularly writing, but translating academic writing to product copy or marketing strategies came with an incredibly steep learning curve.

Kadlec was out for about one year, identifying as queer and starting her new business, although she now mostly identifies with the term *lesbian*. She chose the name Bluestockings after the eighteenth-century Blue Stockings Society, an informal group of intellectual women who ran literary salons in London. She launched her ecommerce business in April 2015 and received a lot of press, in part for her writing skills and ability to talk about representation in lingerie from an academic perspective. Her literary interests and personal identities helped shape the business; that is, she was always the public face of the company and explained that her identity signified that "This is LGBT-owned and I am a queer woman," and "I'm running it, and the reason you [the queer community] can trust the company is because you can trust me." She wanted a space for the community where she had something for everyone; yet, that led to too much inventory. She had begun with as much product as possible in every size but scaled down to include only underwear, trans gear (e.g., packing briefs), bras, loungewear, and sex toys.

FtM Essentials

Searah Deysach (she/her) founded FtM Essentials, a Chicago-based brand that is part of Early to Bed, a feminist sex shop. In 2001, Deysach opened Early to Bed, the first woman-owned sex-toy store in Chicago. Deysach explained that a lot of her early consumers were from her own queer community—she identifies as queer/lesbian—and these consumers included many trans guys asking for trans supportive gear, packers specifically. While packers are different from sex toys, they are penis-shaped, so they do come from the sex-toy industry, since the molds are very similar. She began carrying what was available at the time, which included one company that made only limp packers. As her business grew, her consumers were getting younger, and issues began to arise with the parents feeling nervous about young people accessing a sex-shop website. At that moment Deysach realized she needed a separate website for trans gear, so that parents would feel comfortable with their children shopping there. Thus, in 2012 Deysach began FtM Essentials, with its own website. She explained that the separate website was also helpful for people supporting and affirming trans folks and their identities, such as case workers or family members.

Numerous websites have emerged since Deysach began, but her more than ten years of experience in retail, ecommerce, and business made it possible for her to easily enter the market. She heard numerous stories of consumers having extremely bad experiences with other trans gear companies, because the companies were struggling to fulfill orders due to their lack of experience. Deysach received her undergraduate degree at the Art Institute of Chicago and continued there for a graduate degree in the fiber department. But she quit school to start her business. When she began, she had much experience in food service, and no retail experience; she credits her passion for the business and for serving her community with the business's success.

Deysach described the existing business as growing very organically, and she explained that the business has grown exponentially since she founded it. As her business grew, she started another, Trans Kids, in 2015. Trans Kids emerged out of interactions with parents at the Philadelphia Trans Health Conference, where numerous parents were looking for trans-supportive gear for their five or six year olds. Deysach, who has a gender nonconforming, trans child, related to the parents, frustrated that existing products did not match the children's physiologies. Trans Kids seeks to make parents feel "safe and supported and that this stuff was there for their kids if they needed it."

She chose the name FtM Essentials for ease of searchability. Yet, Deysach now regrets the name because, as she explains, "our language around trans identities is evolving at such a rapid pace that actually FtM, for a lot of people, is a really antiquated term." In retrospect, she would have chosen something more gender neutral. And the name of the offshoot business, "Trans Kids," was not without controversy: while the term *kids* has been problematic, she wanted to make sure the brand obviously targeted a younger market.

The entire business is built around buying wholesale and selling through her three different businesses, either online or at the brick-and-mortar shop. Deysach explained she did not want to get into manufacturing but did work with some of her vendors to improve products based on consumer preferences. For example, she worked with New York Toy Collective to produce smaller packers for Trans Kids. She also works with a manufacturer who produces stand-to-pee devices, and they often want her feedback on the prototypes. Because Deysach and her employees work directly with the consumers, they obtain a lot of feedback about the changing community needs and desires.

Transguy Supply

Scout Rose (they/them) founded Transguy Supply, an ecommerce business that offers products for the transmasculine person—such as binders, packers, stand-to-pee devices, apparel, and packing swimwear—a "one-stop shop" for trans masculine folks. Rose studied philosophy in college and then worked for a coffee company in New York City for about ten years, starting as a barista and working their way up to a director position, building their first ecommerce platform with other responsibilities including product development, product design, and managing leadership at seventeen locations.

They identify as trans and queer, and explained they experienced alienating shopping experiences prior to launching Transguy Supply. Shopping was largely difficult, as they were socialized as a female and said specifically that when they started their transition almost twenty years prior many of the products Transguy Supply offers did not exist. Much of the trans gear (e.g., packers) was marketed as gag gifts, which does not provide a dignified shopping experience for a trans person. The business started as a side project, in 2017, and it officially launched in 2018. Rose chose the name Transguy Supply as the name because it rhymed, and *guy* was more expansive than *man*. During the interview, they reflected that they might have chosen a different name today, but that folks generally use those words to find the products online.

Case Study 4 Beefcake Swimwear and Outplay Swimwear

Beefcake Swimwear

Mel Brittner Wells (she/her) is the owner and founder of Beefcake Swimwear; she grew up in southeastern Idaho and is a fifth generation Mormon who was raised in a "very, very Mormon family and in the religion." Growing up she attended church every Sunday and then attended Brigham Young University. The university's mission centers Mormon philosophies, and religion is interwoven throughout all aspects of the institution, including limitations on academic freedom that violate adherence to Mormon values. Wells studied English, with an editing emphasis.

During college, she went on a mission to Belgium, explaining, "There I figured out that I was queer because I kept having huge crushes on my companions." She came back from the mission, finished her undergraduate degree, left the church, and moved to Portland, Oregon, in 2007. She said, "I have traveled around the West a lot, and I lived in Belgium for a year and a half, but I was a missionary when I was there, so my cultural experiences were limited. Once I got to Portland it was like, woah, new world." She also completed a master's degree at Portland State University in book publishing, and while she does not currently work in publishing, she finds the project management skills useful in her business. Since 2010, she has also worked full time at a nonprofit, Literary Arts, which focuses on youth programming centered on creative writing.

Wells described her gender identity as "tomboy femme." She strongly identifies with women and "not just cis women, of course." She related, "There was like a slight moment where I was like, maybe I'm trans, and then I was like, no, I actually just want male power. That was an interesting moment. I'd say femme tomboy—definitely sort of a jock, but really goofy, I don't know." She identifies strongly with *lesbian* and uses the term *queer* a lot. She said, "I think because I was raised in a really, really conservative culture and it took *so* much to come out that I just use the most basic terms possible with my family. They understand *lesbian*, but they don't really understand *queer*, so *lesbian* is usually what I go for."

Motivation to start the brand resulted from her own surfing experiences. She said, when on vacation in 2012, she tried surfing in a bikini and experienced bad rashes on her stomach, which made her realize the importance of rash guards, but "trying to find a one-piece suit that wasn't really girly was actually really hard." The idea for the 1920s-style suits emerged from a roommate who wanted a 1920s wool, one-piece swimsuit but could not find one to purchase. Wells has extensive sewing skills that her mom taught her. She attempted to make her friend a swimsuit but quickly realized that sewing stretch fabrics is much different from woven and quite difficult. She finished the garment and had a ton of praise from folks, which initiated her interest in seriously pursuing selling inclusive swimwear. However, she knew she would need a manufacturer.

Wells wanted a name with "strong queer roots" without being "gay swimwear." She and her wife disagree about who came up with *beefcake* first, but she settled using the word with *swimwear* because *beefcake* reminded her of being strong and said, "Fuck it, we can all be beefcakes. It's a sexy, strong state of being than it is necessarily the true meaning of the words." Beefcake Swimwear officially became an LLC in Oregon in 2016. The company sells mostly swimsuits and has some smaller products, such as pins and patches. Wells does everything in the business, except the manufacturing. She hired a local manufacturer and sources her fabric from Italy. When I asked her about expanding, she said she wanted to respond to consumer requests—such as built-in bust support and long sleeves—but she has realized how complicated producing garments can be and her product, which is pretty simple, already retails at $99. She cannot afford to chase trends, and, despite loving boobs, she said, "I do not want to make clothing for them. Making bras is so intense." Also, her manufacturer already told her she would have to find someone else.

Outplay Swimwear

Marialexandra Garcia (she/her), born in Venezuela, founded Outplay Swimwear, an ecommerce business that has since closed, which sold through its own website, Amazon, and other websites, such as Radimola, which curates gender nonconforming clothing options. She grew up in various places, including Ecuador and the Dominican Republic, and eventually went to the Savannah College of Art and Design, in Savannah, Georgia, where she earned a bachelor of fine art degree in fashion design and a minor in art history. Afterward, she landed in Miami, where she started her swimwear business. She began her design career at ten years old and made her first wedding gown at fourteen. After graduation from college, she had numerous clients lining up for custom-made eveningwear and bridal gowns, which grew at a pretty healthy rate until 2007, when the economy crashed.

She was selling her products in major retailers such as Saks Fifth Avenue, Neiman Marcus, and small boutiques. Then, suddenly, with the economic downturn, more than 50 percent of the boutiques she worked with closed their doors, many of whom did not pay her for products already delivered. Trying to keep afloat, she thought, "There's got to be something more that I can do. There's got to be something that I can do with my talent that makes more sense." She explained the industry is extremely cut-throat, she was mentally and physically tired, yet was brainstorming business ideas. She said, "I felt there had to be something else I could do where I could still do what I love to do, which is create … these amazing things that I can come up with in my head and make them real, which I thought I could use to affect people's lives for the better." She partnered with Bernadette Smith, an early, gay wedding planner, who owned 14 Stories, a boutique wedding planning firm. The company name reflects the Fourteenth Amendment that allowed interracial marriage and the fourteen state representatives who contributed to changing marriage equality law in Massachusetts. The pair formed the company Fourteen.

Garcia created jackets, vests, and pants that individuals could mix and match for wedding attire. She explained:

> This is different, and this is where I'm helping people fill this gap that doesn't exist in the market. The person who doesn't want to wear a dress is stuck buying a suit where they feel uncomfortable going into the store, then it doesn't fit properly and then they have to spend money on buying that suit that doesn't fit properly and taking it to the tailor to get it fit properly, which costs another fortune. It was too much, so I wanted to offer people this option. We made it mix and match, so it didn't matter where you fall, it was just that if I want the blouse to be really, really girly and the jacket had to be very, very masculine, you could just have it and mix it up. … So we came up with that, and I worked on it for about three years. I actually did almost two years of pure research in order to get it done right and get the fit right. I mean, the fit had to be perfect. I believe that [in] any brand, fit comes before anything else, and if your fit doesn't work, it doesn't matter if you size up. It doesn't matter how pretty it looks or how cool it looks, if fit doesn't work, you're done. You might sell it once, but that's it. So, in order to accommodate the fitting, it took me a year and a half, almost two years of trial and error and a lot of focus groups. I had focus groups for trying on people and fitting people … I sat at these meetings, and I listened to them try the clothes on and I listened to them talking afterwards about it.

In the meetings, Garcia kept hearing that swimwear was difficult to find. So she did research and talked with her business partner about the possibility of adding a line of swimwear. Smith, however, decided that the fashion industry was too hard and pulled out. Garcia then closed Fourteen, because it did not make sense financially as she was "pouring money into it, and it was making no money." She then launched Outplay, her swimwear company, in 2014, with preorders to ensure it would be a viable business. She recalled, "It was just such a huge hit right off the bat, that I knew this was it. I could really make a difference in people's lives with something as simple as swimwear and that's how Outplay came to life."

The name Outplay Swimwear is a play on words. Garcia explained:

> I wanted it to sound like something that it could mean much more than just a name. So, Outplay is the fact that you can Outplay yourself, you can Outplay somebody else—you can be better, you can be a better you, it plays with it, you can see in the font as well, you can go out and play, go outside and play.

The name relates to being open about your sexual and gender identities in the queer and trans communities. She explained, "You can go out and feel comfortable and not have body issues because Outplay's here to help you, that's the—that's the play on the words."

Case Study 5 Play Out Apparel and TomboyX

Play Out Apparel

Abby Sugar (she/her) is the founder and co-owner of Play Out Apparel, an ecommerce underwear and athleisure brand, which is now closed. Sugar grew up in Ann Arbor, Michigan, and moved to New York City to attend Barnard College, where she studied literature and creative writing. She started the brand with her ex-wife, who was "a little bit more on the butch side of the spectrum" and had trouble finding underwear that was masculine leaning, comfortable, and enabled her to feel sexy. Sugar explained that her wife would buy men's underwear that was not flattering. In 2011 they had the idea to start the brand because they could find only European brands making masculine-style underwear for women, and they were very expensive. Play Out officially launched on Valentine's Day 2014, after about three years of development and planning.

Sugar's ex-wife came up with the name. The name itself, a product of intensive brainstorming, encapsulated the essence of the brand—a fusion of playfulness and liberation, symbolized by the multiplicity of meanings behind "Out." Sugar explained, "What we really loved about Play Out was the definition, and the idea behind *Play*, which is having fun, being comfortable, enjoying what you are wearing." They used *Out* for its multiple meanings, like playing outside, being out about one's identities, and as in men's underwear, where the logo-bearing waistband often shows above the pant line.

In 2017, Liz Leifer (they/them) joined the company as co-owner and creative director. When Sugar's ex-wife left the company, it was put on a slight pause. Leifer and Sugar had been friends for a long time, Leifer had experience in fashion, and Sugar was looking for a new business partner. Together, they overhauled the brand in its marketing, mission statement, and goals. Leifer, who self-identifies as a middle-aged Jewish dyke, started apprenticing for artists when they were ten and at twelve started going to fine arts classes at the University of California, Santa Cruz. They attended the University of California, Berkley, but left their third year to birth their first child. They have much business experience and experience in the arts, starting their career as a painter, then moving into film production, and later creative direction in fashion and product styling. Since joining the team, Leifer has brought on many folks including their daughter, who helps with the brand's illustrations. Together, Sugar and Leifer have created a brand that reflects progressive values, which is highlighted on their website:

> Members of the LGBTQ+ community deserve to see themselves reflected in the brands they shop and the clothes they wear; we strive to build a brand founded on a mission of queer visibility and celebration. For queer people, gender nonconforming and transgender individuals, shopping for clothing can

be incredibly stressful and intimidating. We were unable to find sexuality and gender-affirming apparel, and knew that we needed to design and manufacture it ourselves – so we did!

(Play Out Apparel 2023a)

TomboyX

Fran Dunaway (she/her) and Naomi Gonzalez (she/her) founded TomboyX, an ecommerce clothing line that initially focused on providing comfortable and stylish undergarments for women. Their journey into entrepreneurship was shaped by their diverse backgrounds and shared experiences as members of the LGBTQ+ community. Both identify as lesbian, and, at the time of the interview, had been married for two years.

Dunaway, who grew up as an army brat, experienced life in various parts of the United States, while Gonzalez, a first-generation Cuban American, was raised in the vibrant environment of New York City. Their individual paths before founding TomboyX were marked by diverse experiences. Gonzalez started her professional journey as a massage therapist, eventually establishing and later selling her own business. Meanwhile, Dunaway began her career working at a group home before eventually venturing into entrepreneurship herself by opening her own group home. Subsequently, she transitioned into the realm of media, where she engaged in freelance work and pursued her passion for storytelling.

The genesis of TomboyX stemmed from Dunaway's personal frustration with the limited options available in women's clothing, particularly shirts that failed to cater to her preferences and body type. Her persistent question, "How hard can it be to start a clothing line?" laid the foundation for what would become a transformative venture. Despite her appreciation for men's styles, Dunaway found that they often did not accommodate her body shape. This realization, coupled with feedback from others expressing similar frustrations, prompted Dunaway and Gonzalez to explore the idea of creating clothing that embraced a more inclusive and diverse range of body types and styles.

Their journey began in 2011, driven by a desire to fill a gap in the market and provide women with comfortable and stylish alternatives. Initially focusing on shirts, they soon pivoted their attention to underwear after recognizing a glaring absence of boxer briefs designed specifically for women. This shift underscored their commitment to challenging traditional gender norms and empowering individuals to express themselves authentically.

In March 2012, and based in Seattle, Washington, TomboyX was officially incorporated, marking the formalization of their vision. The name TomboyX was chosen not only for its playful and catchy appeal but also for its reflection of their own identities and the ethos of the brand. While they have significant focus on underwear, they also sell products in a variety of categories including swim, lounge, sleepwear, active, T-shirts, and accessories.

Case Study 6 Dapper Boi, Kirrin Finch, NiK Kacy Footwear, and Strapping Sacramento

Dapper Boi

Vicky Pasche (she/her) is the founder and CEO of Dapper Boi, an ecommerce business that sells everyday masculine-leaning products. She grew up in a small town in upstate New York near Albany and went to college in Plattsburgh, New York, where she studied physical education and mass media communication. Afraid to move to New York City because "it was such a scary place for us upstarters," she relocated instead to San Diego, California, where she had some family. She first worked for her family in a postal business. Then, she found a marketing job for the Viejas Casino and Resort; she stayed there for about eight years, eventually working her way up to promotions manager and then moved to another casino as head of the marketing department. Then, she began consulting with casinos in a marketing role.

Pasche explained that her own look originally entailed long hair and feminine styles, which she hated. Then, she had her first lesbian relationship in San Diego and became more comfortable with herself and more immersed in the San Diego gay scene. She recalled:

> I chopped my hair and I was excited to shop in the men's departments. I remember trying on my first pair of jeans in the men's department, and it was crazy because the jeans didn't fit me actually. It's just that it was unflattering, but that was the best—I felt like that was myself, and I could dress masculine, and that's when I really started caring about how I looked and making sure my ties were matching. I had accessories and all kinds of things, and I was just super excited about fashion at that point.

From then on, she only shopped in the men's section, but she realized that men's clothes are not cut for the curves of the female body. She started looking for brands that might fit her needs, realized there were none, and then she was inspired to create her own company. Because she worked in casinos, she had to wear suits, and, in 2012, she wanted to design suits, but since numerous suit companies (e.g., Saint Harridan) were emerging, she decided to focus on casual, everyday wear. She named the new venture Dapper Boi, using *dapper* to mean "the right fit and look" and *boi* because it "is kind of playful, it could go for a man or a woman." She wanted to make numerous products but started with jeans, the first item she tried on in the men's department as part of her journey in self-presentation.

Pasche did not have a background in fashion, and no one responded to her initial attempts to find partners to create her products; in fact, people would often hang up the phone on her. This was 2013, when she decided to take a step back and get her ideas together. Then, in 2014 right before their marriage, she and her fiancée decided to try again. She explained that for months they called manufacturers and "were getting hung up on left and right ... People were like, 'do you even know what you're doing?' Like, 'No, no, I don't. I just have an idea and that's it, and I'm looking for the right people to help us.'" Finally, in the fall of 2014, a manufacturer thought she had an interesting concept and worked with her and her partner to create samples for their first product. They incorporated in June 2015.

Kirrin Finch

Laura (she/her) and Kelly Moffat (she/her), a married couple, founded Kirrin Finch, a New York-based company that produces casual wear with a masculine-leaning aesthetic. Laura "never wanted to wear dresses growing up" and was "very uncomfortable, even as a little girl." Kelly had a similar experience. Growing up she wore dresses when she had to, but, otherwise, she wore pants. Similar to Laura, dresses did not make her feel comfortable. Laura and Kelly both used *tomboy* and *dapper* to describe their current style. Laura grew up in Scotland and moved to the United States for college, on a golf scholarship. She moved to New York City for a PhD in neuroscience but quit the program and went into marketing, which sparked her interest in starting a business. Kelly grew up in New Jersey, went to university in upstate New York, then moved to New York City to be a teaching fellow, after which she taught in the public school system for eight years.

Both explained they did not "know anything about fashion" but wanted to start a fashion business. They were motivated by their own bad shopping experiences. Laura "never really understood why [she] felt terrible after" shopping. Not until she realized that her style just did not exist on the market did she began to understand some of her experiences. She did not want anything feminine and did not like anything in the men's department and largely found the whole experience "demotivating." Her experiences with sales associates also turned her off of shopping at certain stores, especially when the clerks pointed out the woman's section. Kelly felt terrified when she went to buy her first pair of men's jeans. However, she had a positive experience as the sales associate was positive, and found the whole experience "very liberating," and wanted to return because she finally found clothes that allowed her to express herself in an authentic, comfortable way.

Thus, their frustrations were a significant motivation to start the company. Because they had not run a business before, they took numerous courses at the Fashion Institute of Technology and went from "knowing nothing to knowing a lot more." They brainstormed to come up with their company's name, explaining that their own tomboy identities and their different places of origin helped them choose Kirrin Finch. Laura recalled, "We just thought about how I'm from Scotland and Kelly's from the US and Scout Finch is [an] American tomboy and Georgina Kirrin is a tomboy character from a UK book series, and we just put the two names together to form Kirrin Finch." She continued:

> You know, when you read about these tomboys in young adult literature, they're very free for the most part. They're not worried about what they're wearing, and they're just playing and they're just doing whatever they want. You don't really realize when you're that age, that there are these societal constraints. They haven't quite put pressure on you and told you not to do these things, so you just have that attitude of just being yourself. I think that really rings true for the company as well.

Kelly added, "I think that a lot of people hear it and they think that it is actually a person. Kirrin Finch almost sounds like a person's name ... and there's an association with that character notion. You know, it embodies who they were."

NiK Kacy Footwear

NiK Kacy (they/them), who identifies as gender nonbinary, trans masculine, masculine of center, and queer, founded the ecommerce business NiK Kacy Footwear (Figure 5.4). They grew up in New York City and attended Pepperdine University in Malibu, California where they majored in fine arts and advertising and minored in international communications. Following graduation, before starting their own company, Kacy worked in almost every area of advertising. They were an art director, graphic designer, media buyer, quality assurance analyst, and then producer. Then, they moved from their agency to Google to start their project management team in Los Angeles. After some self-reflection, they decided to take a risk before they had a family, and started their own business. They left Google in 2013 and incorporated right afterward. They had transitional surgery in 2014 and took time to heal, and then began talking to folks in the industry.

Kacy started thinking about their business since they were a kid, because of their own shopping experiences:

> So, the reason I actually started my brand was because of my experience. My whole life, since I was a kid, I couldn't find shoes that fit, I guess, my inside? My outside and my inside never matched, you know, being born in the wrong body and knowing that I was in the wrong body, but never really being able to pinpoint what it was exactly, because I didn't understand. But I knew that whenever I saw guys' shoes I would be like "Oh, that's what I want to wear." Unfortunately, I had very average female feet so I could never find shoes in my size that I liked and then, whenever they would have maybe a certain style that they would say that they have in the female sizes, I would put it on and I would look down and I just remember feeling like, "this is not the same shoe." For whatever reason, their female version is always so much more feminized. They never looked right proportionally when I looked down. I just remember I would look down and be like, "I have like baby feet all of a sudden." It was very

Figure 5.4 NiK Kacy sitting behind shoes from their various lines. Photo courtesy of NiK Kacy.

embarrassing and humiliating, I think, to walk into a store so many times and be like, "I would like to try these shoes on," and they would be like, "Go to the women's section." Even though when I was a teenager-to-an-adult, presenting very masculine, still being directed to the women's section was very hard. That's why I started my company.

Kacy asked numerous industry folks why the products they wanted did not exist and repeatedly heard that the niche was not worth it. Kacy responded, "You're telling me and my whole community, that I'm not worth it and that my people are not worth it? So that was when I was really like, I'm really going to go and do this now. I will do whatever it takes now."

They explained the difficulty small businesses like theirs had in competing with billion-dollar companies and how easily they could be pushed out and their philosophical differences. Kacy explained, "They're coming from a place of trying to make money, whereas we're coming from our experience, our history, our hearts, and, you know, our beliefs."

Strapping Sacramento

Susan Stewart (she/her) founded Strapping Sacramento, which has a brick-and-mortar store in Sacramento, California. She was born in in The Bronx of New York City and grew up in Palm Springs, California, a vacation town with many retired and older folks. Her entrance into retail began with her interest in golf. She played as a child and explained that the golf environment is "very masculine" and "very macho, male-oriented." When she went professional, she had a hard time making golf her career, so she transitioned into retail, as a buyer for various golf resorts for about fifteen years, and she began this career right out of high school, without attending college. Stewart described her time as a golf buyer as "boring" but said it helped her channel energy into wanting to start her own store and clothing brand.

Stewart began with an ecommerce clothing line, selling masculine-leaning button-up shirts for female bodies. In 2015, she had an extremely difficult time finding a dress shirt to wear to her own wedding and settled on a woman's shirt that barely fit and kept popping open in the front. She said, "I know how to manufacture. I know where I can go to get things done, like how hard is it going to be to make a pattern." This motivated her to begin her business.

Stewart developed her first prototype in 2016, having spent the remainder of 2015 convincing her wife that going into business was viable. (Her wife, who held a full-time job, did not share Stewart's entrepreneurial spirit.) She also spent significant time finding and then working with a patternmaker who understood what she desired. She told patternmakers she wanted "a woman's shirt with no darting and a slimmer neckline" and explained many of patternmakers did not understand, thus it took some time to find the right person. After five or six months working to get the pattern right, she then launched the line in 2016 via an ecommerce channel. Stewart accredited the name Strapping Sacramento to thinking through gender. She chose *strapping* because it references the common phrase *strapping young man*. She explained the name made much more sense for her clothing line, which included the button-up shirts and other masculine-leaning items like neckties. She eventually chose to focus on a different model and started a brick-and-mortar gift shop that also sells items from her original clothing line. She kept the name for the gift shop, which sells an assortment of quirky gifts and home decor, because of her pride in her initial venture.

Case Study 7 Kipper Clothiers and THÙY Custom Clothier

Kipper Clothiers

Erin Berg (he/him), who identifies as a trans guy, founded Kipper Clothiers, a custom-made suit and suit coordinate company, which has since closed. He grew up in San Francisco, in the Castro district, in an environment where he "thought all men wore leather and had nipple rings" until he was thirteen years old. He also grew up in a very queer-friendly household and then attended Oberlin College, in Ohio, where he studied neuroscience and American studies. Afterward he traveled around the United States, looking for places to live, and after seeing much of the country he realized that as a trans person he wanted to stay in the San Francisco area.

The day after Proposition 8 was repealed, he founded Kipper Clothiers. He explained, "You know, if we're going to do this, this is the moment we're going to do it." He continued that, at the time, San Francisco was the location of many queer weddings. Berg had previously worked at Tomboy Tailors, where he and his former business partner met and "fell in love with the idea and fell in love with the concept." Everything was made to order, and they had a showroom in downtown San Francisco, where consumers would come in to have fittings, review swatches, and talk about their design interests. Berg would request that the consumers build Pinterest boards with visual cues so he could get a sense of their style as he talked them through the purchase process. His former business partner came up with the name by researching older tailoring industry terms. *Kipper* used to refer to a tailor's assistant. He also explained that most people do not know how to pronounce *clothiers* or know what a clothier is, both of which he finds "annoying."

THÚY Custom Clothier

Thúy Nguyen (she/her) founded THÚY Custom Clothier, an ecommerce custom suit and suit-coordinate apparel business. Her parents are Vietnamese refugees who escaped the war when she was just a baby. Her mom, who influenced her heavily, was the eldest in her family and was sent to Saigon to learn a trade, specifically to be a seamstress. After Nguyen's family escaped Vietnam, they landed in Puerto Rico, where her mom worked as a seamstress for Van Heusen. Nguyen explained she got her great style from her dad and her determination from her mom. She recalled feeling like a free spirit at a young age, achieving freedom such as getting a job at fifteen and getting her driving permit. Eventually, her family moved to California, as one of her uncles worked there at U-Haul, and her family members all eventually moved to work at the moving company.

Nguyen studied photography and cinema first at Evergreen Valley College in San Jose, fell in love and did the "U-Haul thing" where she "basically moved up here [San Francisco] for my first girlfriend" and stayed. She then attended City College of San Francisco, meeting numerous people, including teachers, who were extremely influential and who she credits with helping shape her into an artist. Nguyen started her business with influence from her mom because, once the family moved to California, her mother had numerous dressmaking clients coming over all the time for custom garments.

Nguyen had been interested in style and fashion since childhood:

> I've always been a tomboy, and I've always wanted to wear my brothers' clothes, and as soon as I could, I started kind of stealing some of my dad's clothes. I still have a pair of his slacks and vests, and I don't know what he did with the jacket, but I wish he still had it. I would go thrift shopping to buy clothes for myself, and I would learn how to alter them so they would fit me better. I also have this sense, from growing up with a father who's always dressed up. He would always be so sharply dressed, and we would sometimes be like, "Dad, where are you going?" "I'm going to go buy milk." He was such a good-looking guy. And my mom made all her outfits, and so I think that even from a young age, I was very aware of fit and style. I used to shop for my little brother, who is seven years younger than me. I say that my little brother is my first model, because one of my responsibilities was to help raise him, to take care of him, basically. So, as soon as he started school, I would get his little outfits ... and put them out for him. I would be like, "Tomorrow you're going to wear this!" And of course, he's the little kid being like, "No I don't want to wear that!" "No, you have to!" I remember going thrift shopping, and I would be like "[gasps] This would look so good on David!" I was just shopping for myself really, but for him, because it was that he's my little brother, and I'm going to dress him up.

She explained she was a late bloomer and came to terms with her sexuality at twenty-one, yet always felt like a tomboy, growing up with four brothers. Growing up she very much related to males because of her family. She also felt like a tomboy, in part, because, since her family was poor, she had numerous hand-me-downs from her brothers.

The idea for her brand came from her own experiences shopping for suits. She and her first girlfriend loved to get dressed up, but every time Nguyen went shopping, it was hard to find something that fit. She wore boys' suits and tried numerous places to find well-fitting clothes. When she started her business, she began working with tailors in Thailand who understood her queer-centered business, choosing that country specifically for its good labor and LGBTQ+ laws. Like her mom, she wanted to create custom clothing, but suits instead of dresses, and she began her business officially in October 2013. She used her own name for the brand because her mother had done the same. She may eventually cut *custom clothier* from the name because she is quite proud of her name, especially as it is an androgynous one.

Case Study 8 Audio Helkuik and Rebirth Garments

Audio Helkuik

Audio Helkuik (he/him) is the founder of Audio Helkuik, a clothing and accessory brand based out of Omaha, Nebraska, who also holds other jobs; for instance, at the time of this oral history, he was a costumer for a local children's theater. He spent most of his life in Nebraska, living in surrounding states, including Iowa and Minnesota, for short periods but now calls Nebraska "Homoha." After visiting the fashion museum on campus at the University of Nebraska, Lincoln, as an undeclared major, he decided that same day to major in textile and apparel design with a studio art minor; he also has a second minor: entomology.

In college, he focused on the brand ideas, using different class projects to experiment. He explained, "I knew I wanted an androgynous brand. It's weird to say that, because *androgynous* is not quite right." After he graduated, he had more time to focus on producing designs that were not created to earn a grade. At that point, he began selling on different platforms, such as Etsy, and in-person at craft shows. He said, "I just kept making and selling items, and it wasn't super focused, it was just finding fun yarn and making a fun hat. Or I'd pick up a piece of paper and draw an interesting picture. It was very spontaneous. I did that for a long time, but I, I wasn't like a focused brand."

He graduated from college in 2008 and began the brand in 2011, selling designs "without gender in mind." Helkuik has a heavy emphasis on leather accessories, including harnesses, headwear, crowns, chokers, and jewelry. Helkuik has a studio where he handmakes almost all the items and stocks a few other products such as pins and patches. You can also purchase Helkuik's original art, which centers queer love. In November 2023, he had about fifteen different nine-by-twelve-inch colored illustrations available for purchase. Helkuik explained that in regard to his personal identities, he usually says,

> I'm nonbinary, or gender-queer, gender-fluid, gender nonconforming, all of these apply to me. If I'm talking to like a cisgender heteronormative person, who just doesn't totally get it yet, I just say nonbinary, because if I say I'm a femme-presenting, but masculine-leaning, nonbinary queer person, I think their brains kind of explode. All those words make sense to me because I'm in the community and I'm around this vocab and expression all the time. Mostly, I insist that I am not a girl.

His designs reflect his personal gender identity, and he likes to wear his own products, such as the accessories, almost every day, and occasionally wears the harnesses when feeling fancy. As the sole proprietor of Helkuik, he does everything from checking emails from consumers, creating prototypes, sourcing materials, packaging and delivering orders to the post office, and managing social media content, including the newsletter and blog posts. Much of Helkuik's business is direct-to-consumer, via his online storefront, yet he has done some wholesale, consignment, in-person sales, and vending at events.

Rebirth Garments

Sky Cubacub (they/them) founded Rebirth Garments, a radical fashion brand based in Chicago, Illinois, which centers people of color, queerness, fatness, and people with disabilities in its entire business plan. They attended Northside College Prep, a prestigious high school, which paved the way for a full scholarship to the Art Institute of Chicago. Both of Cubacub's parents are artists, and Cubacub has been highly involved with different artists and designers since they were fifteen, and after high school graduation began work on Rebirth Garments. They earned a bachelor's of fine arts degree in fibers, performance, and fashion but was not in the fashion department, because it was "racist and classist and sizeist and ableist and queerphobic." Cubacub wanted to make clothing for people of every size and they related that their professors perceived, for example, their inclusive illustrations as "fat in a negative way."

Their personal clothing style includes colorful, geometric patterns, and they often wear a lot of chainmail. They wear most of the types of clothing that they make; Rebirth Garments is a "completely personal project" that they are sharing with other folks. They explained they started the company because they could not buy a binder or packing garments in high school. And they wanted to make garments that were celebratory, not medical looking. During high school, they initially envisioned the project as two separate lines: one line of undergarments specifically for trans folks and another centering clothing for people with disabilities. But they decided to merge the idea and create an intersectional space for clothing and accessories. They "did a couple of interviews with folks who were more binary-trans and a friend who is a wheelchair user" and made clothes for them.

The brand's name reflects its personal nature: Cubacub explained that they had a rebirthing ceremony for themselves. At the time of the interview, they were four and half years old, since that was the time since the ceremony. They explained:

> I have always had anxiety and like panic disorder for like my whole life and umm, there's times in my life where I'll have panic attacks at least once a day for years. It was just getting to a point where, in one of those rounds of severe panic attacks all the time I could not handle being myself anymore. Later, I found out about this thing that Kate Bornstein says in a book like about suicide, about trying to prevent teen suicide, and being like, "I kill myself to not kill myself" or like, "I kill myself to not harm myself." So, I had a funeral for myself and had this rebirthing ceremony. It wasn't religious or anything. It was just weird performance art goofiness but, it really did help me a lot. I don't think I had a panic attack for like six months after that, which at that time was … not really possible for me to do. So, it yeah, it was just all about

like shedding my skin. And, like, you know, now I understand my anxiety so much more 'cause I have an amazing queer therapist, but uh, at that time I just needed to learn how to, like, let go of some things and not let my anxiety like completely make it so I couldn't function.

They sell their garments online through Etsy and through direct communications. Because of the personal nature of each object, Cubacub interviews each person to meet their needs and then crafts the products.

Case Study 9 Show and Tell Concept Shop, Stuzo, and WE ARE MORTALS

Show and Tell Concept Shop

Alyah Baker (she/her) is the co-founder of Qulture Collective and the owner of the Show and Tell Concept Shop, which at the time of the interview was a brick-and-mortar store in downtown Oakland, California, at 1714 Franklin Street (Figure 5.5). Baker grew up in New Jersey; moved to North Carolina; then lived in New York and Pennsylvania, pursuing a dance career; then moved to Oakland. As a child, she attended various schools, including Shandley High School for its dual program with the Pittsburgh Ballet Theatre. Baker then attended Duke University, and at the time of the interview was interested in doing a master's of fine arts in dance. While dancing throughout her early adult life, Baker also worked in retail and fashion in San Francisco, including employment at The Gap from 1999 until 2011, in roles from sales associate to store manager and then as corporate merchandiser.

Show and Tell emerged because Baker wanted to create a space where people could find clothes that were "not the mainstream." Working at The Gap gave her a solid background, but the Gap environment did not center diversity, and she wanted to expand beyond that. She opened the shop with her previous partner, who was masculine presenting, and the initial interest emerged from watching them continually be misgendered while shopping. Baker witnessed her partner "being told she couldn't shop in certain areas of the store, being followed around the store and then not even being able to find the pieces that she wanted to wear that were made for her body." Baker wanted to create a space where she could "scout out those pieces, or create those pieces, and create an environment where everyone felt comfortable shopping and fully, authentically, expressing what they wanted to show." She's interested in "pieces that have some meaning and stand out." Show and Tell, therefore, has many handmade and one-of-a-kind items, carefully curated into an assortment of products.

Baker opened Show and Tell Concept Shop in November 2011 during Occupy Oakland at Fourteenth and Broadway, directly across from where protestors were camping out. She explained:

> I have an older brother, who passed earlier that year, and then Occupy Oakland was going on, and there was the whole debate about Don't Ask, Don't Tell in the media, so we were having lots of conversations around what we were doing with our lives, how we wanted to live and what our values were. We also were considering, how we can do things that appeal to the 99 percent versus falling into that trap of trying to reach the 1 percent of ethics, sustainability—and all of those pieces culminated in us being inspired to see if anyone would give us a lease, and they did! Which is something that still shocks me. Sometimes I walk around Oakland, and I'm like, "I can't believe I have keys to

Figure 5.5 Alyah Baker, founder of Show and Tell Concept Shop. Photo courtesy of Adya Baker.

all of these buildings in Oakland." It's pretty trippy but, we got lucky. They gave us a lease and [we] ran from there.

Her co-founder, Nicole, left the business, and at the time of the interview, Baker was running it solo. Show and Tell Concept, the original idea, centers community and community organizing. Then, in January 2015 Baker also cofounded Qulture Collective with Terry Sopwilson and Julia Sopwilson, a married couple. Qulture Collective includes community elements, including a coffee shop, community programs, and maker workshops. Its mission is to "drive queer culture" while centering community needs. She explained they chose the name Qulture Collective because it's "*culture* with a *Q* for *queer* and *collective* because there are several businesses now that kind of tie into the space and work to maintain it." I completed the oral history with Baker at the Franklin Street location, and when I walked into the space, I was immediately greeted with a hip coffee shop. There was seating available and numerous people enjoying beverages. Then, to the immediate right was the Show and Tell Concept retail area.

Stuzo

Stoney Michelli Love (he/she/they) founded Stuzo, a lifestyle brand with a brick-and-mortar store in Los Angeles, California (Figure 5.6). Love grew up in New York City, in the Bronx, and at the time of the interview had lived in Los Angeles for about thirteen years. Following high school, they earned an associate's degree in performing arts, specifically acting, and then went on to a bachelor of fine arts in graphic design. They then taught themself to sew, screen-print, and run a business—via YouTube and other informal learning spaces. Before starting Stuzo, Love had upward of fifty jobs, from working retail, to bartending, to serving tables at Buffalo Wild Wings, a popular sports-bar chain restaurant.

Love began thinking about Stuzo in 2018. In the last year of their degree, they started sketching:

> So I couldn't stop, and I started sketching and I was also planning out where I could get the T-shirts and … how much they would cost and all this stuff. So I was just planning out the whole, basically the whole company and what I would need to do to start it. So I need this much and this and that. And most of those designs actually didn't even really make it, to tell you the truth, but it was just the structure, and then that was one day. And then fast-forward maybe a couple months, I had conversations with my mom, and I had conversations with my ex-boyfriend, and they kept asking me if I was still gay and I was just like, Yep, still gay.

Love felt like her family and friends did not believe they were gay, so they designed the first official logo, which many folks like them could relate to. They kept drawing and sketching adding elements of their other identities (Latina, African, etc.) and used their senior capstone project as the vehicle for the logo of their brand at the time, Graphic Queen Apparel. They quickly changed the name, however, because they did not want to steer cisgender men away from the company. Their classmates and professors helped fine-tune the logo. Thus, the brand was born with a focus on expressing one's authentic gender. In particular, their focus on gender related back to their own personal experiences with clothing as they always had found themselves wearing their brother's clothes and mixing and matching men's and women's clothes. They wanted to create clothes "that fit everyone," where they could create their own style based upon their individuality. In 2010, they officially incorporated with a name that used the first two letters of their name and then "grabbed a name from a well-known African name" to put some of their heritage in the name. They explained

Figure 5.6 Love in front of their storefront in Los Angeles, California. Photo courtesy of Stuzo Clothing.

they want Stuzo to be associated with gender free so much that it might end up in the dictionary.

WE ARE MORTALS

Anji Becker (she/her) founded WE ARE MORTALS, an ecommerce clothing line that focuses on challenging the gender binary. She grew up in a working-class family between Milwaukee, Wisconsin and Chicago, Illinois. In college, she studied education because it seemed like a viable path and her mother and grandparents were all teachers, yet she always had an interest in the arts. She minored in Spanish and took numerous electives in women and gender studies, which she said increased her awareness and influenced her path. She moved to San Diego at twenty-one years old and then moved to Los Angeles, where she lived at the time of the interview. She had taught school for a few years, yet felt creatively unfulfilled.

While Becker is cisgender, she identifies as pansexual yet previously related to the terms *bisexual* and *lesbian*. Her past shopping experiences influenced her idea for the brand; she also credits her non-fashion background and the way she questioned the industry and its need for binary men's and women's departments.

She began sewing her own projects and created a fanny pack that sold well on Etsy. That experience motivated her to move to Los Angeles and start her fashion brand, which she officially incorporated in 2014. She named the company WE ARE MORTALS because one week after moving to Los Angeles, she lost her mother to cancer, even though her mom was an extremely healthy person. Also, the name WE ARE MORTALS highlights how we all have something in common. WE ARE MORTALS is a genderless brand with the slogan "The future has no gender."

Case Study 10 Greyscale Goods

Sara Medd (she/her) founded and was the CEO of Greyscale Goods, a styling service focused on the queer and trans communities, which has since closed. Medd grew up in Virginia, near Washington, DC, and then moved to New York City to attend the Fashion Institute of Technology, where she majored in fashion merchandising and management. During school, she worked in retail at J. Crew in Rockefeller Center, and after graduation she took a position at a wholesale company that did private labels for Dillard's. Her lack of desire to work in an office provided motivation to seek other opportunities. She landed a styling internship at the Condé Nast international office, where she worked on shoots for *Russian Vogue* and *Italian Vogue*. Then, she moved to Los Angeles, where she worked as a styling assistant for about five years.

She described her personal style as "hard femme" or "tomboy femme," but she is most comfortable "in a T-shirt and jeans." She identifies as gay, and her partner's shopping experience inspired her to start Greyscale Goods. She explained she often dates women who identify as "masculine of center," and seeing partners struggle to shop for special events or even everyday wear highlighted the need for her service. Medd knows the access that major cities provide but thinks it is "much harder for someone living in the Midwest, even a city in the Midwest." She continued, "There is just the pure lack of options for stores, and then when shopping in the men's department is not an option, just because of the stigma that surrounds that, and the impact it can have on someone's self-confidence."

Since she had styling experience, her friends always went to her for shopping advice. In 2014, her friends were ordering from Stitch Fix, an on-demand styling service that delivers clothing to a person's door. Both members of one couple, a feminine-presenting person and a masculine-presenting person, completed a Stitch Fix order. The feminine-leaning person loved the service, but the "more masculine of center [person], tried ordering and tried her best to put in, on the style profile, all the answers that were the most similar to her style." When the box arrived, Medd's masculine-leaning friend said, "They clearly don't get it. There's nothing in here that I would ever wear, it's just way too feminine." That was Medd's "aha moment," when she realized that this could be a viable business, a mail-order styling service catering to masculine-of-center folks (Figure 5.7).

Medd had never started a company or worked at an executive level, so she spent a whole summer doing online research about how to start, operate, and sustain a business. Then, she incorporated in September 2014. She chose the name Greyscale Goods because "we live in this world right now, where nothing is binary. Gender is not binary, and style is not binary. So I was playing with the thought of like, style is so much more than black and white and there are all these shades in between." Thus, Greyscale Goods. Each customer filled out a style profile, with pictures, then placed an order, which included a $48 styling fee, and they received a box in the mail with hand-selected items, with the option to purchase the items or mail them back. Medd started a modern styling service for the queer and trans communities, particularly for consumers in rural areas and small towns with limited access to clothing store options.

Figure 5.7 Example of styling service ensembles that reflect a masculine-leaning aesthetic. Photo courtesy of author.

Part 3 Positioning Consumer Products

6 Vehicles for Queer and Trans Sensibilities

Products are the tangible embodiments of a brand, the concrete manifestations that entrepreneurs create, market, and sell. Yet, within the realm of queer and trans fashion, these products serve as more than just commodities. They become vessels that intricately convey and embody the multifaceted tensions, ambiguities, and ambivalences surrounding queer and trans identities. The profound questions arise: what qualities within these products allow them to actively resist, subvert, and simultaneously uphold traditional notions of gender and sexuality? How did these entrepreneurs think through these tensions, create the products, and then communicate that to their consumers? In navigating the complex landscape of the twenty-first century, queer and trans fashion brands strategically position their soft and hard assemblages not merely as clothing, accessories, or shoes, but as intentional tools to challenge and support prevailing fashion norms. Exploring the nuances of this strategic positioning unravels the layers that define these products as powerful conveyors of queer and trans sensibilities, shedding light on how they navigate and contribute to the evolution of societal and personal perceptions and expectations.

The Custom Suit Experience as an Identity Journey

The custom masculine-of-center suit is one of the many products queer and trans fashion brands specialize in. THÚY Custom Clothier (Thúy Nguyen) craft made-to-order suits and suit coordinates with a keen focus on intricate details, personalized construction, and an individualized shopping experience. Clients can tailor every aspect of their suits. The clothier offers a diverse range of lapel styles, from notched to peaked, allowing clients to influence their suits' formality and aesthetic. Choices in pocket styles, such as welt or patch pockets, contribute to both functionality and visual appeal. The freedom to select fabrics, choose the suit silhouette, and personalize the lining further enhances the bespoke experience. Nguyen's clients can have suits in any style they prefer. Kipper Clothiers (Erin Berg), while open, also made similar products to Nguyen. The suit may seem mundane, yet so much detail and craftsmanship goes into its many aspects (Figure 6.1).

In her custom-suit business, Nguyen describes herself as the "lone traveling salesman." That is, she often hauls her product samples to and from client consultations, where an initial consultation can take up to three hours. Nguyen, who lives in San Francisco meets many clients in a softly lit, blue-toned therapy room at a small medical clinic when possible, because going to a client's home can be very distracting,

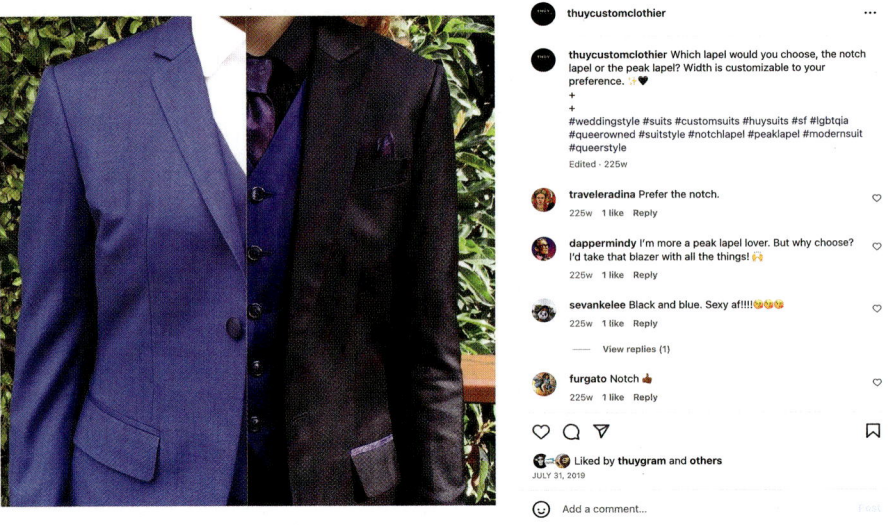

Figure 6.1 Nguyen's social media post highlighting the numerous suit detail options. Photo courtesy of THÚY Custom Clothier.

making the appointment more than three hours. Her product is defined by the one-on-one consultation experience. Nguyen described:

> So, I sit there, and they sit here, and it's funny, because this room is called the therapy room, and it feels like that, too. So, I feel like my consultations, are very personal. I feel that a lot of my clients ... have certain body issues and have certain experiences with going shopping that really make them uncomfortable. I feel like the space already sets the mood. It's very calming, we sit down, there's not a lot of stuff. I'm not like trying to do a sales pitch. I'm more like, I sit down. I'm like, "Oh, what is the event?" Then we look at all the fabrics, and then they choose some and then we go through a process of elimination until they pick their favorite one. There are fabrics for linings that they can pick from, too. When it's still daylight out, we will walk out with the fabrics, so that they can also get a sense of the colors in daylight, and I have some more lights that I actually set up here for just kind of browsing through the fabrics. So, we pick out the fabrics and then I take their full measurements.

It is about personal connection. Nguyen commented:

> So, for me, it's not just about a piece of clothing, it's about, how do I connect with this person and how do I make them feel comfortable through the process? A lot of times, I'm working on outfits for a wedding, a very special event, and I have the one shot to make this right, and to make them feel like a star for their wedding or their event. I want them to feel comfortable. I want them not to not have to think like, "Oh, do I look stupid?" Or like, "Oh, does this look weird on me?" I think, as a butch person, going through life, finding comfort, even in my own body, even wearing certain clothes, I know exactly what that's like. I know what it's like to go to a family wedding and just be like, "Does this look right on me?" I get a lot

of these clients who go through that, so it does feel like therapy. I feel like I do get, again, like when I'm doing a consultation, and they're sharing stories with me, they're sharing personal parts of themselves with me, and I get to be some small part in their wedding. Like, they're wearing something that I, well, I didn't literally make, but it's like I had made something for them. I had created this outfit for them. Even after a consultation, when people leave here, and they are just all smiles. A lot of times my clients will be like, "Gosh that was fun, that was painless, or that was, you know … I didn't expect for it to be so easy."

Berg (Kipper Clothiers) described a similar process: he does not keep any inventory, and everything is made-to-order via custom measurements. However, he opened a showroom for clients in downtown San Francisco that reflected the brand's classic, dapper style. And like Nguyen, Berg does a lot of education in the custom-suit order process, as many folks do not regularly experience made-to-order fashion, whose variety and available choices can be overwhelming. He said:

> I like to do a lot of education in the process, because a lot of queer folk, or masculine-of-center folks, haven't had the experience of getting to know any of this—unless, of course, their like dad has taught them. So, people come in, I give them a little bit of education, show them the fabrics, and then we design it. I measure them, and we do all the fun posture stuff, and then, the garment comes back six weeks later, and we do the round of alterations. So, it's all made to order.

While Berg and Nguyen target the queer and trans communities, they both serve cisgender, heterosexual consumers as well. In every case, the result is not just a suit but unique and personalized garments that resonate with the client's individuality, regardless of their gender or sexual identity. Berg and Nguyen can certainly relate to queer and trans consumers, and they each provide a shopping experience without heteronormative assumptions, a space where clients from these communities can feel seen, understood, and respected. Here the suit then reflects the embodied experience of obtaining it, and the process is wrapped up in the suit's tangible elements. These aspects, in turn, encapsulate and mirror the meaningful journey of the suit's creation, forming a connection between the wearer's own narrative and the craftsmanship behind the garment.

The Button-Up Shirt: Masculine for Folks Assigned Female at Birth

The button-up, collared shirt is a staple item in many people's closets. These versatile shirts not only reflect a sense of classic style but also serve as emblematic essentials that transcend trends, holding enduring appeal in the realm of fashion. Kirrin Finch (Laura Moffat and Kelly Moffat), Strapping Sacramento (Susan Stewart), and Dapper Boi (Vicky Pasche) produced button-up shirts as core products for their brands, with a focus on construction details to create queer and trans space—literally through some of the product construction details.

Laura, Kelly, Stewart, and Pasche all highlighted that they focused on construction details while developing their product. Specific elements that make Kirrin Finch's button-up shirts appealing to queer and consumers include the nine center-front buttons that prevent the fabric from gaping at the chest. They also designed the shirts with structured collars, making them easier to wear with ties (Figure 6.2). They also made the shirts longer than typical menswear so folks can tuck them and fit them around the female body hips. While the shirts work for queer and trans folks, Kelly is very aware of the balance between needing to make money by expanding their audience and staying true to their community. She related:

> I think that's where a lot of the queer-focused brands, have really struggled, because in choosing that market, you're saying, "Yes, there is an unmet need," but that market is inherently smaller than the general mass market. So, we're always fighting this battle of "how do we get a bigger audience without losing our core audience?" It's literally the kind of constant battle we have when we're writing copy on the website, when we're developing product. It's this tension point between making money and satisfying the audience. And they don't always necessarily agree with each other.

Design elements in Stewart's shirt include putting the placket on the right, which is traditional in men's clothing, and to create a square, boxy look, she did not include any fit devices (e.g., darts). She changed the placket to cater to trans masculine folks "so that if I have a trans-fella wearing it, he's not going to feel like, 'I'm in a woman's shirt.'" She also shortened the collar width, because people assigned female at birth often have smaller neck circumferences than those assigned male. Of the shirt, she said, "When it's on, it's got a very crisp, masculine look," reflecting her interest in upholding a traditional masculine aesthetic.

In reference to the color choices and variations and marketing, Stewart expressed how the queer and trans communities are a small market segment and that branching

Figure 6.2 Kirrin Finch product copy, highlighting the structured collars on their button-up shirt. Photo courtesy of Kirrin Finch.

out to other consumers to expand their business brought varying responses. She highlighted that she sometimes withholds that the shirt was designed with the queer and trans community in mind:, "I don't always tell people that it's gender-neutral because some people really get freaked out, and the thing about wearing a queer brand, it scares them; they're like 'Oh, I'm gay.'" Stewart has sold her button-up shirts to cisgender, heterosexual men, by emphasizing how "big and strong" they look in the shirt, playing on the "strapping" part of the store name. She also mentioned that doing trendy prints is difficult again due to the small market segment: "I'm already playing in a market that's so small, and then it's like, "queer," "lesbians" or "transmen," and masculine, so it just keeps getting smaller and smaller, so you have to be as broad as possible to that little baby customer group, because if you go even farther and cater to this kind of person who likes wild, Hawaiian prints, it just keeps getting too small. So mine was about mass appeal."

Pasche designed her button-up shirts while thinking through the curves of the body of someone assigned female at birth. To keep the shirt form-fitting without having a chest gap, she added three snaps to the interior placket (Figure 6.3). This is one of their largest selling points, which they emphasize in their product copy (Figure 6.4). She also described another functional element to the short-sleeve button-up shirt: a sunglass buttonhole slit adjacent to the patch pocket on the chest. The detail allows the wearer to secure their sunglasses in a fashionable position (Figure 6.5).

Thus, through its thoughtful design details, the button-up shirt becomes more than a wardrobe essential. The careful considerations of construction details, such as button placement and collar dimensions, demonstrate a commitment to creating garments that look good while subtly serving the needs of masculine-of-center, assigned female at birth folks. Beyond its aesthetic appeal, the shirt becomes a testament to a meticulous consideration of construction details, where tiny elements serve a purpose to consider the queer and trans experiences while wearing it or getting dressed and undressed.

Jeans: Mixing and Matching Gender Details

Vasche of Dapper Boi started her business around the desire to create jeans. Drawing inspiration from her own preferences, she meticulously curated a fusion of the best elements from men's and women's jeans, seeking to transcend gender norms and cater to a diverse audience. While Vasche lacked a background in patternmaking, her determination led her to collaborate with a skilled professional who could translate her vision into tangible samples.

The cornerstone of her design philosophy was rooted in addressing a longstanding issue: the impracticality of traditional women's pant pockets, notorious for their diminutive size. To rectify this, Vasche and her team meticulously crafted jeans featuring functional pockets, with a particular focus on accommodating the modern essentials of daily life. Notably, her attention to detail extended to the coin

Figure 6.3 Dapper Boi button-up shirt featuring snaps on the placket interior. Photo courtesy of Dapper Boi.

pocket, engineered to comfortably house a bulky smartphone (Figure 6.6). Vasche's vision for improved denim also manifested in the extension of the crotch seam and zipper, coupled with a design that seamlessly embraced and celebrated the natural curves of hips and buttocks. Dapper Boi's jeans aimed to transcend the boundaries of conventional denim, redefining fashion norms and providing a stylish, functional, and inclusive solution for folks assigned female at birth.

Unbifurcated Queerness

In contemporary society, unbifurcated garments—dresses, skirts—frequently carry strong associations with mainstream femininity. These clothing items, characterized by their singular, nondivided structure, have become emblematic of traditional gender norms. Certainly, there are exceptions and nuance to skirts and femininity, for

Figure 6.4 Dapper Boi product copy for its button-up shirt. Photo courtesy of Dapper Boi.

example, the Utilikilts brand, based in Seattle, Washington, markets its kilts to manly, cisgender men (Reddy-Best and Howell 2014). Due to the enduring patriarchal system, the adoption of stereotypically feminine traits (e.g., unbifurcated garments) by men is sometimes linked to perceptions of diminished power or authority.

For WE ARE MORTALS, the Fluidity Dress serves as a symbol of its vision for a future without rigid gender distinctions (Figure 6.7). In her product copy, Becker describes the product: "Chunky straps and metal detail work to balance masculine and feminine on this unisex dress" (WE ARE MORTALS n.d.). Metal, a hard material often associated with masculinity, is incorporated to offer a mix of gendered aesthetics. Similarly, the garment has wide straps, meant to signify notions of masculine essence. This departure from established, slippery-slope norms challenges societal perceptions and represents a conscious effort to create a more fluid approach to fashion that transcends traditional gender boundaries.

Femme and Masc Shoes in Every Size

NiK Kacy (Kacy) focuses specifically on gender-neutral and gender-free shoes. Kacy describes that their unisex sizing system and range of sizes sets them apart from the competition. They shared that most companies have about seven sizes whereas they have fourteen, because they include the entire range of what would be considered "female" and "male." Thus, having the full range of sizes is a way to remove gender from the objects. Kacy conveyed they wanted to create masculine-leaning shoes but also wanted to create shoes for everyone.

Figure 6.5 Dapper Boi model wearing button-up shirt with sunglass slit feature. Photo courtesy of Dapper Boi.

They create classic designs such as oxfords, derbies, and monk boots. However, to make them more inclusive, they have expanded the sizing and subtly added queer and trans symbols: "I can add like accent colors or like signature looks such as adding the equal sign emblem on all of my products in order to modernize it in a way where I can utilize fashion as activism. That's my way of designing" (Figure 6.8). In Kacy's first collection, called Fortune, they created the Chelsea boot, in red, as it is a sign of good fortune in their Chinese culture. They said, "I wanted the idea of, you know, good fortune to be brought to all the people who want to support this concept

Figure 6.6 Dapper Boi jeans with coin pocket large enough to fit a cell phone. Photo courtesy of Dapper Boi.

of equality, right?" Kacy describes the Fortune line as "masculine dress shoes for smaller feet," which has five distinct shoes in masculine-of-center traditional styles (Kacy 2023b).

Kacy named their second collection of shoes Destiny, because "it's the first collection that's going to be not only gender-equal but also gender-neutral, and that's ultimately my destiny to do that." The Destiny collection has five different shoes that are described online: "Not only are the proportion and sizing genderequal, but the design of the shoe in itself is truly gender-neutral and genderfree in style" (Kacy 2023a). One of the styles is referred to as the Georgios:

> I guess the reason he [George Michael] inspired me to do this design in the "First Time I ever Saw Your Face" video. In the video he has boots that are cowboy boots, and I think cowboy boots are something that's so masculine. Like, in

Vehicles for Queer and Trans Sensibilities 101

Figure 6.7 Fluidity Dress by WE ARE MORTALS. Photo courtesy of Sophia Strathearn.

American culture, cowboys—that's the ultimate masculinity, right? At the same time, for the whole time I was growing up, I think George was just this vision for me that was both so beautiful and so masculine. I knew that I loved him because his music was so soulful. His look was so masculine, but there was something about him. I don't know if it was my gaydar, I don't know what it was, but I knew that there was something about him that just encompassed everything that I love about human beings. It's like this blend of masculinity and femininity. So, I knew that I wanted to make a shoe like this because I've always wanted to wear one. Even though it was inspired by the cowboy boot, it's also inspired by Flamenco dancer boots. I'm a huge fan of like watching Flamenco dancers and I love the male dancers' boots. They have like the heel that's like this, you know? It's tapered and higher. It reminds me very much of a cowboy boot and a Flamenco dancer boot, put together. I really think that this is a boot where you can look at it and think that it's neither masculine nor feminine, and yet all of it at the same time.

Kacy also marketed stereotypical feminine-leaning products as gender neutral. In 2018, they developed a high heel for their brand (Figure 6.9). Notably, these heels are not confined to a narrow size range but, in keeping with the brand's ethos, are available in an expansive array of sizes. This bold move not only reflects the brand's dedication to breaking down gender stereotypes but also emphasizes its commitment to providing fashion options that are both stylish and accessible to all.

Figure 6.8 Gender-equal Chelsea Brogue Boots. Photo courtesy of NiK Kacy.

Unisex Swimwear Styles/Supporting or Compressing the Chest

Beefcake Swimwear produces a line of 1920s-inspired unisex swimwear (Figure 6.10). The suits share the same one-piece silhouette with a scoop neckline, thick shoulder straps, and a mid-thigh-length short. However, to add variety, they come in a few different retro-inspired prints. Because the suits are marketed as unisex, Wells encourages potential consumers to compare their body measurements with the brand's size chart, which ranges from extra small to 5X.

Wells jokingly mentioned that she loves breasts because she is a lesbian, but she "does not want to make clothing for them." Her manufacturer confirmed the complexity of making bras and wanted no part in changing the product to include them: "My manufacturer's already been like, No. If you want to do that, you need to find someone else." She certainly has thought about the chest area in her swimsuits, and, in an original iteration, she incorporated a "simple piece of fabric across the front panel, with a little strip of elastic underneath where the breasts would be." The design

Figure 6.9 Gender-equal high heels titled The Borga. Shoe on the left features the red embroidered equal sign. Photo courtesy of NiK Kacy.

feature provided some support but did not provide any lift or compression binding. She received some feedback about the chest area from consumers and decided to line the entire front, which assisted her consumers with larger chest areas. On her website, Wells wrote, "Wearers with full chests have confirmed the compressive fabric offers good support and coverage" and that if they wanted any further support, they should layer "a simple bikini top or sports bra underneath (like you would with a rashguard)" (Beefcake Swimwear 2023). In her product development stages, she also considered the crotch area—and again kept it simple because she "couldn't figure out how to put a penis holder in there."

Marialexandra Garcia (Outplay Swimwear) designed both swimwear and some activewear. One unique product by Outplay was the compression swim tops. The swim tops were available in no compression, light compression, and high compression. She described that consumers wanted binders, yet Garcia emphasized that she did not make swim binders because she was informed it is unsafe to bind during physical activities, although scholarship on safety in this context needs further exploration and anecdotal evidence suggests that folks do exercise or swim with binders—loose and tight (Folx 2022). Garcia made a close compromise by laying fabrics:

> It's layers of fabric that create the compression, and the no-compression is obviously just from the regular spandex that you use in swimwear, it's just the same cut as everything else. Then low compression has the outer layer of fabric, the lining, because everything is lined. I like everything to be really nice on the inside, so, that's my couture side still in my head. Everything needs to be lined and

Figure 6.10 Swimsuits designed by Beefcake Swimwear. Photo by Ashe Walker. Copyright Beefcake Swimwear.

everything has to be pretty on the inside as well. So, it's the outer layer, the lining, and then between the lining, for the low compression, the front of the top has this special mesh material that still stretches but much less than everything else, and that compresses in the front. High compression has that same material in the front and in the back, so it smushes you in as much as possible from every end, so that is what creates the compression and acts as kind of a binder that you can be active and swim in.

For research and development, she listened to the problems folks were experiencing and tried to design solutions. Because she is a skilled patternmaker, she envisions the product and knows that it can work, despite some factories claiming the design might be impossible. She said:

> Everybody kept telling me, "You can't make these swim tops like this," and I kept saying "You can; this is what we're going to do; let's go do it." It was back and forth with several manufacturers until I found a factory that fell in love with the idea and that was completely open to every crazy idea I had, and I finally got to make what I wanted to make. That's how I did it. So yeah, it's a very different process making very functional, very cool looking, swimwear than making beautiful wedding gowns.

Boxer Briefs and Underwear for the Femmes, Too!

Play Out Apparel, Let's Be Brief, and TomboyX specialize in crafting and selling underwear. Their initial focus was on creating boxer briefs tailored for assigned-female-at-birth individuals who identify as masculine of center. However, as their businesses developed, they expanded their product ranges. While they continued to offer boxer briefs designed for the comfort and style preferences of the masculine-of-center community, their product line grew to encompass a more diverse and inclusive range of undergarment styles. This evolution reflects their commitment to providing a broader and more comprehensive selection in the realm of intimate apparel.

Although Naomi Gonzalez and Fran Dunaway from TomboyX initially thought they would focus on button-up shirts, they realized quickly that they would have success as an underwear company, specifically starting with the boxer brief. They did presales, sold out in two weeks, tripled their sales in six months, and stayed with underwear, since that seemed to be their niche. Since the beginning, they have expanded from the boxer brief and sell everything from a bikini-style to a nine-inch inseam boxer brief and period underwear (Figure 6.11). They also sell various bras, including soft and racerback bras. While their name reflects a masculine-leaning aesthetic, and they have a core LGBTQ+ consumer group, they also wanted to create "underwear that any body could feel comfortable in, regardless of where they fell on the size or gender spectrum" (TomboyX 2023c). They sell a traditional masculine-leaning boxer brief in various styles. They describe their 4.5-inch inseam trunks as the "classic gender-neutral boxer brief, now soft as a kitten," and that

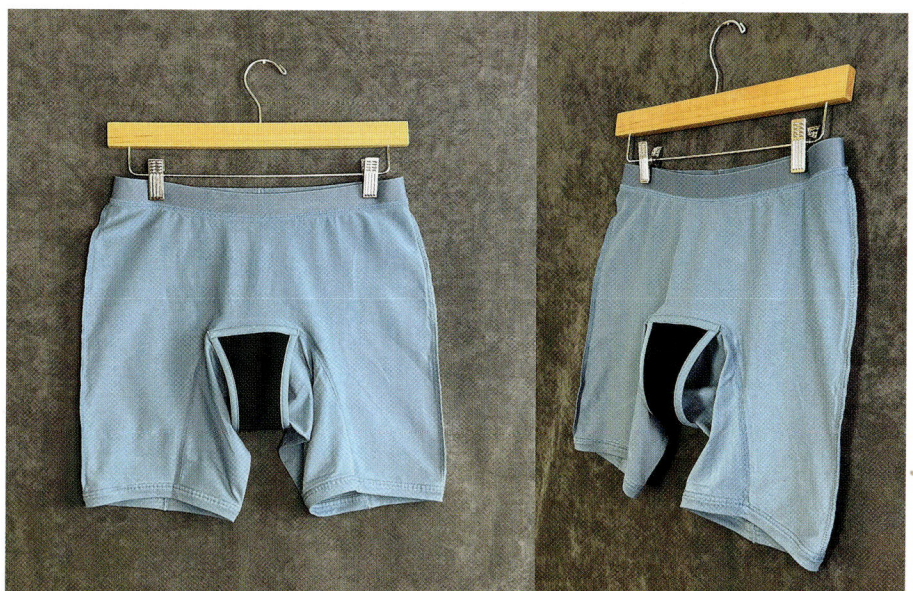

Figure 6.11 TomboyX period underwear with a floating gusset that can fit a pad with wings. Photo courtesy of Sophia Strathearn.

they "took a classic and made it into a TomboyX icon, the first truly gender-neutral boxer brief" (TomboyX 2023a). However, beyond the self-identified label, it is difficult to distinguish the gender-neutral boxer brief from a gendered boxer brief. The bikini cut underwear is not labeled as gender-neutral, but, similar to the brief, the product copy says it was "fit-tested on all body types, sizes XS–4X" (TomboyX 2023b). The company also produces a line of thongs, which are described as stretchy enough to fit any body type.

Lindsay Krakauer (Let's Be Brief) produced printed underwear in four different cuts: thong, hipster, brief, and boxer brief. However, her most popular item, and the impetus to start the brand, is the boxer brief. She related: "The number one seller for a long time has been this, this boxer-brief cut. This was really the bread and butter of why I started this business. It was the most masculine-inspired underwear, and it had a fit for people that were more female-bodied, even people that were transitioning." She did not discuss much of the design beyond the boxer-brief cut in general, but her focus was comfort for all bodies. She said, "I just always thought about people [being] comfortable in their skin, but looking for something that fits them … and not them trying to fit something that's on the market." Krakauer's commitment to creating a space where individuals feel comfortable in their own skin, rather than conforming to preexisting market offerings, encapsulates her vision and the driving force behind her business.

Play Out Apparel (Abby Sugar), like the other companies, started with the masculine-style boxer brief. The company originally designed its boxer briefs with a flat front. Yet consumers requested more crotch space, for a penis or packer. Sugar articulated:

We would have people that did have the equipment who really loved our stuff that were buying the flat-fronted, sort of traditionally female-cut, if you will, and they were like, 'These are uncomfortable, but we loved them so much, but I need space for what I have.' So, we decided to make two different styles … one with the extra fabric and extra space and one without.

As the brand evolved, its owners thought more about inclusivity. Liz Leifer said they "weren't speaking as much to our femme audience, and we didn't have a strong offering for them." Thus, they began thinking about expanding to bikinis and thongs and including two versions while being mindful of their marketing. That is, on their website, they aim to create a "gender-equal shopping" experience that is "not about erasing pronouns/gender identity; it's about removing the categories that tell you what you should or should not wear based on them" (Play Out Apparel 2023b). They describe their bottoms as either flat-front or pouch-front (Figure 6.12 and Figure 6.13). Sharing product details about fit for different bodies is essential to how Play

Figure 6.12 Play Out Apparel underwear, featuring Low Rise Flat Front Boxer Brief in Anthem Stripe Print. Photo courtesy of Play Out Apparel.

Figure 6.13 Play Out Apparel underwear, featuring Pouch Front Bikini in Anthem Stripe Print. Photo courtesy of Play Out Apparel.

Out is unique. For their pouch bikinis, they emphasized to their consumers their attention to detail: "After significant testing, we've created a new shape with fewer seams, more room and support in the pouch, and a fuller fit around the butt. This new shape was also tested with, and better fits and supports packers" (Play Out Apparel 2023c).

Trans-Supportive Gear: Functional, Fleshy Body-Shifting Fashions

A few of the brands focused on trans-supportive gear, or *trans gear* for short, which encompasses a diverse range of items and accessories designed to affirm and support the gender identity of individuals identifying on the trans and nonbinary gender spectrums. This can include clothing such as binders, or chest binders for chest compression, packers for creating a more masculine appearance, or tucking devices for more feminine silhouettes. Additionally, trans gear may include accessories like pronoun badges, gender-affirming jewelry, and other items that contribute to an individual's expression of their authentic self. Beyond physical items, trans gear also extends to emotional and psychological support resources, such as books and websites that foster a sense of belonging and understanding for those navigating the journey of gender identity. Here, I discuss trans gear that changes the shape of the body (binders, packers, tucking undergarments) and that helps perform different bodily functions (stand-to-pee devices, also referred to as STPs).

Trans gear is a little more obvious in how it actively resists, subverts, and simultaneously upholds traditional notions of gender and sexuality as compared to the garments already discussed. That is, these products work to change the shape or use of reproductive organs and sex characteristics, which are so often tied to gender. These brands navigate unique and multifaceted tensions, ambiguities, and ambivalences when producing and selling these objects.

All is Fair in Love and Wear (AFLW), FLAVNT, and gc2b focused much of their business on one product especially considered trans gear: binders, specifically those worn as undergarments. Binders are compression garments designed for transgender individuals, those assigned female at birth, who seek to present a more masculine or gender-neutral appearance. Composed of fibers like spandex and nylon, binders work by flattening chest tissue, creating a silhouette that aligns with the wearer's gender identity. They come in various designs, such as tank tops or full-length styles, resembling sports bras or undershirts, and may include features like adjustable straps or zippers. Binders can offer psychological comfort and help alleviate gender dysphoria or gender unease, yet prolonged or improper use may lead to health issues, including breathing difficulties, skin irritation, or damage to breast tissue. Thus, to ensure both effectiveness and comfort while minimizing potential health risks, it is essential to select the right size, which the brands emphasize in their product copy. For many trans and nonbinary individuals, wearing a binder contributes to improved mental wellbeing, allows them to authentically present themselves, and increases feelings of safety despite the related physical body issues (Reddy-Best et al. 2023a).

In prototyping the binders, Marli Washington of gc2b focused on fit and compression to help his consumers achieve their "ideal form" (gc2b 2023b). He emphasized the careful balance between comfort and constriction when designing binders:

> There was a lot to consider, because it has to bind, but it also can't restrict it. So, I think that evolution of how to actually get that done, and then, what pieces to put together, was when I figured out that all I really needed was a non-stretch front, instead of trying to completely restrict people. That was my moment, and from then it was mostly tweaks and material research. I needed something non-stretch, that's not itchy, and doesn't shrink when you wash it, but the inner material can possibly shrink, so [that meant] buying something sturdy enough that's going to hold the rigidity in the form in the front, but not be too solid.

Washington patented his design that "uses a double panel binder made with a nylon spandex blend and cotton for extra flattening effect" (gc2b 2023a: para. 7). The binder is snug against the body, with a specific functional purpose. Thus, gc2b offers multiple sizes, from XS to 5XL, yet suggests "getting sized by one of our Customer Care Team members before making a binder purchase" (gc2b 2023a: para. 8). Focus on fit and its impact on changing the body's physical form challenges prevailing norms surrounding bodies and gender through use of the binder.

In developing their binders, Peregrine Honig and Christian Dominique, of AFLW, considered sizing, language, fit, and consumer use. For instance, number (band) and letter (cup) sizing systems are used for traditional bras, so they thought carefully about how to describe their binder sizes. Honig stated, "Sizing, you know, was difficult too, because you're still dealing with … different aspects, but you want to be respectful of the person's identity. That was also really like, 'Oh, you know, we can't do numbers.'" Domonique, who works closely with fit models during development related:

> Even in fitting sessions, it's a lot easier, it's so much easier to just ask what bra size are you and then find a binder based on that, because there is so much information there. But that triggers a lot of individuals who have gender dysphoria, so there is the—despite the fact that it is probably the easiest way to collect that information—starting from the very beginning and saying "What is your top chest measurement, what is your under bust measurement, what are both of these measurements?" It neutralizes that conversation a lot, and makes it a lot easier.

In the silhouette, too, they think through subverting norms. Domonique mentioned that they are working on prototype development to create binder styles that would not be visible under a V-neck shirt, crop top, or top that stops mid-chest. They also carefully considered the closure, incorporating a side-seam invisible zipper on the compression material at the chest area, to make it simple for the wearer to don and doff the garment (Figure 6.14). To keep the compression tight, they needed a way for wearers to easily get in and out. Honig commented the choice for zippers over hook

Figure 6.14 AFLW binder prototype. Photo courtesy of author.

and eyes was crucial to center affirming gender identities: "Moving conceptually away from an eye and hook—as you have on a commercial bra—was incredibly important as an emotional and functional shift. Removing standardized ritual behavior was evolutionary."

Packers, another trans gear item, are prosthetic devices designed to provide a sense of comfort, confidence, and alignment with gender identity. That is, packers mimic the appearance and feel of male genitalia, helping to alleviate dysphoria and enhance the overall experience of gender expression. These devices come in various shapes, sizes, and materials, allowing individuals to choose the options that best suit their preferences and comfort levels. They also are worn in a variety of ways, including in the packing brief, which includes a small pocket to hold the packer; a packing harness; or small packing pouch that attaches to the interior of undergarments. FtM Essentials, Transguy Supply, and Rebirth Garments either work with manufacturers to help them modify their packers per consumer requests or develop and sell their own packers.

Scout Rose of Transguy Supply, who started their business completely wholesale, curating an assortment of products specific to trans needs, turned to research and development to improve the available products, specifically prosthetics, including packers. They said, too, that earlier versions of various trans products often were not intended for the trans communities. When Rose began their transition processes in the early 2000s,

> [t]he products just simply didn't exist. I think at the time, Fleshlight had created one … it wasn't a packer actually. It was intended as a gag gift—Mr. Limpy was supposed to be something funny that people gave to each other at bachelor parties. Trans masculine folks saw that product and thought, "Oh wait, we can use this for our own purposes." So there was that, I mean, but that shopping experience, it's not a dignified one, where you're buying something that is a gag gift. That's how 100 percent of the products were when I first started my transition. All of the products that were available to us were things that were designed for other people and other bodies that trans folks realized that we could use for our own purposes as well.

Rose worked on prosthetic product and development to create packers that were soft, not sticky, and did not pick up much hair or lint. They developed the #1 Trans Packer—Cut 4," which does not need to be powdered to reduce stickiness against the skin. They transformed the offensive gag gift into an intentional, celebratory, trans-centered, gendered-affirming object.

Searah Deysach of FtM Essentials began stocking trans gear in response to community requests. Similarly to Rose, she carried what was available, which was initially quite limited. She said, "In some ways, 2001 was a really long time ago and also not that long ago, but, when it comes to this stuff, it was hugely different situation. There was only one company that was making, for the most part, limp packers that you could buy. So, there wasn't that much to get." While she operates as a retailer who buys wholesale, her connections with the packer manufacturers helped her influence product design based on what her consumers were requesting. She remarked: "I'm able to say to them, 'Like, lots of people are asking for this; can you do anything about this?'"

She did not want to go into production, because running her business was already complex, yet she also believed: "We're not making anything, but I feel like we sell enough of stuff that we can actually help kind of influence what people are making sometimes."

The packers developed by Sky Cubacub (Rebirth Garments) stand out in contrast to other available options. That is, those sold at Transguy Supply and FtM Essentials realistically depict genital anatomy typically associated with individuals assigned male at birth. Cubacub's packer design diverges from the conventional flesh-colored models shaped like a penis with accompanying testicles. Cubacub's chain mail packer, crafted from interconnected metal rings, is an alternative for those seeking to create a bulge in their attire without opting for the conventional silicone penis packer (Figure 6.15 and Figure 6.16). This design challenges conventional norms, embodying and reflecting queer ideologies. It disrupts preconceived notions of what is traditionally used to achieve a noticeable crotch bulge. The interlocking chains in this design symbolize the fluid and interchanging nature of gender identities—ranging from masculine and feminine to androgynous, female, male, agender, and more. Each link created serves as a disruption, reshaping our understanding of anatomy. Simultaneously, the design empowers individuals, giving them agency in expressing their sense of self through bodily practices.

Transguy Supply has an abundance of gear to help secure the packer while one wears it. Specifically, it sell boxers briefs for packing and for use with an STP. The company designed its STP briefs with much consideration for wearing and using in multiple situations. The product copy describes the product and informs consumers how to use it when in public and in private:

> Construction Details: Our STP underwear has a 3-layer construction.
>
> The inside layer has a slit that acts as a barrier between your body and your STP device when it is not in use. Tuck the cup of your STP into the slit to give your junk some breathing room.
>
> The middle layer has a reinforced round hole through which you can pull the shaft of your STP device. Once pulled through the hole, position the head and shaft of your STP in a downward position.
>
> The outer layer of these briefs has an opening with two buttons. This layer keeps your STP hidden from view when you're changing or just lounging in your underwear. When ready to use your STP, unbutton this layer, pull the shaft out, and take your aim.

Similarly, the STP product copy also instructs the consumer in its use:

> This STP packs easily and can be packed up or down. While it is very soft to the touch, the shaft will retain its shape when not compressed for easier bathroom use. For this reason, you will need to use a harness or STP underwear to keep the shaft from poking your neighbor's eye out. For first-time users, we strongly recommend you practice in the shower before attempting to use it in public. Even if you have had success with other STPs in the past, every STP is different and requires some getting used to.

(Transguy Supply 2023b)

Figure 6.15 Ensemble created by Sky Cubacub with chain mail packer inserted in the packing shorts. Photo courtesy of author.

Figure 6.16 Chain mail packer created by Sky Cubacub. Photo courtesy of author.

Rose mentioned that another core component of their business was blogging. On the blog, they have one post on essential tips for using an STP. Their blog is arguably a one-stop-shop for information about trans identities, trans politics, and bringing light to trans representation.

The brands also integrated absorbency (e.g., menstruation, sweat, urine) features into their trans gear product designs. Transguy Supply's Cake Bandit underwear line, for example, features a Cake Bandit—Neptune—Absorbing Boxers. Product copy on the website carefully considers gendered language when discussing the body and absorbency:

> Introducing the first-ever absorbent packing underwear. Neptune briefs are designed with a pouch for packing and a leak-proof absorbent liner. Double your confidence when you need it most. Keep the bulge, and don't worry about blood, sweat, or pee. No bulky pads or liners, no surprise leaks, and less dysphoria. Even if you don't get your period anymore, this underwear will protect against any kind of flow.
>
> (Transguy Supply 2023a)

TomboyX similarly produces masculine-leaning underwear and has integrated menstruation into its design. Yet, while TomboyX has begun producing much trans gear, including binders, packing underwear, and tucking undergarments, it did not integrate packing and periods. Its period underwear comes in numerous cuts, including bikini, boy short, brief, and nine-inch inseam boxer briefs. Each pair can hold up to six teaspoons of liquid in the crotch liner and allows the consumer to also wear a pad with wings that can wrap around the floating gusset if needed, thus considering different period flow needs.

The brands also feature other trans gear in addition to prosthetics and garments. For instance, both FtM Essentials and Transguy Supply stock scar cream for folks post top surgery, which is produced by Upper Case Chase, a trans YouTuber who creates much trans-related content, including trans-focused product reviews (Streck and Reddy-Best 2023). Transguy Supply also stocks hormone-related items, such as an inject-ease, a medical product to help with injections, in addition to a shot kit that can hold all hormone-related needs: testosterone, syringes, bandages, and alcohol wipes. So, while garments are a central component to appearance and identity, companies also prioritize their embodiment in relation to the physical fleshy body through different products (Entwistle 2000).

Genderfuck Styles: Fucking with Gendered Fashion or a Big Fuck You to Gender Styles

Some of the brands included in this study embody genderfuck, or intentionally challenge and disrupt gender norms and expectations. Genderfuck is a form of expression that often involves "fucking with" elements traditionally associated with both masculinity and femininity. Both Audio Helkuik and Rebirth Garments create products in this provocative aesthetic.

In particular, Helkuik's Queer Scouts collection pushes an incendiary agenda, which he produced for the fifth queer fashion show hosted by DapperQ at the Brooklyn Museum. The line pulls elements from historic and contemporary scout uniforms, he related: "I researched uniforms through history, and different accessories that are worn in scout troops, and the culture and all that. So I researched and then blended it all and spit out in [a] cool new way" (Figure 6.17). The looks encompass the traditional khaki-and-green color of scout uniforms. The collared button-up shirts, neck scarfs, berets, sashes, and badges (in the form of pins) provide a clear connection to both the Boy and Girl Scouts. Then, Helkuik "fucks" with it, which is certainly controversial given the history of sexual abuse and queer and trans discrimination within the Boy Scouts organization (Ring 2024). That is, the designs feature lace-up seams revealing bare skin underneath on the legs, hips, waist, and chest. The ensembles also feature leather harnesses and other leather details, such as a crossover bowtie with its brass snap closure. Also featured are knee flashes, or straps worn just below the knee, which scouts traditionally wore as garters to keep socks in place. The flashes here, though, reference bondage, as they are made from leather and worn without socks.

The collection also features some highly provocative details. For instance, the Queer Scouts group is signaled through the bright red patch featuring the troop number 69, a reference to the slang term for when two partners orient their bodies to perform oral sex on one another. Additionally, Helkuik has included badges that

Figure 6.17 Audio Helkuik queer scouts collection. Photo courtesy of Hannah Cohen.

overtly refer to queerness (Figure 6.18). One reads "knot tying" and features a black body silhouette tied up in a red rope-like restraint. While scouts can earn knot-tying badges, this interpretation centers provocative sex acts. Another pin reads "tent pitching" and includes a naked body with prominent breasts and erect nipples laying on the ground, wearing a jock strap and a tent over the genitals. The line also features a "pet care" badge that features pet-play fetish masks.

Cubacub of Rebirth Garments explores bold aesthetics in their designs by revealing diverse bodies, embodying genderfuck principles. For instance, midsections on all individuals are exposed, either uncovered between crop tops and bottoms, or draped with sheer fabric. Large breasts are unsupported and frequently revealed, either one or both at a time, while commonly concealed aspects of human skin, such as cellulite, puckering, and sagging, are showcased on bare arms and legs (Figure 6.19). Contrary to conventional fat fashion norms, which favor dark colors, the outfits are crafted from brightly colored, elastomeric fabrics, consistent with the rest of Rebirth Garments styles. In their designs, Cubacub challenges the assumption that fat bodies should be concealed and deliberately celebrates fat individuals.

Furthermore, as demonstrated in their manifesto, "Radical Visibility," Cubacub centers fatness as one of the many marginalized identities their audience must navigate. It's a perspective embraced by those following the Rebirth Garment philosophy of dress reform and radical visibility. Here, queerness and fatness are intertwined, and the section of the manifesto on "'radical visibility" advocates for rejecting "passing" and assimilation. Cubacub confronts fatphobia within queer communities, challenging the notion that fatness contradicts beauty and sexiness.

Figure 6.18 Pins from the Queer Scouts collection by Audio Helkuik. Photo courtesy of Audio Helkuik.

Subtle and In-Your-Face Pride

The brands also centered some of their business on the so-called traditional Pride gear that was either in-your-face, obvious Pride, or had the subtle queer messaging, for those in the know. These phrases or queer Pride imagery were printed on T-shirts, pins, sweatshirts, pants, bags, jewelry, hats, and other gear. Some of the owners founded their brands with Pride gear central to the business (e.g., Queer Supply, FLAVNT Streetwear, Stuzo), whereas others (e.g., TomboyX, NiK Kacy Footwear) incorporated overt and subtle queer Pride in their product lines.

Queer Supply founders Kit and Sade centered their business on "making a statement in regards to gender identity and sexuality." In their home-based business, they did all their screen-printing by hand. Their work incorporated such phrases as "fuck your gender-binary"—as seen on their original T-shirt—in addition to others such as "high-anxiety queer" and "magic Black femme." Kit discussed inspiration for the original phrase:

Figure 6.19 Cubacub design that reveals the midsection and emphasizes stretch marks on the body. Photographer: Colectivo Multipolar. Model: C'est Kevvie. Clothing: Rebirth Garments.

The concept came out of a conversation with my friend Key Thomason, who's actually a musician in Canada, in Toronto. We both definitely have lots of thoughts on gender, and couple years ago, we were on the cusp of lots of transitions literally and figuratively, and we're talking about it. I think we were just really upset that we had to spend all this time kind of pushing back on these things that [are] just all due to the gender binary, essentially. We were just, "We should just make a shirt that says, 'fuck this!' and then everybody can read, and they'll understand how we feel." Then we kind of talked about between "fuck the gender binary" and "fuck your gender binary," but we settled on, "fuck your gender binary" to distance ourselves even further from the binary, and the "I don't even want it," and, yeah, I think, it can be powerful.

Kit continued on that their experiences wearing the first shirt confirmed their motivation to make it and share it with the world:

The first couple times that I wore it out I remember people were very, either really positive or quite, negative or confused, just not understanding, the positive reactions made me feel really good, and I think that was kind of the motivation to share it, because I think printed graphic tees can be really helpful because when you see another person who agrees with it, you can kind of have that moment where you're, making eye contact, and you're, like, yeah, you get it, that's cool. I'll say, "Nice shirt," and he'll say, "thanks," and then you're on the same page, and [it] creates that sense of comradery with strangers, yeah, that's the story behind that print.

In a similar fashion, Stuzo (Stoney Michelli Love) and Dapper Boi (Pasche) created and stocked graphic tees that communicated their lived experiences. Love remarked that when planning her business, her mom and ex-boyfriend kept asking if she was gay and she replied that she was. She continued:

I was like, "What in the hell is going on? And why did they keep asking me this?" Apparently, they don't believe you. I was born that way. And so, ... the lightbulb went off, and I sketched that, and that was the official first logo because I just felt like there's a lot of people that probably relate to this because of the whole theory that you're not born that way ... And it's, like, so I wanted it [to be] something to speak to that message and also maybe wear it so they just not ask me again. And so I sketched that on the T-shirt and then I just kept going from there because the first sketches were loose, too; it wasn't really things that I resonated with.

Thus, Love's lived experience informed this particular overt queer messaging (Figure 6.20). She emphasized her experiences in the product copy: "For those who still wonder, let them know in this gender free tank" (Stuzo 2023).

Pasche from Dapper Boi also had similar experiences; others thought she was a male due to her masculine-leaning presentation. So in part of her company's Kickstarter phase, she produced shirts and hats that read "I'm not a boy." She related,

Figure 6.20 "Yup, Still Gay" T-shirt by Stuzo. Photo courtesy of Stuzo Clothing.

I based it off of my own personal story. I get that all the time, when I go to the grocery store. When I walk into the women's restroom, I get the double glances. I get the "Hey, you're not supposed to be in here," and for the most part, I've been lucky in the fact that people usually feel bad when they say that, and then it makes me feel bad, because I'm like, "It's okay, I'm okay with it. Don't worry." So, that was the premise behind the "I'm not a boy." I put on that hat, and I'm like, "Hey it's all good. Okay, like, we're human beings that make mistakes, and it's fine." Others are not so lucky, and I know that we've had a lot of people share their stories, and some people take the hat very seriously and they wear that with pride, actually, when they're going to the restroom. That's something that they can easily point out without having to explain anything. They're like, "Listen, I'm not a boy. I'm allowed to be here." So, we've gotten a lot of emails and stories from people thanking us for our T-shirt that says the same thing. Yeah, that's something we're actually really proud of, and we decided to look into it a little bit further with other products.

Pasche continued that two consumer stories about the "I'm not a boy" T-shirt resonated particularly with her. One was from the mother of a masculine-leaning daughter:

A mother ... emailed us, and it was [about] her little girl, she was eleven years old. We've actually featured them quite a few times on our Facebook now. She told us her daughter dresses like a boy and has short hair, and when she goes to school, she is scared and gets bullied, and because of, not only the hat—of course she wanted the hat, and she wore that with pride—but, just having our brand out there, in general, for her, she just knew that there's people out there like her and especially knew that there were people to look up to. We're not necessarily a kid brand, but she follows us now on Facebook, and when we posted her picture, the love that outpoured from the story that I posted with her picture was like, "Stay strong." All these people were reaching out. It really was just a community reaching out to her, and her mom was just overjoyed. She told us that that meant the world to her, so later I see orders coming in from her—the little girl now—and she gets our, like, "extra, extra small" shirts and it's adorable. I love it. It was definitely moving, and it just let my wife and me know that we're doing something good here. It feels amazing.

Other in-your-face Pride manifested in different brands' collections, with various imagery and colors. Outplay Swimwear, TomboyX, and gc2b all have incorporated Pride-themed collections into their merchandise assortments. TomboyX includes rainbow-themed prints in its iconic waistbands and in all-over patterns and gc2b had a collection of binders that also incorporated the various queer and trans flag colors. Kacy included some subtle queer nods throughout their products. An embroidered equal sign is one signature in their shoes. Thus, the sign is meaningful to those in-the-know and looking closely. Similarly, "break the binary" is embossed repeatedly in small font on the soles of select shoes.

Krakauer at Let's Be Brief incorporated another subtle insider Pride element in her underwear prints. One of the company's prints had a toaster. She shared, "We wanted our images to really appeal to the LGBTQ customers, so we created designs like 'Toaster Heaven.' We all just get it … it's funny … and it's cute!" (Guest Authors 2011). The "toaster" joke is a playful and humorous reference within lesbian culture, often used in a lighthearted manner. The joke's origins are a bit unclear, but it has become a popular meme and inside joke within the LGBTQ+ community. The joke is based on the idea that when someone comes out as a lesbian, they receive a toaster as a "welcome to the club" gift. The concept likely plays on the stereotype that kitchen appliances are traditional wedding gifts, and it humorously subverts this notion in the context of coming out. Over time, the toaster joke has taken on a life of its own. It's often referenced in memes, social media posts, and conversations among lesbians as a way to share a laugh about the shared experience of coming out. The humor lies in the absurdity of the idea that one's sexual orientation would be celebrated with a household appliance.

Queer Styling Services

If you previously did an internet search for "lesbian stitch fix" then Greyscale Goods likely appeared in your search results. Styling or personal shopping has been a long-time profession in various forms, and a Harvard Business School student developed Stitch Fix in 2011, largely revolutionizing styling services. The online personal styling service blended technology with personalized fashion expertise. The dedicated stylists handpick curated selections of clothing and accessories, and then items are delivered to the consumer. The business model features flexibility: the person can keep items they love and return those that do not match their style. Sara Medd, founder of Greyscale Goods, drew on this business model and expanded it to center queerness. She offers the same kind of service, yet focuses on serving queer folks. She noted that she pulls from a variety of brands when shopping, with a "mix of everything," but when she can, she incorporates queer and trans fashion brands; for instance, she worked with Kipper Clothiers and had developed a community with others brands, including NiK Kacy Footwear, Sharpe Suiting, and Sloane & Tate. She explained many of her consumers are "female-bodied queer people who have a slightly more masculine style" and that through trial and error and her experiences as a stylist she "found brands that work well on a female body" or those who are more gender neutral. Medd wrote on Greyscale's Kickstarter page how she thought, through queer styling, to create a new way to shop that goes beyond traditional retail stores:

> The current dichotomy between traditional men's and women's departments in stores is no longer relevant to so many of today's customers. Many customers like to shop in both departments, because contemporary style has become more and more gender-neutral and androgynous. Greyscale Goods searches for the best styles in the market, regardless of intended department, and offers them to customers in a brand new shopping platform.
>
> (Greyscale Goods 2015)

Queer Makers and Queering Product Copy

Show and Tell Concept Shop (Alyah Baker) and Bluestockings Boutique (Jeanna Kadlec) functioned as retail entities, specializing in the curation of products sourced from wholesalers, manufacturers, and artisans. Their approaches involved selecting items based on the maker's identity, in certain cases, and also acquiring products and subsequently emphasizing a unique perspective by queering the product through inventive copy and strategic positioning within their business model. This dual strategy allowed the businesses to showcase the origin of their products but also to add a distinct and inclusive dimension to their brand identity, setting them apart in the competitive retail landscape.

Bluestockings Boutique, unlike the other underwear-focused companies, operated as a wholesale ecommerce business that did not do any fashion production. It purchased numerous product types wholesale and focused heavily on product copy to create a shopping experience centered around fit, not gender. Kadlec described her process:

> The copy is something that's always been really important to me. Like, having size guides that consider trans folks, and having product descriptions that have fitting notes for different kinds of body types, which is something that I've always had.

Also, product descriptions that are not heteronormative or that use pronouns. My site's basically gender neutral. You're not going to find a product description about how this bra helps you look cute for your boyfriend [laughs]. You know, things like that.

She emphasized that while she wanted to carry certain products, some brands only did direct-to-consumer, to manage their brand identity. She explained:

gc2b debuted, I think, a year into Bluestockings being open. I have talked to them a little bit. I very much wanted to stock gc2b once they debuted, because they got such rave reviews from friends who wore them and just uniformly well-viewed. They offer them in so many colors. It's just very fashionable looking. I really like how it looks. It's well made. I think it's made in the US; they tick all the boxes in being ethically made. They look great, etc., and are comfortable, all of the things. That's a whole other piece of being a retailer is contacting a bunch of indie brands, like gc2b, who only work direct-to-consumer and do not actually work with retailers.

Washington, of gc2b, related that because of his emphasis on trans-consumer needs he believes wholesale would be bad for his business, despite the potential financial gains:

We run through Shopify, and orders come in, and in the backend we ship them out, and then customer service just deals with any inquiries and order issues and size help. We've had a lot of people ask for wholesale prices, but I think the nature of the product, with the knitting, custom sizing, and the high possibility of needing exchange doesn't lend itself to wholesale ... If I let other stores sell it, then it will kind of take away from the brand. I don't want people having issues and not having our customer service handle it, which is great. We have a 90–99.7 percent size factory rating, so I don't want to tarnish that, or our reputation.

Here Washington relates how so much of buying a binder is personalized, and an important element of his brand is allowing for returns, due to the nuance in fit and sizing of a binder. Kadlec's queer and trans consumers wanted different brands, such as gc2b, yet she relates the nuanced difficulties in buying practices:

Often, I'll get feedback from the community ... like, "Why don't you have this brand? We want this brand." But of course, there's this whole behind-the-scenes conversation of, like, "I've been talking to them and they don't do it!" It's looked at as, like, "You know, why don't you have everything?" And it's, like, "Actually I would love to, but either they don't do it, or like the minimum order is too high." There are some brands who are like, "Well, your first order has to be over $1,000 or you have to order a certain number of pieces." And I'm, like, "That is so out of my budget," and it's just not a feasible conversation.

Baker, of Show and Tell Concept Shop, focuses much more on the makers. She prioritizes makers from marginalized communities, including women, people of color, queer and trans folks, and formerly incarcerated folks. If she sources products made on a larger scale, she prioritizes ethical and sustainable production. So her products vary widely from month to month, as do her prices. Yet, she believes it is important to think through making her products accessible, while honoring the makers and their labor. To offset the high costs on unique items, she sometimes works with customers:

> This one older Black women on a fixed income really wanted this quilt, and she was like, "Okay, can I put like $25 down on it today and come back and like pay for it, and I was like, "Yeah, totally, we'll hold for you as long as you need," and she bought it, she ended up paying it off, but it took her—she came for a couples months and she didn't come for a couple months and then she came back again, she did what she needed to do to be able to have this piece that she really loved and wanted and, you know, that feels good to me, to be able to work with customers that way.

She described how these interactions fueled the mission behind her work:

> It's maybe not like, always the smartest bottom-line decision, but I don't think I opened either of these places to really be about like making money and the bottom line. It kind of, I mean if I wanted that life, I would have stayed at my corporate job, because that's the life I had then, I could do pretty much whatever I wanted to do because I had a good steady income.

Are My Socks Then Queer Fashion Socks? And Who Decides?

These fashion brands engage in a nuanced and intentional exploration of queer and trans issues, deftly balancing multiple intersections throughout the entire lifecycle of their creations. These brands produce commodities and interweave layers of queerness and transness into different aspects of product development, distribution, and consumption; of course not all at once. That is, the brands' narratives embody care and sensitivity toward queer and trans identities, manifesting through a diverse array of approaches and possibilities: consumption, making, options, messaging, makers, and educational hubs. Each brand adopted different approaches at different times for different reasons while drawing on their strengths and acknowledging their limitations. These fashion products intentionally navigate the realms of ambivalence and ambiguity. They disrupt conventional categories, deliberately blurring lines to foster a space where ambiguity is accepted and celebrated. This challenges normative expectations, encouraging a more inclusive and expansive understanding of fashion—one that allows for the coexistence of multiplicity and complexity.

In the realm of consumption, these brands revolutionize shopping experiences by adopting gender-equal practices, transcending traditional labels to focus on diverse styles that resonate across the spectrum of identities. Further, they redefine the very essence of products by queering the accompanying copy, transforming it into a medium for expressing the richness of queer and trans experiences.

These brands pay meticulous attention to construction details in making their products. They mix and match heteronormative elements of garments, challenging preconceived notions and embracing a spectrum of possibilities. The very shape of the body becomes a canvas for expression, with options ranging from compression to additions, allowing individuals to assert, explore, and embrace their identities through clothing.

In further options, these brands go beyond conventional sizing systems that root back to the early twentieth century, embracing an expanded approach that accommodates the diverse bodies and identities within the queer and trans communities. This inclusivity extends beyond mere measurements; it becomes a testament to the brands' commitment to cater to the varied needs and expressions of their audience.

Messaging becomes a powerful tool in the hands of these fashion brands. They overtly express pride, celebrating queer and trans identities with bold statements that resonate with authenticity. Simultaneously, they weave subtle pride into their communication, creating a sense of belonging and recognition for those in the know, which has a long history in the LGBTQ+ communities, for example, gay men's use of bandanas to communicate with other gay men—sometimes called flagging (e.g., see Reilly and Saethre 2014). This layered approach to messaging reflects a deep understanding of the diverse ways individuals experience and express their queerness and transness.

Behind the scenes, the maker plays a crucial role. These fashion brands actively seek queer makers and designers, ensuring that the creative process is deeply rooted in the lived experiences of the community. By doing so, they not only bring authenticity to their products but also contribute to the visibility and empowerment of queer creators.

Finally, these brands are more than mere fashion entities; they evolve into queer and trans education hubs. Not just purveyors of clothing or accessories, they become platforms for fostering understanding, dialogue, and community building. By embracing this broader role, they transcend the boundaries of traditional fashion brands and contribute to the empowerment and visibility of queer and trans communities on a larger scale.

Despite their disruptive influence on the traditional fashion system, these innovative products and brands, with all their transformative potential, remain inherently rooted in the capitalist framework. Despite their avant-garde approaches and commitment to reshaping the industry, their ultimate objective is often profit-driven, a necessity for sustaining operations and fueling further innovation. In essence, these enterprises, while introducing novel ideas and challenging established norms, navigate within the broader landscape of neoliberal capitalism. The system they aim to redefine is the one they must operate within to survive. The quest for profitability and market dominance propels them forward, even as they strive to revolutionize fashion paradigms.

It is crucial to recognize that these companies' participation in capitalism does not negate their positive impact on the industry. They might challenge conventional standards; however, the fundamental structure within which they operate often demands adherence to market principles, shareholder value, and competitive strategies, aligning them with the broader capitalist ethos. In this complex dance between disruption and conformity, these enterprises become both agents of change and products of the system they seek to transform. As they push boundaries and redefine the fashion landscape, they simultaneously underscore the resilience and adaptability of capitalism, absorbing and co-opting even its most radical challengers. This paradoxical relationship highlights the intricate interplay between innovation and the persistent economic structures that shape the fashion industry and society at large.

Thus, to consider the question, are my socks then queer socks and who decides? Arguably, these brands create opportunities for queer and trans moments to exist. Kaiser and McCullough's (2010) knot metaphor (where varying parts of our identity are hidden and visible at different times, that is, when a knot loosens and exposes more of the rope, the parts of the rope relate to different parts of one's identity) is a useful tool to contemplate how truths about queer and trans products (thus, queer socks) can be temporarily obscured by the very limitations the fashion brands are navigating, only to be unveiled as the knot is loosened and is perhaps retied when leaning on their self-defined successful business practices centering queer and trans identities. In essence, this dynamic interplay between societal perceptions and the evolving strategies of these brands underscores the knotty entanglements of queer and trans identities in the realm of fashion and fashion products. That is, the brands expose the complexity in trying to define queer fashion within boundaries on a particular idea, maker, body, and/or product.

Part 4 Production, Pricing, and Media Considerations

7 An Ethical Balancing Act: Production and Pricing

No doubt these queer and trans fashion brands have centered justice in their business philosophies. In their media, they heavily considered intersections with race, gender, sexuality, body size and shape, and ability. Of course, other intersectional issues plague the globalized industry, such as its negative environmental impact, which some of the brands discussed extensively.

The fashion industry contributes to natural resource consumption and damaging environmental pollution during each phase of a textile's lifecycle—from fiber production to manufacturing processes, consumer care, and product disposal (Chen and Burns 2006; Palamutcu 2015). The fashion industry has been labeled as a considerable contributor to greenhouse-gas emissions and climate change (BSR Staff 2009; Drew and Yehounme 2017; Zaffalon 2010). In the United States alone, consumers spend nearly $400 billion on apparel and footwear each year, fueled by fast fashion (inexpensive and easily disposable throwaway items, offering new inventory on a weekly basis), leading to overconsumption and over-disposal habits, where approximately 7.6 percent (10.5 million tons) of all landfill materials are textile-based (EPA 2019; Kozlowski, Searcy, and Bardecki 2018). This high product turnover further exacerbates undesirability and obsolescence and an increasingly unsustainable fashion industry.

Since the 1992 Rio de Janeiro Summit, the United Nations General Assembly acknowledges and is actively working to form agendas to progress sustainable paradigm shifts. The summit goals encompass a list of seventeen sustainable development goals (SDGs) (with 169 targets) for the world to address by 2030 (United Nations 2015). Many of these can be traced to interdependent units of the fashion industry, including good health and wellbeing (SDG#3), clean water and sanitation (SDG#6), and responsible consumption and production (SDG#12). Additionally, there is much research and attention needed on the ways these SDGs *must* center decolonization philosophies (e.g., how the fashion industry continues to occupy and destroy Indigenous lands) and environmental racism (e.g., how communities of color are disproportionately affected by health hazards through policies and practices forcing them to live near landfills or polluted waters). As the world's population is set to rise to 9.7 billion by 2050 and natural resources will be severely under threat, shifts from linear models of fashion design thinking and production to those with ethical and just considerations is essential (Radhakrishnan 2020). Thus, how and where the queer and trans fashion brands were producing, the materials they sourced and used, and other parts intersecting the product lifecycle were addressed in the oral histories.

Producing Here or There?

Production location brought up a lot of conversation for the queer and trans fashion brand owners. Should they produce in the United States or could or should they go elsewhere? What factories do they choose, and why? Many factors went into these decision-making processes. Not one person I interviewed said that sustainability did not matter, and in fact they often discussed it as extremely important but something that was complex and multilayered.

Many of the brands related that they had major desires to produce in the United States, as that was viewed as the clearest way to demonstrate their commitment to sustainability justice. Marli Washington (gc2b) said he was "making sure everything is made in the USA." Abby Sugar (Play Out Apparel) pledged to "try to do what we can, made in America." Similarly, Alyah Baker (Show and Tell Concept Shop) focused on curating her shop with "American hand-made production." One of the major criticisms some brands received was that they did not produce in the United States, which many people prefer, for reasons such as helping the local economy and perceived superior quality of US-made products (Salfino 2021, 2022).

While producing in the United States was a major goal, the brands had to make tough choices. For instance, both Vicky Pasche (Dapper Boi) and Susan Stewart (Strapping Sacramento) wanted to produce in the United States, but ultimately they went elsewhere due to the required minimum purchase orders and the related costs. Stewart wanted to prioritize a lower price for her consumer. She explained:

> I had the designs or the pattern made here in the US, and then I had my samples made in China, and I use a factory in China, and that was simply because, my thoughts as an entrepreneur who is, I guess I like to think of myself as a business-minded human, I'm like, why does the GAP get away with using factories overseas, and why does everyone get away with it, but the second that you say that I'm a small business, "Oh, you have to be the most ethically sourced person," and I definitely checked my factory to make sure if there was any weird child labor. They had to be accredited, you know?

Pasche explained that she manufactures different products in different countries and also found a compromise where the manufacturer is based in the United States and operates its factory overseas:

> Yeah, it's really hard. When we first started, I wanted everything US made and, to be honest, it's really hard for a start-up. It's really hard. Minimums come into play, and the prices are astronomical—we would never be able to survive. This was the way to do this, and it was kind of a happy medium when we met this particular manufacturer because they were half here and half there. They have people that are constantly overseeing the operations from here. So that kind of made me feel a little bit better and, of course, seeing the prices were a little bit better was better too. We also still choose, even though it's cheaper than the United States, premium fabrics, because something that is really important when it comes to

fitting body styles, is getting that particular soft, stretch fabric. So, we still get the premium products, but we're able to get it at better pricing.

To keep her prices reasonable for the already expensive suits, Thúy Nguyen (THÚY Custom Clothier) chose production outside the United States: "If I were to use American tailors the price would be really high, too, and it's not like I'm paying them poorly, but also, I pay for the materials, and I pay for what they ask for, and so I feel like I'm contributing to another small business."

Factory conditions were also at the forefront of much of the brands' considerations of environmental justice. That is, they chose factories with good working conditions, that considered their impact on the environment from byproducts of the production process, and also had ethical employment practices and humane working conditions. Many brands visited potential factories to ensure working conditions were to their standards. NiK Kacy (NiK Kacy Footwear) said they visited a factory and opted for another because of the poor conditions: "When I was in Italy, unfortunately, my experience was that the factories I went to had poor environmental standards or there were none. Like, there was no venting, there were no fans, there was no protection of any kind. I walked in and I could barely breathe, you know, because of the fuzz." Marialexandra Garcia (Outplay Swimwear) was also adamant about visiting the factories where her products were being made and had significant interest in how they treated women:

> I know every single factory that I work with. I've been to every single factory I work with. I've seen how they work, how these people work in the factory. That's another thing that's very important to me. I practice what I preach. I will not sell product produced in a factory that I haven't been to, and that I don't know where they're working or how they're working or what conditions they're working in. The factories I work with actually have daycares for the mothers that have kids, and they have educational programs for the mothers that work there.

Kacy (NiK Kacy Footwear) described a unique experience when looking for a manufacturer and how it was compounded with racial discrimination. They explained, "When I first started with the research part, I went to like the shoe fairs, you know, and, and met shoemakers from literally around the world." They continued:

> If there was, just a rough number, like a thousand manufacturers from around the world at this trade show, I would try to talk to maybe 80 percent of that number. Out of the 80 percent …, only 10 percent of those people would even comprehend what I'm talking about. Out of that 80 percent, not even to the 10 percent yet, maybe only 5 percent of the people would even bother to talk to me, because I'm nobody, right? So, it's a very old industry where everyone has been in the industry for many, many years, and they all know one another. It's a very old industry where everyone—I was so surprised like everybody knew everybody. So, I come along, and nobody would talk to me because they were like, "We don't know you." Understandably, too. I found that later it's because 1) I'm Asian, so they thought I was trying to, like, go and like steal ideas, and then 2) I wasn't

represented by like an agent or like anyone who knew them. So, it was very hard for them to want to communicate with me, right?

Others also experienced confusion about their products. For instance, for FLAVNT Chris and Courtney Rhodes wanted to be close to their production facility because binders are not a product that the average person understands: "A lot of people don't know what a binder is or have never seen a binder or aren't in the community, so we wanted to be able to visit."

The brands also chose production facilities for practical reasons. That is, some of the products could not be produced in the United States because no US facilities can cater to their market or could not handle the brands' capacities. Both Sugar (Play Out Apparel) and Lindsay Krakauer (Let's Be Brief), who produce underwear, faced these issues:

> I was dead set on manufacturing in the US. And I did everything I could to see if I could find underwear manufacturing in the US. And there was nothing. There was nothing, there were no resources. Every time I would find a company I thought could produce it, somewhere in the middle of America, to be honest, because that's where they were located, I'd call them, I'd try to talk to them, there was no way they could produce what I wanted.
>
> (Krakauer)

> One of our goals was to do as much as we could in United States, but even then, and this was six—five—six years ago, you ran up against the problem that so much of the industry has moved overseas and people do not even have the machinery anymore. They don't have machinery to stitch the flat stitch or to measure out the waist band, in the way that it needs to be done to make manufacturing possible.
>
> (Sugar)

The brands also chose factories that would give them the highest quality product, which led them to produce in countries that specialized in a specific product or material. For instance, Erin Berg (Kipper Clothiers) had their suits produced in Hong Kong because of the country's history of and specialty in producing high-quality tailored suits. Nguyen (THÚY Custom Clothier) also related that high-quality tailors are hard to find in the United States: "I don't think I've come across any good American tailors, unfortunately." Kacy (NiK Kacy Footwear) chose a shoemaker in Portugal for its quality and Garcia (Outplay Swimwear) produced her swimwear in Columbia because they have "the best spandex in the world," and she wants her product to be "top notch." She emphasized that she did not go overseas because it was cheaper—it was not cheap— but that her whole focus was on product quality that would last for the consumer.

Audio Helkuik (Audio Helkuik) and Sky Cubacub (Rebirth Garments) discussed their ambivalence related to sustainable fashion practices and how they operate their businesses. They both used controversial materials, yet focused on small-scale, slow-fashion production.

I usually hesitate to talk about sustainability because I do use leather, and that's just a huge red flag for people. But I can address it in the way that I've made it feel okay for myself. So leather and the leather industry is bad for the planet. No one is going to say it's not. But cotton is also terrible for the planet. And so is polyester, and dyeing fabric, and fashion manufacturing in general. Anyway, everything is bad for the environment, and if you can just find a way to reduce your carbon footprint, or just be responsible for what you make, that's like the best option for this industry. But, I do make a high-quality product that's going to last, so that's my way of being sustainable. Slow fashion. For example, I have a pair of high quality leather boots that I've been wearing for over fifteen years. Or instead I could buy cheap synthetic boots, but have to replace them every year or two. So with my harnesses, that's how I've come to terms with working with leather, a faux pas for some. I only buy the amount of material I need; I make each product to your requests; the harnesses will last and last. I make just a small number that are going to exactly the people that want them and will wear and wear and wear them. Slow fashion.

(Helkuik)

I have been on a couple of panel talks for sustainable fashion, even though I make clothing out of petroleum products, which is oil, which is the evilest thing in the world. I think about it a lot, but it's also like the material that works best with my own body. I'm allergic to wools, and I want to source some cotton things, but then I just haven't figured it out correctly, yet. I guess people include me in those green fashion talks from an angle of getting something hyper-custom made for yourself and having it for a long time and not being like, "Oh, I need an entire million-piece wardrobe." Unless you need to, because no other clothing is accessible to you, just having a couple of key pieces and not having excessive amounts of clothes is ideal. I mean, I know myself, I have excessive amounts of clothes, but I also make clothes, so I feel like I feel like it makes sense. I don't think that people should have, like, piles and piles and piles of clothes in general. I think people should be more choosey or just buy stuff from the thrift store.

(Cubacub)

The brands also thought through sustainability with the materials being used in their products. They highlighted their use of recycled materials. They also highlighted their attention on zero-waste production. For instance, Kelly Moffat (Kirrin Finch) related:

When we make a button up shirt, there's lots of little pieces leftover, and maybe a marker—you have an extra foot or whatever here. So we would make pocket squares and bowties out of that extra fabric. We make them into pockets in some of our other shirts and on our T-shirts. So, we're just getting creative, about the ways that we can make sure we use the resources that we have.

Cubacub similarly thought about the scraps left over and either used them in future projects or donated them for arts and crafts at local schools.

Beyond production, the brands also thought through packaging materials and shipping, how they treated their own employees, and ultimately expressed a desire to continue to do better. Because Washington (gc2b) hires many trans folks, he implemented specific policies to create a positive and sustainable work environment:

> It's in the office itself, no one is paid minimum wage, everyone is paid above that. Everyone that is full time has the option to get healthcare. It's not dependent on how long they've worked here, or their salary. We recently added a policy, because we actually haven't had any of our employees get surgery until this year, so we needed a policy to allow employees go live somewhere for any gender affirming surgery, for a paid two weeks.

Washington focused on thinking through environmental sustainability, but at the forefront of his discussion, too was the safety, comfort, and livelihood of his queer and trans employees.

Pricing Tensions: Social Good in Capitalism

In conjunction environmental justice concerns, brand owners were acutely conscious of the pivotal role socioeconomic status played in their decision-making processes. This awareness extended beyond mere acknowledgment to a nuanced consideration of how pricing strategies could affect the accessibility of their products within the context of the income levels of queer and trans individuals. The intersectionality of socioeconomic factors, coupled with the commitment to inclusivity, prompted a reevaluation of conventional business models. For these brand owners, business sustainability was not solely a matter of profit margins but rather a delicate balance between financial viability and social responsibility. They grappled with the ethical imperative to ensure that their products were not priced beyond the reach of marginalized communities. This conscientious approach involved thoughtful pricing structures that considered the economic disparities faced by queer and trans people.

Many of the brands were continually criticized for being expensive. In many ways, the brands were serving a much-needed purpose that relates to making people feel good about themselves and helping them find their identities through fashion. However, this noble mission unfolded within the complex dynamics of a capitalist marketplace. The brand owners found themselves grappling with how to receive and respond to feedback from consumers who were often unaware of the intricate influences shaping business decisions. Balancing the pursuit of positive societal impact with the financial realities of their industry became a continual challenge, requiring a delicate dance between values and market demands. Pasche (Dapper Boi) related:

> We hear all the time, "You guys are expensive," "expensive." I'm sure a lot of other small brands like ours are saying the same exact thing. We just can't compete with Target, Walmart, Forever 21—any of those brands, because, again, our minimum quantities are—I'm lucky if I get three hundred of one shirt and that's the minimum. I feel defensive, and I take things very personally, so when I'm responding or not responding to something like that, I have to really think that through and consider what they [customer] can relate to and understand.

Similarly, Fran Dunaway and Naomi Gonzalez (TomboyX) explained that it is hard or nearly impossible to compete with big-box retailer prices:

> If we have negative feedback it's usually just around the price point. And again, people just don't understand how expensive it is to run a business, pay wages, and use fabrics that are ecofriendly and processes that are ecofriendly. It all costs money. You know, Fruit of the Loom might buy in mass quantities. So, there's massive cost savings buying such huge volumes, and we just can't do that.

There was an overwhelming sentiment that the brand owners were aware that they were creating change, yet surviving under capitalism was exceptionally difficult. Berg (Kipper Clothiers) explained: "Running any kind of business under capitalism—it's like, surviving, working under capitalism, and to also help the queer community, that is the biggest struggle." Nguyen's (THÚY Custom Clothier) friends thought she priced her made-to-order, custom suits too low:

> Yeah. So, for a two-piece, single breasted suit I start it at $600–$650, which is really cheap for a custom suit with a three-hour consultation, and a fitting. A lot of my friends were like, "You need to price your things higher. Think about your time." Even my tailors are like, "What are you pricing your stuff at?" They're like, "You should price them higher, this is also your time."

Despite her extensive consultations with each customer, she still keeps her prices low and described that she's there for "literally, a movement, for changing and creating social impact. So, hopefully, that's what it will do."

Cubacub (Rebirth Garments) thinks critically about their prices and folks who cannot access their products. Recognizing the financial constraints faced by some individuals, particularly disabled individuals and queer-trans teens, they implement alternative payment options, including a sliding scale. This approach allows customers to pay within a range that accommodates their financial circumstances. They explained,

> There is some sort of sliding scale. I try to be more reserved about it, of course for folks who just like don't have the funds and that are disabled folks, and, I don't know, queer-trans teens. It is actually surprising I don't have as many people take me up on it as I figured would. I think people are trying really hard to respect my prices for the most part and that is really nice.

Baker (Show and Tell Concept Shop) also highlighted her commitment to fostering a customer-centric approach, prioritizing the connection with individuals over strict financial considerations.

The willingness to work with customers on a personal level, even if it might not always align with the most financially prudent decision, resonates with the brand's ethos. Baker's motivations extend beyond profit, emphasizing the intrinsic value of making meaningful connections and enabling people to acquire pieces that hold importance to them.

8 Queer and Trans Media: For Us and Them, Too

The power of media is undeniable. It transforms and influences how and what we see in the world. As these queer and trans fashion brands produced their products, many thought critically about representation and media. These brands recognized the power of media as a tool for reshaping societal perceptions and promoting inclusivity. By consciously considering representation, they aimed to challenge norms and foster a more diverse and accepting narrative beyond the actual products. In essence, the power of media, wielded by these queer and trans fashion brands, became another catalyst for dismantling stereotypes.

Representation Matters and Doesn't

Examining visuals is significant in comprehending the impact of an image's messages or meanings. According to Alan Branthwaite, "The effectiveness of imagery in terms of communication and persuasion lies in its ability to transcend the boundary between the external world and our internal experiences" (2002: 165). Thus, the observed image can elicit both emotional and physiological reactions in the observer (Kätsyri, Ravaja, and Salminen 2012; McManis et al. 2001), rendering imagery a compelling mechanism. Stocchetti and Kukkonen (2011) contend that it is not solely the image's inherent power that wields influence; rather, it's the utilization of the image—the transmission of social values by the agents involved (which may include image creators, distributors, and viewers). Of note is that the selection of imagery and how and where it is positioned can shape perceptions of individuals, politics, and current events (Corrigall-Brown 2012).

Scrutinizing the representation of individuals in visuals is crucial because exposure to these images and messages molds perceptions of our societal environment. That is, examining visuals through various channels can wield a substantial influence on the observer and their understanding of themselves and others (Chidester 2008). Iteratively observing a similar category of visual representation might lead the observer to accept that the portrayal faithfully mirrors reality, even if it is somewhat distorted (Gerbner, Gross, and Morgan 2002). Visuals in the media serve as a source of socialization, contributing to the process of acquiring behaviors, values, and norms (Arnett 1995a). Socialization sources enable the cultivation of meaning and what is deemed significant or valuable (Arnett 1995b: 618). Although there exists various agents of socialization, such as family, peers, school, and communities, the media plays a crucial role in shaping meaning and influencing how individuals perceive and construe their surroundings (Arnett 1995a).

Researchers have determined that even brief exposure to related media can impact the user's thoughts, concepts, and subsequent judgments and attitudes (Bargh, Chen, and Burrows 1996). Nonetheless, extended exposure to an image enhances the likelihood of developing a stronger fondness for it (Winkielman and Cacioppo 2001). While different forms of media exert distinct short- and long-term effects on viewers, Gerbner, Gross, and Morgan (2002) noted that media like television contributes to the extensive, persistent, and shared exposure of diverse audiences to centrally generated, broadly distributed, and repetitive narrative systems. Numerous scholars have investigated the specific influence of various media messages on self-perceptions. For instance, recent findings have revealed that the "observation of sexualized images" led to heightened self-objectification among women (Linder and Daniels 2018: 37). Researchers conducting a meta-analysis of studies on exposure to slender bodies in media discovered adverse effects on women, including "concerns about body image" (Grabe, Ward, and Hyde 2008: 460). Additionally, studies have shown that individuals respond more positively, gravitate toward media that mirrors their diverse identities (Harwood 1997; Ogle et al. 2023), and avoid content that does not align with their identities or portrays them negatively (Abrams and Giles 2007). Additionally, some nonbinary folks explained that in their journey to positive body image, they reframed negative body image information by challenging the prevailing norms and actively comparing themselves to those who are more like them (Ogle et al. 2023).

Over time, there has been much more diverse representation and a shift away from the white, heterosexual, cisgender, able-bodied, thin aesthetic dominating media spaces. In particular, there has been much growth in queer representation. Das and Farber provided a definition for queer media as media specifically aimed at queer individuals and/or crafted and disseminated by individuals who identify as queer. Historically, mainstream media has marginalized and underrepresented queer people, making queer media an avenue for them to establish their own visibility (Das and Farber 2020). However, scholars have argued that, in utilizing queer media to construct their narratives, queer individuals often unintentionally perpetuate prevailing norms. For instance, in its inaugural season, *The Androgynous Model*, a reality show competition created by an androgynous Black model, and an example of queer media, showcased five Black androgynous-identifying lesbians in its inaugural season. While the models were encouraged to embrace their androgenicity, some challenges required them to compartmentalize their femininity and masculinity. For instance, each participant had to create a Photoshopped image presenting themselves as conventionally feminine alongside another in which they dressed and posed in stereotypically masculine styles (Blake 2019).

Web series like *Between Women* (nonfiction) and *The Peculiar Kind* (fiction), both produced by and featuring Black queer women, have explored tensions between constructing alternative narratives and perpetuating existing power dynamics and stereotypes. However, these series have elicited mixed reactions within the community. The portrayal of dating violence in *The Peculiar Kind*, for example, frustrated some Black queer female viewers, who believed it did not challenge dominant notions of aggressive Black masculinity in butch women. At the same time, other viewers praised the series for realistically depicting gender expression for Black queer women (Day 2018).

Reactions to *Between Women* and *The Peculiar Kind* also highlighted the internet's crucial role in facilitating social relationships for queer and trans individuals (Day 2018). DeHaan et al. (2013) found that the majority of LGBT youth use the internet for communication, while Erlick (2018) emphasized its importance in community-building and activism-organizing for trans individuals. Websites created by trans woman escorts, showcasing their services and using language emphasizing specific ethnic and/or feminine features to attract potential clients, exemplify the internet's role in this regard (Vartabedian 2019).

Additionally, YouTube serves as a platform for community-building through sociability, shared purpose, interaction (including emotional and practical support), culture (such as shared experiences), and face-to-face interactions (Rotman and Preece 2010). O'Neill (2014) identified five main categories of trans YouTube videos: DIY gender, transitional videos, trans video blogging, trans anti-bullying videos, and celebrity trans video blogging. These videos primarily guide and model techniques for manipulating one's gender presentation, fostering a sense of social interaction. The DIY gender category, for instance, features videos where individuals or friends demonstrate the best way to present as the opposite gender. These are often created by trans youth, showcasing practices like shaving legs or concealing breasts, although some cisgender individuals produce similar content for cross-dressing activities, such as swapping clothing between boyfriends and girlfriends (O'Neill 2014).

Overall, the literature highlights the profound impact of visual representations, bringing forward the persuasive and communicative power of imagery in eliciting emotional and physiological responses. The examination of media's role in shaping socialization has underscored its influence on behaviors, values, and norms, with enduring effects on self-perception and body image. The evolution of diverse representation, notably within queer media, recognizes the nuanced interplay between fostering inclusivity and inadvertently perpetuating prevailing norms. Thus, the literature emphasizes the internet's pivotal role, particularly platforms like YouTube, in fostering social connections for queer and trans individuals, affirming its crucial contribution to community-building and activism within contemporary society. The queer and trans fashion brands in this research produced much queer and trans media in varied and nuanced ways, with many varied reactions from inside and outside the communities.

When Representation Works and Doesn't at the Same Time

Overall, the fashion brands thought critically about representation in their imagery. They certainly wanted it to be relatable. That is, they wanted their consumers or potential consumers to see themselves in the images. They understood that consumers are more likely to engage with and feel a connection to their products when they can see individuals in their marketing materials who resemble them. For example, Chris Rhodes from FLAVNT said, "We love that people can see people that look like them on our site and our look-book and that we have models that are all from the community." Similarly, Sara Medd from Greyscale Goods explained her models included "friends and people in the community, because it's important to me for it to feel relatable." The relatability aspect of model choice influenced these brands to use everyday folks, not professional models, who so often have bodies that diverge completely from those of the average person. Additionally, they mentioned, too, that using everyday folks was certainly due in part to expense: as small businesses, finances were at the forefront of their minds. While there was much intentionality in model choice, Kit and Sade from Queer Supply explained that they used their friends as models and that they just happened to all be queer; they said, "So, we weren't actively trying to make that the case, but I think that was a nice thing, that it was maybe just for queer people, and that the models in the shirts kind of like had a connection in some way to some of the shirts they were wearing."

Scout Rose (Transguy Supply) was intentional about imagery and emphasized the significance of creating beautiful images and representation for the trans community. They explained:

> I think it is incredibly important from a community perspective. I think that creating a space where transmasculine folks of all bodies and races—and ... even under this larger sort of trans-umbrella—can see themselves, can see themselves represented, and to see themselves looking, like, fucking great. We love being able to ... one of our favorite parts of the businesses are the photo shoots that we've done, and being able to create beautiful images of trans people, which I think is fantastic for people to have of themselves, but also, I think it feels great for people to see ... for the world to see just how gorgeous we are as a community, yeah. Yeah, so I would say it's not incredibly important in terms of sales, but I think it's a big piece in terms of ... I think it's very important for the community.

They continued, "I really wanted to create a shopping experience that felt ... where people feel safe, where they feel seen, and that feels beautiful."

Discussions surrounding the story being told through marketing media brought up questions related to who their consumers were and how to authentically capture that in imagery. The brands' underlying emphasis is, or at least at the start, centered around queer and trans identities. Some of the brand owners wanted to be as inclusive as possible yet struggled sometimes with how they positioned their products. The struggles resulted from others responding with confusion to the brand or thinking through what it means to be inclusive. For instance, Stoney Michelli Love (Stuzo) said, "I'm very intentional about that [models in the imagery] because I think we all deserve a chance and we all have a beauty to us that should be shown," and continued, "the requirement [to be a model] is very broad and it starts with you being a human being." Despite using anyone to model for the brand, Love further explained that sometimes getting cisgender men to view the product as for them was challenging. She explained:

> Typically, guys are just, when it comes to fashion, it depends. For the most part, I think society has a lot to do with it, where it's like I want them to allow themselves to be more free and not tie it [clothing] to sexuality and tie it to certain things and emasculating or anything because we're as humans, masculine and feminine energy. So you wear what you want, you wear it your way, and no one can say anything about it. So that's the agenda that I continue to push. And I have seen the rise of men now like, "Wow, okay, great." Of all sorts. I get it. And it is helping me come out of this shell where I'm not worrying about what anyone else is looking at because I know who I am inside and it just looks great. You can't deny it when you put it on. So it's just one of those things.

Vicky Pasche (Dapper Boi) shared a similar experience. Models Pasche has used thus far include mostly her friends who looked like her, with a masculine or androgynous leaning aesthetic. She continued, "I'm having trouble here, because I never want to forget our initial audience [queer or nonbinary folks], and because they have the least amount of options available, I think. So, that's been a real challenge. Probably the most challenging aspect is like, 'Who do we target, how do we target, and how do we do that sensitively, too?'" This line of thinking made her question how she targets her consumers and then expands to men and feminine-leaning women. She suggests that one path forward for her brand may be to think about it through body type, not gender. Similarly, NiK Kacy (NiK Kacy Footwear) said his Kickstarter ad campaign specifically was very purposeful but that it was "hard to include everyone" because "*everyone* is subjective." Thus, his models included, "trans people, cis people, queer people, straight people, everyone." For his photoshoot, he reached out to his community and "was like, whether you're straight, gay, male, female—whatever you are, this is what I'm doing, and if you believe in supporting this, then come." Fran Dunaway (TomboyX) practiced similar philosophies related to who they featured. She explained:

> It's a real challenge marketing-wise to be a gender-neutral underwear company because it's just so engraved in our minds that it's either "boy" or "girl." And so, we think it's going to take some time. We have a lot of male customers, we have a lot of trans customers—our customer base is just really across the spectrum. We're trying to be all-inclusive. I wouldn't say that we're exclusive. It's not like we sit around and talk about who we shouldn't choose. It's about, how do we find somebody to tell the next cool story about.

This thinking brings up critical questions about what it means to do diversity work versus justice work related to inequities.

It was clear, though, that the brands were interested in rejecting dominant beauty ideals by featuring people of color, fat people, people with cellulite—and they did not want to alter the images. In her swimsuit photos, Mel Brittner Wells (Beefcake

Swimwear) featured models wearing sizes from medium up to 4X. When talking to her models, she asked them: "So, if you have cellulite and stuff, are you going to be mad if I don't Photoshop you?," highlighting her commitment to portraying real bodies with all their nuances.

Jeanna Kadlec (Bluestockings Boutique) operated and Searah Deysach (FtM Essentials) operates retail businesses and initially relied on the wholesalers' images. Thus, Kadlec was intentional about which brands she partnered with:

> I did not have any imagery of my own to use, and something that was important to me when I was choosing brands was based on which brands had what images. Like, who was conscientious about their models and about how they represented themselves in a very thoughtful and smart way. I didn't want to be partnering with brands who were exploitative about how they represented women, and how they represented people. Queer-inclusive imagery is hard to come by on a good day in lingerie, so I wasn't necessarily hoping for that, although I did make a point to stock a few queer designers, like Play Out, which is Abby's brand, and, like, FYI by Danny Reed.

Deysach either used the stock images from the wholesaler or took her own photos (Figure 8.1). She explained that Underworks, which sells binders, did not originally intend its product for the queer and trans communities. It started making medical products, for example, for people with hernias. Therefore, their original product imagery focused on heteronormative people. Yet, when Underworks realized who was buying its product, it changed its advertising approach to include trans masculine folks; Deysach then began using Underworks' imagery on her website.

The brands also grappled with media imagery by featuring the products alone, not on the body as a context. Deysach explained,

> I take a picture of everything in my own hand because I am a very cheap model, but also because I feel like, well, one, it's really easy for me to take a picture in my own hand, but also, then I feel like there's a consistency of scale even though no one knows what my hand size is, and it's a pretty average hand size, but that if I have two different sizes of packers in the same hand it hopefully gives them some perspective.

Deysach employs an innovative method to assist clients in understanding the appropriate size for their packer, minimizing the likelihood of unfavorable comparisons customers might draw between themselves and the selected model.

While the brands thought critically about their imagery, they experienced critical feedback via social media. TomboyX encountered scrutiny in March 2020 when it featured a trans-man model for its women's celebration underwear print. @Trinity, the model, shared their experience on Twitter (now X):

> I'm very disappointed in Tomboy X. I just recently worked with them again, and within a minute of me arriving they informed me that they cast me to model their WOMEN'S CELEBRATION print and reactively I said, "No I'm not, I'm a trans man, legally male, and a year on testosterone."

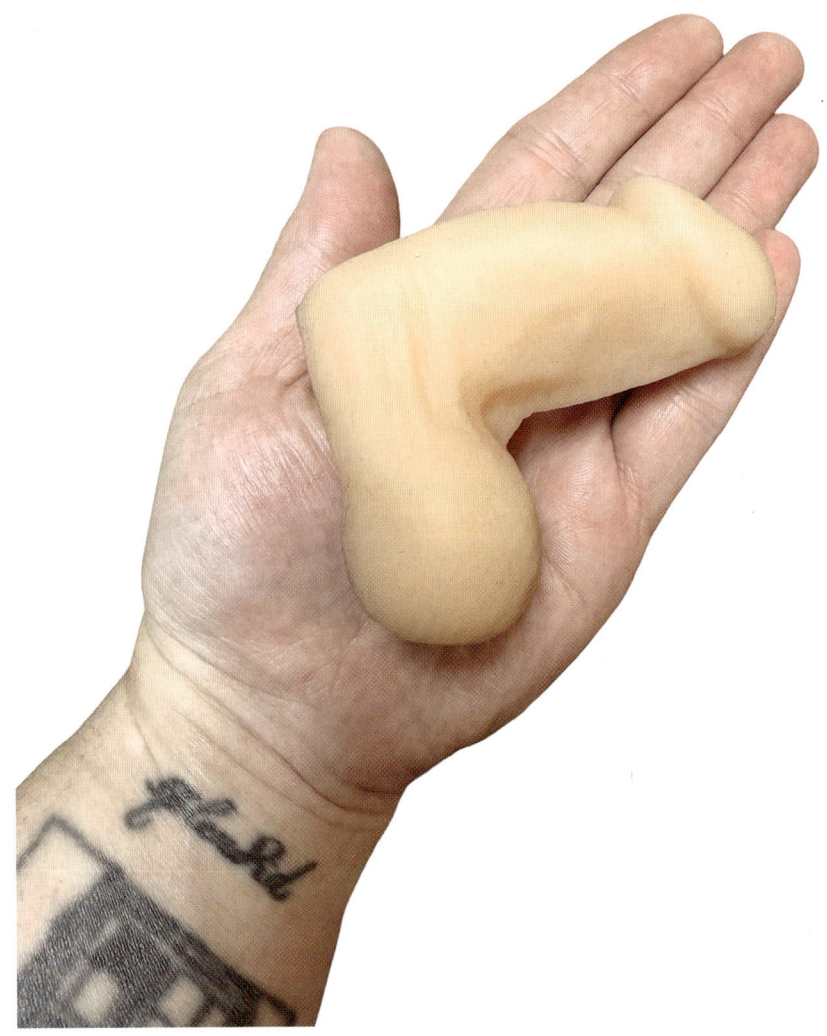

Figure 8.1 Packer sold by FtM Essentials. Photo courtesy of Searah Deysach.

I arrived (completely unprompted on the print) and was immediately put into an unsafe environment, being reduced down to my genitals, and continued to get misgendered throughout the entirety of the day on set even after being corrected. The transphobia did not end there.

They had a sign that read "We the *insert cat photo*". I asked them about it to which they responded "We the Pussy." I explained how that excludes trans women from the celebration, and to try and include me, a trans man instead purely because of what genitals I have was wrong.

This severely impacts their authenticity as an LGBT company. They thanked me for educating them, to which I replied, "It was not my job to educate you. I am a model". There were so many oversights regarding this casting and it was unfortunately at the expense of my safety.

(@tomboyX)

Post-incident, TomboyX released underwear and packing underwear with the trans flag colors (blue, white, and pink stripes). In response to the images on social media, someone referenced @Trinity's post, labeling the company "transphobes" in the comments. Another criticized TomboyX supporters after harassing a trans model, "Damn … people really still out there supporting you after u harassed a trans model?" TomboyX publicly responded, expressing self-reflective sentiments on Twitter (now X). "Our CEO sat down with Trinity this week and they agreed to work together to establish a protocol for ourselves & other agencies to ensure the trans community feels welcome, cared for, & respected on photoshoot sets. We are dedicated to learning & getting better every day" (@TomboyX 2020).

TomboyX directly addressed criticism of the imagery, asserting it was not intentionally transphobic. Other brand directors responded to criticism differently. For instance, Kadlec faced emails criticizing a photoshoot with a trans woman alongside cisgender models because the trans woman was featured in the back, which caused the uproar. Kadlec chose not to engage directly, stating, "There is nothing to be gained from being in this." Instead, she focused on positioning models in future photoshoots. She said, "Someone on the internet will always respond to a tweet being upset and you have to let it go as a brand," and she learned to be critically aware of Bluestockings Boutique's imagery. Despite acknowledging social tensions, she recognized the inefficiency of reacting to every negative customer comment, considering the extensive emotional labor involved.

9 DapperQ, Qwear, and Contemporary Queer Fashion Shows Emerged on the Scene

Alongside the rise of these queer and trans fashion brands and their own media production was the development of a few prominent queer-focused fashion media outlets, such as DapperQ and Qwear, which both specialize in the intersections of fashion, style, and queer and trans communities creating both digital media and in-person events. Like, the fashion brand Dykes in the City previously described, queer fashion community-making in other forms, such as in-person fashion events, certainly existed prior to major media platforms such as DapperQ and Qwear creating their own.

For example, Tania Hammidi, a scholar who engages much with queer culture and politics, contributed significantly to late twentieth-century and early twenty-first-century queer fashion community-making. In particular, Tania produced UCLA's "Queerture Fashion Show" as part of UCLA's Queer Fashion conference, organized by the LGBT Studies program (Williamson 2011). The inspiration for the fashion show stemmed from a previous runway event, "INVINCIBLE: Back from the Ruins," held at the Butch Voices LA conference. Hammidi explained that the show aimed to showcase clothing tailored to LGBTQ communities, leveraging shared talent, platforms, and resources to spread the message widely. The show highlighted diverse influences shaping the Los Angeles' queer fashion scene, including the impact of the movie industry, subcultures such as punk music and the Chicano/a community, as well as the presence of LGBTQ artists and university populations. Throughout, the show emphasized that LGBTQ fashion had influence from various factors, including subcultural values, politics, acceptance, economic conditions, gender norms, and practical elements like weather and transportation habits (personal communication with Tania Hammidi 2023).

Similarly, at Porter College, a residential college in the University of California, Santa Cruz, students organized the Queer Fashion Show (QFS). The event's origins trace to the mid-1990s, when Porter students initiated a showcase promoting the integration of diverse queer identities. Their aim was to spotlight pressing social issues within the community, and they donated all ticket sales revenue to local organizations supporting LGBTQ+ individuals. Over the years, the QFS has served as a bastion of innovation for the queer community on campus. Initially dubbed the "Alternative Fashion Show," in 1997 the event became the QFS, signifying a broader embrace of queer culture. The show, originally hosted in the Porter/Kresge Dining Hall, incorporated fashion, music, spoken-word, theater, and burlesque performances. In its early days, the QFS featured students modeling attire from their own wardrobes, in front of an audience of approximately two hundred people. The event still exists today and remains entirely student-driven, with students volunteering both as organizers and performers (Navarrete 2021).

Of course, drag balls have a longstanding history as vibrant and empowering fashion spaces within the LGBTQ+ community, dating to the early twentieth century. Emerging in urban centers like New York City, these events provided a haven for individuals to openly express their gender identities and sexual orientations at a time when societal norms rigidly enforced traditional roles. Particularly during the Harlem Renaissance of the 1920s and 1930s, drag balls gained prominence within African American LGBTQ+ communities, serving as platforms for creative expression and talent. These gatherings allowed participants to challenge societal expectations by donning extravagant, gender-nonconforming attire, blurring the lines between traditional gender roles and celebrating their queerness. In the post-Second World War era, drag balls continued to flourish, evolving into organized events with various categories and competitions. These gatherings played significant roles in shaping queer culture, fostering a sense of belonging and solidarity among marginalized communities. Drag balls served not only as fashion spectacles but also as vital spaces where individuals could assert their identities, paving the way for the vibrant drag culture we recognize today (Mamp 2021; Newton 1979; *Paris Is Burning* 1990), in addition to the cultural spaces created by the queer and trans fashion brand entrepreneurs of this research, Qwear and DapperQ.

Qwear

Qwear, one of the prominent contemporary queer fashion platforms, describes itself as "dedicated to queer fashion and its impact on health and wellness" (Qwear n.d.d: para. 1). Similarly, DapperQ is described as:

> one of the world's most widely read digital queer style magazines and is a preeminent voice in queer fashion and beauty. We inspire people of all sexual orientations, gender identities, and gender presentations to think differently about both queer fashion and beauty as art and visual activism, and ultimately have a deeper, more fulfilling relationship with style. In the words of Anita Dolce Vita, "dapperQ is a queer fashion revolution, one of the most stylish forms of protest of our generation."
>
> (DapperQ 2019: para. 1)

Both Qwear and DapperQ serve as a hub for the queer and trans communities, providing an incredibly important space for individuals to explore, celebrate, and redefine notions of fashion and style. In addition to showcasing the latest trends and styles from queer and trans fashion brands, these platforms play a crucial role in fostering a sense of community and empowerment.

Sonny Oram (they/them/none) founded Qwear in Boston in 2011, originally named Dyke Duds, in the form of a Tumblr blog (Figure 9.1). Now the platform has multiple people on the team and is co-owned with Ru, Oram's partner, who is Qwear's fashion director. They publish a variety of content documenting personal queer styles, fashion brands, and Qwear "educates the mainstream fashion industry about queer identities" (Qwear n.d.a: para. 4). Like many of the fashion brands, Oram founded Qwear, in part, due to their own experiences. Oram explained how through their

Figure 9.1 Sonny Oram, founder of Qwear. Photo courtesy of Sonny Oram.

journey through depression, assault, and transphobia, clothing was an integral part of their healing process:

> One day I was in the Downtown Crossing T station (Boston) and spotted what appeared to be a secret door that lead into the Macy's guy's department. I opened the door and walked right in. The store was definitely open, but no one was there watching me as I thumbed through racks of beautiful garments. I tried things on in their tiny changing rooms. I looked in the mirror wearing a boxy T-shirt and just felt ... amazing. I loved how flat my chest looked in it. I could stand two inches taller. If I angled myself the right way it almost looked like my chest was completely flat. I tried on everything in si[ght]. I left with a considerable dent in my graduation gift money ... but it was the best money I'd ever spent.
>
> Wearing the right clothing was the best antianxiety medication out there. Though I faced increased bullying, I was thrilled with how I looked and wouldn't trade that for anything.

Oram continued to explain that the connection with clothing helped them come to understand their gender identity more intimately—"It was the clothing I wore that lead me to recognize my trans and nonbinary identity"—and that the heteronormative representation in media stifled Oram's ability to explore an authentic self: "I wasn't aware that there were other clothing choices for me aside from baggy tees. Had I seen people like me in the media, I might have come out years earlier" (Oram n.d.b: para. 24).

Oram also related that before starting Qwear they had an affinity for queerness and media; as children, Oram and their friend created fashion magazines, *Radical Fashion* (Figure 9.2). In their oral history, Oram explained, "We would cut up fashion magazines and then I would write my own articles, so that was pretty cool. A lot of them were parodies, and a lot of them were playing with gender. I would cut off a man's head and put it on a woman's body, and it was a way of exploring gender and also consumerism."

In addition to the digital platform, Qwear also produces in-person fashion shows and performances. Oram explained that once Ru came on board, Qwear began doing fashion shows. Ru had a degree from the Rhode Island School of Design and brought prior experience in the fashion industry. Instead of the conventional method, where clothes dictate the choice of models, Ru envisioned a reversal—models first, outfits later. They would meet with each model beforehand and discuss their style and gender expression. In many fashion shows, models show up to the event and are told what to wear, which, Sonny explained, is turning "models into vessels rather than active agents." This paradigm shift became the hallmark of their fashion endeavors.

Their first venture into this unconventional fashion world was in Oakland, for the "Dismantle Me" show featured in Queer Fashion Week in 2015. They went to California with a suitcase filled with an eclectic mix of clothing, and Ru declared: "No white models. All models of color." Oram said they made an exception, though,

Figure 9.2 Pages from *Radical Fashion* magazine that Sonny Oram created in childhood. Photos courtesy of Sonny Oram.

for their friend Alexis. The intent was clear—subverting norms. It was an inclusive process, with models trying on various pieces, discussing preferences, and expressing their gender identities. The creative process unfolded in hotel rooms and studio spaces. Ru, armed with a vision, spent days adapting, sewing, and crafting new outfits. The morning of the fashion show witnessed a flurry of activity: models donned their unique ensembles, last-minute adjustments were made, and the unconventional runway took shape. Ru had exhibited two unique designs:

> The show premiered two of Ru's unique concepts: the bandana built into a shirt collar, and a tie drawn through a hoodie [Figure 9.3]. We expanded on the bandana theme, dressing several models in bandana-patterned pants and throwing the bandana textile into other aspects of the outfits. Bandanas were used during historic protests as early as the Black Liberation Army and are still seen at race riots sparked by the assassinations of Trayvon Martin and Michael Brown.
>
> (Qwear n.d.b: para. 4)

In 2016, they created a second fashion show, "Femme Desire," held in Boston at the Institute of Contemporary Art, as a part of DapperQ's event "VERGE" (Figure 9.4). In this show, the models and performers were invited to collaborate with Ru, the designer, in the creation of distinctive pieces that diverge from their typical femme fashion expression. Through "Femme Desire," they sought to challenge preconceived notions surrounding gender identity, sexual orientation, and assigned sex at birth. The patterns in this collection evoked historical class and rebellion ideologies, exploring themes of gender and sexuality. Of importance is that "Femme Desire" involved a groundbreaking, model-driven approach to the process of crafting and presenting fashion collections. This endeavor encompassed the entirety of the fashion designer's creative process, ensuring a departure from the conventional dominance of designers and the inclination to solely please the audience (Qwear, n.d.c).

In 2018, Qwear produced an exhibit at the Boston University Art Galleries, titled "Forms & Alterations," with a fashion show they named "Legendary Children." This event featured designs by Ru, who created ensembles for each performer; that is, the models again were the designers. Qwear worked with a student-run shelter for unhoused young folks, who had a table at the event and worked with Qwear to identify one of their residents who might be interested in modeling (Reynolds 2018).

Then, during the pandemic, Qwear orchestrated a virtual fashion show. It invited participants to send in videos of themselves walking the runway, be it in their homes or outdoor spaces. Oram edited them together, and the result was an array of diverse expressions and a unique way to unite the community. The Qwear team explained, "[Neither] we, nor anyone else to our knowledge, had done a fashion show quite like this before and we were pleased with the results" (Qwear n.d.e: para. 3).

Figure 9.3 Ru adjusting model's top backstage at Qwear's 2015 "Dismantle Me" fashion show. The model's top is one of Ru's original designs that features a tie as the drawstring for the hoodie. Photo courtesy of Qwear.

Figure 9.4 Model who participated in Qwear's 2016 fashion installation at the Institute of Contemporary Art, Boston. Photo courtesy of Qwear/Jaypix Belmer.

DapperQ

Sterling Cruz-Herr founded DapperQ in 2009 as a website to address the lack of representation and visibility for individuals who identified as masculine-of-center, genderqueer, and nonbinary in the fashion world. That is, Cruz-Herr initially wrote about "their experiences navigating the world as a masculine-of-center woman, centering conversations around androgynous style for readers who were assigned female at birth (AFAB) and wanting to transgress 'men's fashion" (Devin-Norelle 2019: para. 2). A year into the project, Anita Dolce Vita, a Black femme, joined the team and shifted the direction and focus of the platform to explore the multitude of aesthetics and styles that queer and trans communities embrace. Dolce Vita explains:

> There was definitely a dearth of content and visibility for [femmes] in queer fashion. Femme style was getting lost in the conversation. Often times, people conflate femme style with white, binary, heteropatriarchal beauty and fashion that does not represent a wide range of queer femmes who have been at the forefront of challenging mainstream fashion's norms around size, race, ethnicity, able-bodied privilege, and pretty much anything that isn't deemed sexually desirable by heterosexual cisgender men.
>
> (Devin-Norelle 2019: para. 4)

DapperQ's impact extended beyond the digital realm. The platform organized and participated in various events, including fashion shows, runway presentations, and parties that showcased and celebrated queer fashion. These events not only highlighted the diversity of gender expressions but also provided a much-needed platform for queer designers, models, and stylists to showcase their talents. As the years progressed, DapperQ continued to evolve and grow. The platform became known for its commitment to diversity, featuring a wide range of individuals across different races, ethnicities, body sizes, and gender identities.

One major contribution DapperQ made to the queer fashion space is its live fashion shows. One of its earlier shows, held on April 15, 2012—"Gladiator: The Etymology of Female Muscle"—took place at the LAB in downtown Brooklyn in New York and "showcased the fashion and lifestyles of butch lesbians" (Dolce Vita 2012: para. 1). From there, the shows expanded and moved into the Brooklyn Museum; since the 2012 show, it has produced eight events, each with a different theme and group of designers. In 2014 the show "(un)Heeled: A Fashion Show for the Unconventionally Masculine" at Brooklyn Museum, which they term their inaugural show, featured work by Sir New York, Saint Harridan, Goorin Bros., Sharpe Suiting, Jag & Co., Angie Chuang, and Bindle & Keep (Dolce Vita 2014). This show occurred in the midst of the Black Lives Matter movement, and intersectional politics were woven throughout the evening. That is, Saint Harridan had models walking the runway while carrying Black Lives Matter signs, and the event's production team, including Dolce Vita, closed the show with the infamous "hands up" pose, and then the sea of folks in the audience did the same (Figure 9.5). Dolce Vita explained their solidarity as related to fashion: "We cannot extricate style from politics in the queer community. Fashion

Figure 9.5 "(un)Heeled: A Fashion Show for the Unconventionally Masculine" at the Brooklyn Museum in 2014. Events producer Anita Dolce Vita and models from Sharpe Suiting at the end of the show with the "hands up" sign. Photo courtesy of Steve Prue/Team Rockstar Images.

is not just fashion. For some, simply wearing a suit is a radical and political act. DapperQ is a queer fashion revolution, one of the most stylish forms of protest of our generation. We stand in solidarity" (Dolce Vita 2014: para. 3).

The shows continued each year with new themes and different designer participants. On September 17, 2015, DapperQ produced "VERGE" at the Brooklyn Museum, strategically on the final day of New York Fashion Week and "highlighting queer and gender non-conforming designers" including LACTIC, Not Equal by Fabio Costa, KQK by Karen Quirion, Fony, MARKANTOINE, SAGA by Sandra Gagalo, SunSun, and Jag & Co. (Brooklyn Museum 2015). Again, in 2016, this time on the opening day of New York Fashion Week, September 8, it produced the show "iD: a queer New York Fashion Week" at the Brooklyn Museum and described the event as featuring "independent designers exploring gender diversity and fashion as a means of resistance" (Brooklyn Museum 2016: para. 1). The show featured eight designers: Angie Chuang, NiK Kacy Footwear, Sharpe Suiting, Sir New York, Stuzo Clothing, The Tailory, and WE ARE MORTALS (DapperQ Team 2016). In 2017, the DapperQ team named the show "R/Evolution," "in defiant resistance to the attacks being waged against our community and our stylish unified resistance against those attacks," and the show featured Audio Helkuik, Bindle & Keep, by Nicole Wilson, Clio Sage, SDN Brooklyn, Sir New York, Stuzo, Kris Harring, The Tailory New York, and a collaboration with TomboyX and Clear Coated (Dolce Vita 2017: para. 1). This was the first year TomboyX helped sponsor the show, specifically in support of lighting.

In 2018 and 2019 the shows were also held at the Brooklyn Museum. In 2018, DapperQ presented the show "Dress Code," which "examines clothing as a coded language and one of the first visible markers of our identities, inviting you to consider the way garments uphold or challenge rigid stereotypes" (Brooklyn Museum 2018: para. 1). Designers included THÙY Custom Clothier, A/C Space by Angie Chuang, Audio Helkuik, By Nicole Wilson, SALT, Stuzo, Jag and Co., TomboyX featuring Squirrel vs. Coyote, and The Phluid Project. Before the pandemic hiatus, they produced "Pursuit" on September 5, 2019, with designers Cilium, Claire Fleury, DEVONATION by Devon Yan, HALZ, LANDEROS NEW YORK, Shane Avenue, Sharp Suiting featuring Goorin Brothers, Stuzo Clothing, Travis Oestreich, and, as the show's official sponsor, TomboyX.

The shows returned in 2022 and 2023. In 2022, the show was titled "Bloom," with Transguy Supply as the official sponsor and featuring designers LANDEROS NEW YORK, DEVONATION, THÚY Custom Clothier, Stuzo, Freemen by Mickey, LLESSUR, Transguy Supply, and Hesta by Hester Sunshine. Dolce Vita highlighted the continued importance of creating space for these queer-focused fashion events:

> We are extremely honored to work with Brooklyn Museum for the seventh year to create a platform that celebrates queer bodies and queer style. LGBTQ and POC communities have a rich legacy of being creative visionaries in beauty and fashion, but our ideas are often co-opted without any credit or visibility. Bloom is for us and by us, bringing our talents, bodies, innovations, and voices to the forefront under one roof in Brooklyn Museum's 10,000 square foot, artfully designed Beaux Arts Court. The all queer DapperQ production team also notes that the production and support of shows such as Bloom are critical in a political climate that continues to target LGBTQIA+ identities through banning LGBTQIA+ books, attacking drag performances, and "Don't Say Gay" legislation and bathroom bills. Our shows are both an act of defiance and self-love. Our oppressors try to bury us, and yet we bloom for the entire world to see.
>
> (DapperQ Team 2022: para. 7)

Like previous shows, elements of overt political agendas graced the runways. For instance, Stuzo featured a model with "protect trans kids" written in marker on their arms who posed with the phrase prominently visible for the photographers at the end of the runway.

Muse, DapperQ's most recent show, which I attended, held on September 7, 2023, featured new work by designers Buckethead Productions, DANITHREADS, FreeMen by Mickey, Hesta by Project Runway's Hester Sunshine, Kirrin Finch, LLESSUR NYC, Soid Studios New York by José Gonzalez, and SUN SUN. Kirrin Finch focused its theme on the phrase "give me flowers while I'm here"; the models wore Kirrin Finch suits with powerful political messaging and flowers from a local florist. The seven looks included the phrases "give me flowers while I'm here," "our existence is resistance," "respect all families," "more color, more pride," "wear your truth," "we will not be erased," and "trailblazer." The models featured "queer resistance" leaders of color from the Human Rights Campaign, Family Equality, SAGE, and Callen Lorde. For instance, Crystal Hudson, the first openly gay Black woman, elected to the New York City Council in 2021, modeled a look. Amber Hikes—an activist who in 2017 designed and introduced the Philly pride flag which features black and brown in the rainbow assortment—also modeled. Barbara Adams, a resident at Brooklyn's Stonewall House, an LGBTQ+ friendly adult center, closed out the show. Adams strutted down the runway in a suit and bow tie with her walker covered in flowers and a sign that read "trail blazer" (Kirrin Finch 2023). The audience roared when she came out, and it seemed obvious that she, too, was likely having a great time, as she was all smiles and stopping multiple times for people to applaud.

A few of the queer and trans fashion brands in this research had participated in the DapperQ shows and had extremely positive experiences. Anji Becker (WE ARE MORTALS) participated in the "iD: a queer New York Fashion Week" and felt very positive about it:

> So, I just thought that that was a really epic location when they contacted me. It's just so different from anything else as far as fashion weeks go, because it's just, like, it has a purpose. Again, it's not just the fashion it's also a very celebratory night, very joyful and empowering, because they're doing this. The organizer is very, like, just a super activist in that realm and so it's just important to her to have that voice heard. So, she puts so much time and effort into creating this fashion show once a year and giving a voice to all those designers that really cross, it's a big range because a lot really fits into that broad category of like queer fashion. So, there were designers like myself that just did genderless clothing, but then there was also designers that were specifically making like suits for queer women, trans individuals, things like that. That are more specific products for, like, the LGBT community. So, it was a big mix, but all together the message was definitely like different and unique than any other fashion show. So it was really cool to be a part of that.

Scout Rose (Transguy Supply) also related that the event was important for their brand:

> We showed at New York Fashion Week last … not for the one that just happened in March or February, but fall, winter, September. We had a small pop-up shop at the event, so it was this runway show put on by DapperQ. If folks are familiar, it's the largest queer runway show in the world, and we were really honored to be a part of that and had a tiny little pop-up shop.

Similarly, Helkuik (Audio Helkuik), when asked what he was most proud of in his career thus far, responded that his involvement in DapperQ's fashion shows stood out:

> I think I'm most proud that for two years I've shown at the DapperQ runway event at New York Fashion Week. To be a fashion designer, New York Fashion Week is a goal. Even if people don't know about fashion, they know of that. That's

been really exciting to show there and also to do it in an all queer setting. That day is one of my favorites of the year. I love being surrounded by queer stylists, photographers, models, and celebrat[ing] queerness in fashion.

Fashion Events as Queer and Trans Community Making

Other events emerged in addition to those Qwear and DapperQ produced. For instance, Kacy founded and produces Equality Fashion Week in Los Angeles, with events in 2018, 2019, and 2024. The mission of these week-long events is to "uplift our LGBTQ+ community through visibility, representation, inclusivity and equality" (Equality Fashion Week 2023: para. 1)

In the vibrant landscape of queer and trans fashion, the emergence of dedicated media platforms such as DapperQ and Qwear has played an instrumental role in reshaping narratives around style, identity, and community. Qwear focuses on the intersection of queer fashion and wellbeing with an aim to subvert fashion industry norms by giving all the power to the models. That is, it has created a space where the models move about the space however they please and come out on stage whenever they are ready. DapperQ, a pioneering voice in digital queer style magazines, has brought much queer commercial fashion into view using the traditional fashion runway format. Each has become more than just an outlet for style; they stand as pillars of empowerment, offering safer havens for individuals to explore, celebrate, and redefine their relationship with fashion and were directly connected to and supporting the queer and trans fashion brands in this research. Sonny Oram's founding journey of Qwear, rooted in personal healing through clothing, and DapperQ's evolution into a revolutionary force that transcends the digital realm with radical fashion shows underscore the transformative power of fashion as a tool for self-discovery, activism, and solidarity within the queer and trans communities.

Conclusion

There Will Always Be Haters ... and Lovers!

Despite the ups and downs, the challenges and successes, the brands all explained that what they were doing had positive impact on people's lives, based on their consumers' feedback in various spaces. That is, the consumers feel better about themselves, they feel more authentically themselves, they feel seen and represented, or they used the products to learn about their identities. They also feel more confident wearing the products, they are able to leave their house now that they have these products, or they feel prouder wearing the products. Additionally, their life is changed for the better, they feel more comfortable with themselves, the products saved their life, or the product helped them feel safer. Throughout the sometimes-emotional rollercoaster of dealing with the so-called haters, the brands create moments of pure, emotion-filled joy and love.

> It is pretty amazing when you have somebody that calls you and says, "My son is getting better grades and he's actually like going to school, because he feels better." I had no idea going in that it would be mostly young people. Having young people come in and just be proud—they come in and you can tell they are wearing their binder, and you can tell they're feeling good and they're having a better day.
>
> (Peregrine Honig, AFLW)

> People say like the first time they put on our underwear they started crying, because it's the first time they could feel like it was the right thing for them underneath what they're all wearing.
>
> (Fran Dunaway, TomboyX)

> A lot of the feedback is about my model casting. I hear the comment over and over, "I've never seen someone with my body type on the runway before."
>
> (Audio Helkuik, Audio Helkuik)

> I've gotten emails from women who are like badass swimmers who are like, "This is the best swimsuit I've swum in, in years," and that was awesome! It's mostly people who struggle with body dysphoria that send emails that are really, really positive and really awesome.
>
> (Mel Brittner Wells, Beefcake Swimwear)

I think the community that has come up around it has been a great success. There are a number of people I know who have like met each other through Bluestockings. I have gained a lot of friends through Bluestockings. I have friends who met their wedding photographers through Bluestockings. It's just when people just also coming into their sense of style and feeling, and seeing for the first time, and I'm extraordinarily proud of that. So ... the sense of confidence and the community people ... is a very, an ephemeral thing, but I'm very proud of it.

(Jeanna Kadlec, Bluestockings Boutique)

So, we have these "I'm not a boy" hats and "I'm not a boy" shirts, and they went crazy for them. It was supposed to be a lighthearted kind of thing, and, again, I based it off of my own personal story. I get that all the time, when I go to the grocery store. When I walk into the women's restroom, I get the double glances. I get the "Hey, you're not supposed to be in here," and for the most part, I've been lucky in the fact that people usually feel bad when they say that, and then it makes me feel bad because I'm like, "It's okay, I'm okay with it. Don't worry." So, that was the premise behind the "I'm not a boy." I put on that hat, and I'm like, "Hey it's all good. Okay, like, we're human beings that make mistakes and it's fine." Others are not so lucky, and I know that we've had a lot of people share their stories and some people take the hat very seriously and they wear that with pride, actually, when they're going to the restroom. That's something that they can easily point out without having to explain anything. They're like, "Listen, I'm not a boy. I'm allowed to be here." So, we've gotten a lot of emails and stories from people thanking us for our T-shirt that says the same thing. Yeah, that's something we're actually really proud of.

(Vicky Pasche, Dapper Boi)

It is so crazy to me that we can make that impact because I feel so small, I guess. He [a consumer] felt like he could relate and that there were other people and that he wasn't alone. I think that's the most amazing thing right there, that people don't feel alone. There are people, just like everybody else out there. I didn't expect that at all.

(Vicky Pasche, Dapper Boi)

I'm proud of what we get to give in that binder to other people. They're like, "This gives me confidence," and that sort of stuff. That kind of ties into my other answer, which is maybe not what I'm most proud of, but it's why I do this, is the kids that reach out to us and say like, "Your Pretty Boy shirt gave me the confidence to come out to my parents." We get like really cute messages like that. So, that's really, really validating.

(Chris Rhodes, FLAVNT)

We've talked to people who are like, "I can't leave the house until I get this," and I'm like, "Okay, well, sorry it's the mail. It's just going to take a couple days."

But you know, it is just such an important part of folks lives and the best part is hearing from folks who are kind enough to share with us that, after they've gotten something that embodied how they feel, how transformed they feel in a sense, and for the first time they finally feel like, "You know, this is who I am. This is so right." And that makes up for all the people who challenge us and who don't understand how the postal system works, or who, you know, think that coming at us mean is the way to go.

(Searah Deysach, FtM Essentials)

[It's meaningful to me] that it changed their lives for better, and I really like getting stuff from parents, because I [like] seeing that there's accepting parents out there. I think back to my own history with my parents, knowing what these parents are going through, and creating an environment where their kids can be healthy and independent. [I enjoy] just seeing the beginning of that and seeing that the parents are beginning to see that their kids are smiling now, and feel like they are able to leave the house.

(Marli Washington, gc2b)

The feedback is what keeps me going every day, because, you know, I'm doing this to help people, essentially and I'm doing this to make a difference in people's lives. So, … I'm getting feedback from someone saying, "I have never found jeans that fit me. You must be a magician that you found these jeans that fit me perfectly." … It's stories like that that keep … me going every day.

(Sara Medd, Greyscale Goods)

Oh my gosh! I had a client in here yesterday put on her garments and started crying. Like, I get that a lot. Happy tears! [Laughs] You know, people tell me that they've always wanted to do this and never thought it was going to be possible, especially for people in the older age range. Then, in the younger age range, it's that they've always wanted to try something like this, so they wanted the perfect wedding suit, and I gave it to them and then [I] get … the feedback of just them having a place to come be themselves and really think about their gender identities.

(Erin Berg, Kipper Clothiers)

I was thinking about someone who's modeled for us and also is a friend and is helping us out with a pop-up at the DapperQ fashion show this past week, and they were saying that one of the things they really love about our brand is that when someone tries on that shirt, it's a moment that you see in their face. It's "this was me. For me." I want there to be more of that for the people that our brand speaks to.

(Kelly Moffat, Kirrin Finch)

I remember the first time I put on my own design, and I was in Europe, I was in Portugal, and I put on my design for the first time and I remember the joy of having it just fit me. It fit me without extra insoles, without anything else. I just started tearing up and walking so proudly on the streets, even though they were cobblestones, and it was the first sample, so they hurt like hell because they hadn't been perfected yet, and we were still figuring out the nuances, but at least it fit, and it was my design! It was so amazing. Whenever I get an email or a social media post from my clients, it's that same—I understand. I understand what they're trying to say, because I've been there, I've experienced it, and it's this joy. One client was like, for the first time they felt like they didn't have children's feet because they were finally wearing shoes that look proportionate to their body. Or someone else … felt they walked differently, you know, they felt that they walked proudly and with confidence. Yeah, I mean the stuff about being comfortable, or they look super cool or are great quality—those are all great and I'm super happy to receive that kind of feedback, but … the stuff that is so powerful are the things that impact the way they see themselves. That's the stuff that I really love to hear.

(NiK Kacy, NiK Kacy Footwear)

This one says, "Trans-Masc guy here, this top changed my life. I refused to swim for years because of the dysphoria and not being able to feel comfortable in anything. This top doesn't make me even think twice about swimming, and it doubles as an excellent workout binder"—and then he explains what size he got and how it fits and the whole thing.

(Marialexandra Garcia, Outplay Swimwear)

Looking at people who are going to the pop-up shops and the markets … is when you get to see who's actually getting the shirt, and they're talking more about their experience and lives. I think, in terms of people who don't identify as queer, it's been a lot of, like, family members, people being like, "Oh my child, came out as nonbinary, so I'm going to get this shirt for them," or like, "My friend is a Magic Black Femme, so I'm just going to buy this shirt for her," things like that—where maybe you don't identify with the shirt, but you have people in your lives at the very least, that do. I think mainly the people who buy are queer.

(Sade, Queer Supply)

I've had about a bajillion people come out [about their sexual or gender identities] to me and say that they would never have come out without my visibility. I think that's the thing that keeps me going the most, and I always say that that's what's keeping me alive.

(Sky Cubacub, Rebirth Garments)

I didn't know that I would be affecting people's lives so deeply. I wanted it and it wasn't like … while it was a mission, it wasn't, "I have to change the world." I started with me first and then people around me, and it kept growing, and I'm just like, "Oh, this is bigger than me. This touched people, and this is affecting people too … . This is really touching them deeper than I thought, resonating a lot more than I even thought."

(Stoney Michelli Love, Stuzo)

I've had people straight-up break down. I've had moms break down, because, especially here in Sacramento, there's a lot of young, queer teenagers that are transitioning from female to male, and, if nothing else I make them feel comfortable in here, but also they can get their shirt for prom. I do have a white, plain, basic shirt, I should preface [with] that—they're not going with flannel for prom, and moms have cried, just because their kid feels normal and accepted.

(Susan Stewart, Strapping Sacramento)

In the early days, when I first started, I got this sweet email from this woman saying, "I have a gender-neutral child, and they want to go to prom, and we also want to get them a suit for their sister's wedding." Just to hear a mom be so genuinely supportive of their child, and that she went out of her way to find something for their child, I was like, "Oh, anything I can do to help!"

(Thúy Nguyen, THÚY Custom Clothier)

We get so much feedback from people … I used to say that we're not saving lives. I mean, I get emails from folks on a regular basis saying "This product saved my life" or "This product changed my life," or "This product makes me feel so safe … Now, I know what gender euphoria feels like" or "This product changed the way that I have sex"—I mean, things that are deeply personal and impactful in someone's experience and how they relate to themselves and their bodies and their health.

(Scout Rose, Transguy Supply)

These quotes highlight the profound impact that gender-affirming brands have on individuals' lives. Through various testimonials, we witness the transformative power of inclusive and identity-affirming products. Despite facing challenges and negativity from society, these brands create a sense of community, confidence, and acceptance for their customers. The emotional stories shared by individuals who found joy, comfort, and a renewed sense of self through these products underscore the significance of the work these brands are doing. From enhancing confidence to providing a lifeline for those struggling with dysphoria, the positive feedback demonstrates that in addition to these brands selling products, they are making a tangible difference in the lives of their consumers. The sense of belonging, self-discovery, and empowerment generated by these brands exemplifies the impact of fashion and visibility on LGBTQ+ communities.

Closing Thoughts and Opening Questions

After thinking through the elements of fashion brands, one clear theme emerges: starting and sustaining any fashion brand is hard, ever-changing, and fast-paced, and involves numerous factors requiring careful decisions. There is no one-size-fits-all approach, and the mountain of existing brands makes for difficult decision-making processes to make any fashion brand successful and unique.

Specifically, I asked what these fashion brands collectively contribute to the fashion system. They entered the system and thrived in many different ways, and I argue they embody and engage in various forms of fashion disrupting. Additionally, because of the constant state of flux with the tangible, social, economic, and embodied aspects of styling-fashioning-dressing, one way to think through these tensions is via the entangled meanings and moments they create and created throughout the fashion system.

Queer and Trans Fashion Brands' Collective Contributions to the Fashion System: Fashion Disrupters and Fashion Disrupting

The narratives these entrepreneurs shared reveal the complexities and nuances in the production, distribution, regulation, and consumption of queer and trans fashions but also underscore the roles of these pioneers as agents of change, actively challenging the entrenched heteronormative norms that have long prevailed in the fashion landscape. The resilience, creativity, and cultural contributions of these entrepreneurs emerge as focal points in their narratives. As agents of change, they navigate the challenging terrain of a capitalist industry that historically upholds traditional notions of gender and sexuality. Boiled down, they commodified identities that could certainly be the subject of much ethical debate, particularly from a neoliberal capitalist perspective. However, they expressed much ambivalence about all the intricate moving parts that were in constant flux.

Through the accounts of these entrepreneurs, it is evident that these fashion disruptors actively resist, subvert, and even uphold traditional notions of gender and sexuality. Their brands become vehicles for challenging societal norms and fostering inclusivity. I discussed how the consumer products offered by these brands serve as vehicles for queer and trans sensibilities. From product design to marketing strategies, my findings uncover the deliberate efforts entrepreneurs made to foster a sense of identity and belonging through their merchandise.

The primary reasons for the emergence of these brands were deeply influenced by individual identities, the processes of coming out, and journeys of self-discovery. The brands sought to create products, marketing strategies, and shopping experiences centered around trust, with a specific focus on catering to LGBTQ+ individuals by members of the LGBTQ+ community. Nearly every brand had a personal connection with the LGBTQ+ community, either through the founders' own queer and trans journeys or those of their partners. These entrepreneurs faced challenges, often times since childhood, in finding products in the market that resonated with their identity negotiations through fashion, leading to often negative shopping experiences. Consequently, they aimed to establish a space where queer and trans communities could feel acknowledged and heard through embodied practices, a space that many of them lacked in their own personal lived experiences growing up.

The cultural context of same-sex marriage and the desire to offer products to these consumer segments who have been left out of the fashion system, coupled with crowdfunding initiatives, provided these entrepreneurs with some means to test market viability and raise capital funds. Simultaneously, the integration of social media into everyday life, starting with Facebook in 2004 and followed by platforms like Instagram and Twitter (now X), granted easy access to Kickstarter campaigns, contributing to their success. All these factors played a pivotal role in influencing the emergence of these brands, shaping the how, why, and where of their development.

These brands emerge as fashion disruptors or perhaps more appropriately as engaging in fashion disruption at different moments in varied spaces, challenging the status quo. They created spaces for reimagining shopping experiences to be more inclusive and affirming for diverse identities. They introduced innovative construction details that challenge traditional norms and celebrate diversity. They redefined product silhouettes and sizing systems to cater to a broad spectrum of body types and identities. They crafted product copy and media representation that is not only relatable but also features diverse bodies, celebrating the beauty of all individuals. They also navigated the complex landscape of capitalism while aiming to stay true to the mission of serving queer and trans communities, thereby dismantling the exclusivity often associated with the fashion industry.

In crafting their fashion products, these brands engaged in a nuanced exploration of queer and trans meaning, skillfully balancing multiple intersections throughout the entire lifecycles of their creations. The narratives of these brands demonstrated care and sensitivity toward queer and trans identities, manifesting through diverse approaches in consumption, making, options, messaging, makers, and educational hubs. Each brand adopted different approaches at different times for various reasons, leveraging its strengths and acknowledging limitations. These brands intentionally navigated the realms of ambivalence and ambiguity, disrupting conventional categories to foster a space where ambiguity is embraced and celebrated, challenging normative expectations and encouraging a more inclusive understanding of fashion.

Moreover, these fashion brands thought critically about representation in their imagery, striving for relatability and authenticity. Intentionally featuring people of color, individuals of diverse body types, and resisting alterations to images, they rejected dominant beauty ideals. Some brands showcased products alone, divorced from the context of the body. Addressing environmental justice concerns, brand owners were not only aware of socioeconomic factors but also considered how pricing strategies could affect the accessibility of their products to queer and trans individuals. This conscientious approach involved thoughtful pricing structures that accounted for economic disparities within these communities, reflecting a delicate balance between financial viability and social responsibility.

In the dynamic landscape of queer and trans fashion, dedicated media platforms such as DapperQ and Qwear also played pivotal roles in reshaping narratives around style, identity, and community intersecting with these brands. These platforms were more than outlets for style, standing as pillars of empowerment and safer havens for individuals to explore, celebrate, and redefine their relationship with fashion.

While facing challenges and enjoying successes, these brands emphasized their positive impacts on people's lives, based on consumer feedback in various spaces. Dealing with negativity from detractors was countered by moments of pure, emotion-filled joy and love created by these brands.

Entangling and Disentangling the Ever-Fluid Queer and Trans Fashion Brands: Meanings and Moments

In the shifting landscape of queer and trans fashion, the definition of what constitutes a queer and trans fashion brand undergoes continuous transformation. This evolution is reflective of the fluid nature of identity itself, acknowledging that expressions of queerness and transness are not fixed but rather adapt to the ever-changing sociocultural context. Within this perpetual state of flux, these fashion brands find both their challenge and their potency. These brands transcend the conventional fashion boundaries by becoming agents of cultural expression, empowerment, and identity formation. They navigate the intricate interplay between personal identity and collective representation, acting as catalysts for a broader societal conversation on diversity and inclusivity.

Queer and trans fashion brands carve out spaces where meanings and moments are not predetermined but co-created. Through intentional curation of shopping experiences, the design of products, and the dissemination of media, these brands construct immersive environments that go beyond the transactional act of purchasing. Instead, they become platforms for storytelling, self-discovery, and communal celebration, allowing individuals to actively engage in the creation of their own queer and trans meanings.

The significance of these brands lies not only in the products they offer but also in the narratives they weave. They tell stories in a visual language, crafting tales of resilience, rebellion, self-expression, and everyday life. By doing so, they contribute to the ongoing narrative of queer and trans histories, challenging stereotypes, and amplifying voices that have traditionally been marginalized.

Moreover, these brands play a crucial role in fostering a sense of community. By providing spaces and opportunities for individuals to engage with and contribute to queer and trans cultures, they create a sense of belonging. In these moments of opportunity, the act of shopping transforms into a communal experience, where individuals adorn themselves not only with clothing but also with shared meanings and collective identities.

These queer and trans fashion brands are not merely purveyors of style, they are architects of cultural landscapes. Their meaning derives from their capacity to evolve alongside the nuanced understanding of identity, to create spaces for self-expression, and to empower individuals to actively shape their own narratives.

In creating moments of opportunity, these brands become conduits for the continuous celebration and redefinition of queer and trans identities within the broader facets of society. Overall, the essence of what makes a queer and trans fashion brand meaningful lies in its ability to transcend the mere production of clothing and accessories.

Where Do We Go from Here or There?

How we think about the intersections of fashion, identity, capitalism, and social justice has so much potential for future thought. This research may help the consumer think through ethical shopping decisions: What are you buying, from where, and why? There is so much behind-the-scenes knowledge that the average consumer knows nothing of, but this research can open new avenues of thought for how one approaches consuming. Reflecting on these brand owners' journeys may shed more light on the how, why, and wish-I-could in fashion brand development, with a justice angle. It can potentially help the consumer understand that these businesses are complex, and decision-making may not be the brand owner's ultimate goals. As a consumer, after reading about these brands you are probably a little more equipped to think through where you spend your money with an ethical perspective.

This research certainly has some practical implications for current and future fashion entrepreneurs looking to center justice-related philosophies. Here are some questions to think through if you are looking to become a fashion disruptor or contribute to fashion disruption in the capitalist economy. This is not meant to be a laundry list that magically earns us the "fashion disruptor" title but a way to think through the complexities involved in fashion, consumption, the capitalist economy, and social justice.

1. What are my personal identities, and how do they relate to privileged and marginalized groups?
2. How do my identities relate to the consumer I am looking to focus on as part of my target market?
3. What are the power dynamics of my own identities in relation to those who I am looking to target?
4. What is the history of my consumers?
5. Why am I the person to build this brand?
6. Am I prepared for the criticisms and how to navigate those criticisms in a self-reflective context that centers accountability and structural change?
7. What am I actually disrupting and why?
8. How are my products disrupting, and how is this considered in the following?
    a. Physical aspects of my products
    b. Product maker or designer

- **c** Product materials
- **d** Product positioning and product copy
- **e** Product sizing
- **f** Product fit

9 How are local communities affected by the production, distribution, and consumption of my products?

10 What measures does my brand have in place to address and rectify issues in its social justice efforts?

11 How are the consumer's experiences disrupting the following?

- **a** Shopping experiences in person
- **b** Shopping experiences online
- **c** Return or exchange policies
- **d** Customer interactions

12 What imagery and content am I using to promote my products?

- **a** Who is represented?
- **b** Who is not represented?
- **c** How are people represented?
- **d** How was potential harm considered in developing promotional materials or experiences?

13 How are my products priced, and how am I considering the past and current experiences of my consumer in relation to pricing?

14 How is intersectionality woven into the business?

15 How does the brand genuinely consider community needs?

16 How is profit being prioritized over consumers?

17 How are consumers being prioritized over profit?

18 Who works at the brand, and what are their identities?

19 How much are employees paid, and how much is the brand leadership paid?

20 How are employee needs of marginalized communities centered?

21 How are microaggressions and discrimination related to employees accounted for in my brand?

22 How is potential trauma and harm accounted for in decision-making for employees, consumers, and the community at large?

23 Who financed the brand, and what do they represent?

24 Who else sells my products, and what do they represent?

25 How transparent am I about various practices in running my business?

These questions will help explore various dimensions of the intersections between fashion, capitalism, and social justice, providing a framework for thoughtful reflection and action by the fashion producers and distributors.

Lastly, reading about the varied experiences, diverse fashion aesthetics, and personal journeys of these queer and trans fashion brand owners can help folks to foster empathy. These entrepreneurs not only navigate the intricacies of running businesses but also share profound narratives of resilience, self-discovery, and agency. Their fashion aesthetics challenge societal norms, encouraging a more inclusive perspective on self-expression. By delving into their stories, readers gain insight into the richness of human existence, breaking down stereotypes and providing space for a deeper understanding of the LGBTQ+ communities. Through these personal and artistic revelations, readers may be inspired to embrace authenticity and to reflect on the universal themes of love, acceptance, and the transformative power of celebrating diversity in fashion and the broader human experience. Ultimately, engaging with these narratives facilitates a broad and compassionate appreciation for the shared humanity that connects us all.

Appendix

The Method

I drew on the historic research method and utilized a critical cultural analysis. Specifically, I completed oral histories of twenty-four queer- and trans-focused fashion brands and another with Sonny Oram (he/they/none), founder of Qwear, a prominent queer and fashion-focused media platform. The oral history method involves gathering and preserving historical information through recorded interviews with individuals who have knowledge or experience of a particular time period, event, or cultural context (Ritchie 2003). I focused on capturing memories, perspectives, and lived experiences to document fashion brands and media from the participants' viewpoints in the context of the early twenty-first century.

I completed the oral histories in a semi-structured interview style and aimed to elicit detailed accounts and narratives about specific topics, such as significant historical events, social movements, personal experiences, and cultural practices related to the development of these fashion brands. I asked participants about their own backgrounds, experiences with clothing, the beginnings and general overviews of their companies, their inspiration and design process, challenges and successes, consumer feedback, advertising and public imagery, funding, sustainability, consumers, trends, and final thoughts. I began conducting the interviews in 2017 and completed the most recent one in 2023. The interviews lasted between forty-five minutes and about three hours. My questions varied slightly for Oram's oral history, but they similarly focused on their background, lived experiences, and Qwear's beginnings and evolution.

To select the fashion brands, I made a comprehensive list of all fashion brands that sold clothing, accessories, shoes, and/or other body-related products. I created the list in a few ways: by reviewing news articles published by popular queer media outlets (Qwear, Autostraddle, DapperQ, etc.) that highlighted queer- and trans-focused fashion brands (e.g., Bernard 2022; Dolce Vita 2013); through Google searches using keywords such as, for example, "queer fashion"; also through word of mouth as I interviewed the fashion brands. I sent invitations to seventy-seven brands. Some never responded, and some did but indicated that because they were small businesses, they did not have time to participate.

Validating the accuracy of oral history interviews involves assessing interviewees' credibility and trustworthiness. To increase validity, I aimed to establish rapport and trust by first introducing myself to interviewees and asking how they were doing, encouraging them to provide honest and accurate accounts while acknowledging potential biases. I also cross-referenced their oral testimonies with other historical records, such as photographs and media, to help corroborate or challenge the information provided. I also asked prompting questions such as "Can you tell me more?" and "Can you tell me why?" which helped the interviewees provide rich answers. I also paused after they responded to questions to allow them to think through their answers and add any additional details. I also provided the questions beforehand so participants could think through their answers and also see the questions as they answered them. At the end of each interview, I asked respondents if they had anything else to share, in case I missed any important points or they thought of something to add. Transcribing the interview verbatim also ensured I engaged with accurate data. After each interview was transcribed, my research assistant listened to the interview and read through the transcript to ensure that everything was accurate. At that stage, I sent the transcript to the interviewee and asked if everything was accurate. Interviewees provided any necessary changes or they approved the transcript to be uploaded to the oral history repository (Reddy-Best, Goodin, and Streck 2023).

Reliability, or consistency, in oral history research can be enhanced through careful planning and methodology. To increase reliability, I developed an interview protocol to ensure consistency across different interviews. This facilitates the comparison and analysis of data collected from multiple interviewees. I also maintained consistency by using consistent prompts, follow-up questions, and recording techniques. However, I did allow for flexibility if interviewees moved away from the interview script, though I often brought them back on track if they got too far away from the purpose of the oral history (Creswell 2014).

To analyze the data thoroughly, I employed a combination of open, axial, and selective coding techniques. These methods are commonly used in qualitative research to organize and interpret data obtained from interviews, observations, or documents. Each approach offers a unique perspective and serves specific analytical purposes. In open coding, the initial stage of coding, data is broken down into smaller, meaningful units called *codes*. During this process, I examined the data without any preconceived categories or theoretical frameworks. I carefully read through the data and identified organically emerging patterns, concepts, and themes. By coding the data openly, I ensured that no relevant information was overlooked and I achieved a comprehensive understanding of it.

Axial coding establishes connections and relationships between the initial codes identified through open coding. This technique involves categorizing and organizing the codes into broader themes or categories. It helps in identifying the relationships among different concepts and subcategories, enabling a more structured analysis. Through axial coding, I created a framework that allowed me to see how various codes were interconnected, helping me develop a deeper understanding of the data.

In selective coding, the final stage, I focused on refining and selecting the most salient and relevant codes to develop a coherent narrative. This involved identifying the central themes and patterns that emerged from the data analysis. I carefully selected codes that best represented the essence of the data and organized them into a coherent storyline. Selective coding helps to synthesize the findings and create a meaningful interpretation of the data that can answer research questions or provide valuable insights.

By employing open, axial, and selective coding techniques, I ensured a rigorous and systematic analysis of the data. These methods allowed me to identify patterns, establish relationships, and develop a comprehensive understanding of the themes present within the data. The combination of these coding techniques helped me to organize the data effectively and provided a solid foundation for drawing meaningful conclusions from the analysis (Creswell 2014).

Lastly, the documentation and archiving of oral history interviews are crucial for both validity and reliability. Therefore, I cataloged and preserved the recordings, transcripts, and related materials to ensure that future researchers can access and evaluate the data. This documentation facilitates further analysis, replication of findings, and comparison with future research.

In oral history research, obtaining informed consent is an ethical requirement and a fundamental cornerstone of respectful and responsible practice. This embodies a commitment to understanding, empathy, and transparency; consent should always be voluntary, free from coercion, and fully comprehensible to the narrators, who should be made aware of their rights to withdraw at any stage without consequences. Therefore, when engaging with the interviewees, I first clearly explained the study's purpose, the topics to be discussed, and the potential implications of sharing personal stories. I informed the participants that they could withdraw at any time, even after their oral history was published in the online database. For instance, one brand contacted me to withdraw and I honored their request without hesitation. Additionally, establishing a trusting relationship is vital; I actively listened, addressed concerns, and was receptive to the participants' boundaries.

Limitations of the Research

While rich in data and approach, there are certainly limitations to the research. For example, I analyzed the perspectives of just twenty-four fashion brand owners, thereby offering a narrowed viewpoint of the industry. For example, Chrysalis Lingerie, a brand for trans women (Pajer 2019) was not included. I did not include some brands, such as Torrid, whose product assortment and sizing works for some trans women (Moon 2018), as I limited this work to brands that openly target LGBTQ+ folks as consumers. I also focus on the North American context, yet want to recognize that other brands (e.g., The Butch Clothing Company in the United Kingdom) also certainly deserve further inquiry. Another perspective that this book does not address is the seeming imbalance of brands overtly targeting the LGBTQ+ communities that center masculine versus feminine aesthetics. Future scholars could examine this potential imbalance, and, for example, brands catering specifically to trans feminine women or gay men who adopt a feminine aesthetic. Additionally, the exclusion of employee perspectives limits the holistic understanding of the fashion brands' dynamics, potentially overlooking valuable insights from those directly involved in the businesses' operations and interactions.

The study captures a specific moment in the evolution of these fashion brands. As the business landscape is dynamic, the findings do not include long-term changes and adaptations. Thus, the research does not account for potential evolution.

Additionally, this research predominantly examines the business facet of fashion brands, excluding the consumer side of the interaction. The absence of consumer perspectives restricts the analysis of how individuals engage with these products or brands and the data on consumer behaviors, preferences, and feedback. Further research could offer important insights into how folks in the queer and trans communities embrace and/or push gender boundaries in ways that could have implications for health and wellbeing.

The narratives presented in this study are subject to the limitations of human memory. Interviewees' abilities to accurately recall specific details might be influenced by factors such as time elapsed since the events occurred, emotional states during the interviews, and personal biases. The study also heavily relies on the viewpoints of fashion brand owners. While these perspectives provide valuable insights, they are inherently biased by the owners' experiences, beliefs, and objectives. This subjectivity may influence the portrayal of certain situations, potentially leading to skewed representation of the challenges and successes these brands face. Ethical considerations, such as the potential for interviewees to present curated or idealized versions of their experiences, pose challenges. Interviewees might withhold sensitive information or present a more favorable image, subconsciously or consciously, which can affect the authenticity and depth of the data collected.

In light of these limitations, readers are encouraged to interpret the findings of this research within the specified scope and context. Recognizing these constraints is vital for a nuanced understanding of the study's outcomes and implications. Future research endeavors should consider addressing these limitations to provide a more comprehensive and inclusive analysis of the fashion industry and its stakeholders.

My Positionalities

As a researcher, I recognize the importance of acknowledging and reflecting on my positionality, which encompasses various intersecting identities that shape my experiences, perspectives, and biases. It can be important to disclose and critically examine these aspects to foster transparency and ensure an inclusive research process. By disclosing their positionality, researchers establish credibility, trustworthiness, and ethical considerations in their work. Doing so enables them to critically reflect on their own backgrounds, assumptions, and privileges, fostering inclusivity and enhancing the representation of diverse perspectives. Moreover, a positionality statement informs research design choices, encourages reflexive analysis and interpretation, and contributes to a deeper understanding of the researcher's role in addressing power imbalances and promoting ethical research practices. Overall, it facilitates a nuanced, inclusive, and impactful research process (Massoud 2022).

First, I identify as white. This racial identity informs my worldview and privileges, rooted in historical power structures. I am mindful of the inherent advantages associated with my racial identity and its potential influence on my understanding and interpretation of research findings. I have been married to a Black cisgender man since 2009, and this has provided me with a firsthand perspective on the systemic challenges, racial inequities, and social injustices that he and others in the Black community encounter. This intimate connection and everyday experience have heightened my attention to racial issues, and I approach the research with a deep sense of empathy, urgency, and commitment to dismantling systemic racism.

Furthermore, I identify as a cisgender woman and have largely never swayed from this identity. That is, I have always felt comfortable in my gender identity and gender expression. As a result, I have not experienced a need to seek out specific clothing that aligns with my gender expression. It is important for me to recognize that this lack of personal experience may influence my perspective on the significance and impact of fashion choices for individuals within the queer and trans communities. However, it is worth noting that I have purchased products from some of the queer and trans fashion brands included in the research because their style and aesthetic align with my taste. Through my interactions with these brands, I have appreciated their creativity and design choices through the embodied practice of fashioning my identity through clothing.

Moreover, my queer identity contributes to my positionality. As a queer person, I have experiences and knowledge of LGBTQ+ communities that may shape my approach to research topics related to sexuality, identity, and social dynamics. It is essential for me to recognize and affirm the diversity within queer communities and avoid generalizations or assumptions. It is also important to note that I am a queer person in a heterosexual-appearing relationship, which affords me certain privileges. While I identify as queer, my current relationship may grant me the privilege of heterosexual passing, or heteronormative assumptions by others. This privilege can result in a reduction of overt discrimination or challenges that those whose relationships are visibly non-heteronormative may face. It is essential to critically reflect on and acknowledge the advantages and societal acceptance that can come with a heterosexual-appearing partnership, as it can affect my own experiences, perceptions, and potential biases within the research process. By recognizing this privilege, I am committed to amplifying the voices of marginalized queer communities and challenging heteronormativity within the research context. I aim to center diverse perspectives and work toward dismantling systemic inequities that affect queer individuals regardless of their relationship appearance or visibility.

It is also important to acknowledge that I grew up in a middle-class environment, which significantly influences my understanding of socioeconomic factors and class-related dynamics. Having been raised in a middle-class household, I have developed a particular lens through which I perceive issues of inequity, access to resources, and social mobility. At the same time, while I currently live comfortably and am able to more than make ends meet, my journey to this point has been challenging. I have experienced a long road of personal and emotional growth, which included becoming estranged from my toxic immediate family.

I also identify as able-bodied: I do not have any physical disabilities or impairments that significantly impact my daily functioning. As an able-bodied individual, I acknowledge the privileges and advantages that come with being able to navigate the world without substantial physical barriers. I strive to approach the research process with sensitivity and inclusivity, recognizing the importance of considering the diverse experiences and needs of individuals with disabilities.

Furthermore, in terms of body size, I would generally be described as thin. However, my relationship with my body and weight has been complex and has undergone significant changes throughout my life. As a child, I carried a higher weight, which led to various challenges and experiences that shaped my relationship with food and my body. During that time, I engaged in some disordered eating practices as I navigated societal expectations and pressures. These experiences have given me a unique perspective on the complexities surrounding body image, weight stigma, and the intersection of mental health and physical wellbeing. It is through this lens that I approach the research—with empathy, compassion, and a commitment to fostering body positivity, inclusivity, and understanding.

By acknowledging and reflecting on these aspects of my positionality, I am dedicated to conducting research with openness, empathy, and critical self-reflection. I strive to mitigate any biases that may influence the research process, interpreting findings in a manner that honors and respects the experiences of all participants involved. Last, I remain receptive to learning from diverse perspectives and commit to employing ethical research practices that promote inclusivity, social justice, and equity.

References

Abad-Santos, A. (2018), "How LGBTQ Pride Month Became a Branded Holiday: And Why That's a Problem," *Vox*, June 25. Available online: https://www.vox.com/2018/6/25/17476850/pride-month-lgbtq-corporate-explained (accessed October 30, 2023).

Abrams, J. R., and H. Giles (2007), "Ethnic Identity Gratifications Selection and Avoidance by African Americans: A Group Vitality and Social Identity Gratifications Perspective," *Media Psychology*, 9: 115–34.

Allen, M. P. (2010), "Connecting Body and Mind: How Transgender People Changed Their Self-Image," *Women & Performance*, 20 (3): 267–83. https://doi.org/10.1080/0740770X.2010.529248.

Anawalt, P. R. (2007), *The Worldwide History of Dress*, London: Thames & Hudson.

Andreasen, A. R. (2003), "The Life Trajectory of Social Marketing: Some Implications," *Marketing Theory*, 3 (3): 293–303.

Arnett, J. J. (1995a), "Adolescents' Uses of Media for Self-Socialization," *Journal of Youth and Adolescence*, 24: 519–33.

Arnett, J. J. (1995b), "Broad and Narrow Socialization: The Family in the Context of a Multidimensional Theory," *Journal of Marriage and the Family*, 57: 617–28.

Artavia, D. (2020), "House Passes Amendment to Reverse Trans Military Ban; Senate Is Next," *Advocate*, July 31. Available online: https://www.advocate.com/transgender/2020/7/31/house-passes-amendment-reverse-trans-military-ban-senate-next (accessed October 2, 2023).

Bargh, J. A., M. Chen, and L. Burrows (1996), "Automaticity of Social Behavior: Direct Effects of Trait Construct and Stereotype Activation on Action," *Journal of Personality and Social Psychology*, 71: 230–44.

Barnes, K. (2023), "Transgender Athlete Laws by State: Legislation, Science, More," *ESPN*, August 24. Available online: https://www.espn.com/espn/story/_/id/38209262/transgender-athlete-laws-state-legislation-science (accessed October 30, 2023).

Barrow K. M., and K. R. Allen (2014), "Defense of Marriage Act," in L. H. Ganong and M. Coleman (eds), *The Social History of the American Family: An Encyclopedia*, 330–1, Thousand Oaks: SAGE.

Barry, B., and D. Drak (2019), "Intersectional Interventions into Queer and Trans Liberation: Youth Resistance against Right-Wing Populism through Fashion Hacking," *Fashion Theory*, 23 (6): 679–709. https://doi.org/10.1080/1362704x.2019.1657260.

Barry, B., and B. J. Phillips (2016), "The Fashion Engagement Grid: Understanding Men's Responses to Fashion Advertising," *International Journal of Advertising*, 35 (3): 438–64.

Beefcake Swimwear (2023), "Size & Fit Guide." Available online: https://www.beefcakeswimwear.com/pages/sizing (accessed December 4, 2023).

Beemyn, B. G. (2015), "Genderqueer," *GLBTQ: An Encyclopedia of Gay, Lesbian, Bisexual, Transgender, and Queer Culture*. Available online: http://www.glbtqarchive.com/ssh/genderqueer_S.pdf (accessed October 2, 2023).

Bernard, R. (2022), "85 LGBTQ+ Owned Businesses and Queer Shops to Support This Holiday Season!" *Autostraddle*, December 6. Available online: https://www.autostraddle.com/lesbian-owned-businesses-to-support-359864/ (accessed October 2, 2023).

Brajato, N. (2020), "Queer(ing) Tailoring: Walter Van Beirendonck and the Glorious Bastardization of the Suit," *Critical Studies in Fashion and Beauty*, 11 (1): 45–72. https://doi.org/10.1386/csfb_00009_1.

Brajato, N. (2023), "Masculinity, Identity and Body Politics in the Interzone: A Queer Perspective on Raf Simons's Critical Fashion Practices (1995–2005)," *Fashion Theory*, 27 (1): 115–47. https://doi.org/10.1080/1362704X.2021.1982191.

Brownski, M. (1984), *Culture Clash: The Making of a Gay Sensibility*, Boston: South End Press.

Besel, A., T. S. Zimmerman, C. A. Fruhauf, J. Pepin, and J. H. Banning (2009), "Here Comes the Bride: An Ethnographic Content Analysis of Bridal Books," *Journal of Feminist Family Therapy*, 21 (2): 98–124. https://doi.org/10.1080/08952830902952267.

Best, J., and S. Neiss (2014), "Chapter 1: Crowdfunding: A Historical Perspective," in S. Dresner (ed.), *Crowdfunding: A Guide to Raising Capital on the Internet*, Hoboken: John Wiley.

Blackman, I., and K. Perry (1990), "Skirting the Issue: Lesbian Fashion for the 1990s," *Feminist Review*, 34 (1): 67–78. https://doi.org/10.2307/1395306.

Blake, D. A. (2019), "'It Ain't He, It Ain't She, It's We': The Politics of Self-Definition and Self-Valuation in the *Androgynous Model* Web Series," *Dress: The Journal of the Costume Society of America*, 45 (1): 1–21. https://doi.org/10.1080/03612112.2019.1559529.

Boden, S. (2003), *Consumerism, Romance and the Wedding Experience*, New York: Palgrave Macmillan.

Branthwaite, A. (2002), "Investigating the Power of Imagery in Marketing Communication: Evidence-Based Techniques," *Qualitative Market Research: An International Journal*, 5 (3): 164–71.

Brier, J. (2004), "AIDS and People with AIDS," in M. Stein (ed.), *Encyclopedia of Lesbian, Gay, Bisexual and Transgender History in America*, 27–34, Detroit: Charles Scribner's Sons.

Brooklyn Museum (2015), "Fashion Show: VERGE." Available online: https://www.brooklynmuseum.org/calendar/event/fashion_show_dapperq_september_2015 (accessed December 16, 2023).

Brooklyn Museum (2016), "DapperQ Presents iD." Available online: https://www.brooklynmuseum.org/calendar/event/dapperq_presents_id_september_2016 (accessed December 16, 2023).

Brooklyn Museum (2018), "DapperQ Presents Dress Code." Available online: https://www.brooklynmuseum.org/calendar/event/dapperq_presents_dress_code_september_2018#:~:text=This%20year%2C%20E2%80%9CDress%20Code%E2%80%9D,uphold%20or%20challenge%20rigid%20stereotypes (accessed February 14, 2024).

Brown, E. H. (2019), *Work! A Queer History of Modeling*, Durham: Duke University Press.

Brown, R. M. (1998), "Lavender Menace," in W. P. Mankiller (ed.), *The Reader's Companion to U.S. Women's History*, Boston: Houghton Mifflin.

BSR, Staff (2009), "Apparel Industry Life Cycle Carbon Mapping," June 30. Available online: http://www.bsr.org/en/our-insights/report-view/apparel-industry-life-cycle-carbon-mapping (accessed December 16, 2023).

Burke, P. J. (1980), "The Self: Measurement Implications from an Interactionist Perspective," *Social Psychology Quarterly*, 43 (1): 18–29.

Burke, P. J., and D. C. Reitzes (1981), "The Link Between Identity and Role Performance," *Social Psychology Quarterly*, 44 (2): 83–92.

Burke, P. J., and J. Tully (1977), "The Measurement of Role Identity," *Social Forces*, 55 (4): 881–97.

Burton, K. (2016), "Lesbians Invented Hipsters," *New York Times*, December 31. Available online: https://www.nytimes.com/2016/12/31/opinion/sunday/hipsters-broke-my-gaydar.html (accessed October 6, 2023).

Cahill, D., and M. Konings (2017), *Neoliberalism*, Hoboken: Wiley.

Carbado, D. W. (2017), "From Stopping Black People to Killing Black People: The Fourth Amendment Pathway to Police Violence," *California Law Review*, 105 (1): 125–64.

Carrington, B., and J. Boykoff (2018), "Is Colin Kaepernick's Nike Deal Activism or Just Capitalism?" *Guardian*, September 6. Available online: https://www.theguardian.com/commentisfree/2018/sep/06/colin-kaepernick-nike-activism-capitalism-nfl (accessed October 30, 2023).

Carter, D. (2004), *Stonewall: The Riots That Sparked the Gay Revolution*, New York: St. Martin's Press.

Carter, J., and S. Duncan (2017), "Wedding Paradoxes: Individualized Conformity and the 'Perfect Day,'" *Sociological Review*, 65 (1): 3–20. https://doi.org/10.1111/1467-954X.12366.

Catalpa, J. M., and J. K. McGuire (2020), "Mirror Epiphany: Transpersons' Use of Dress to Create and Sustain Their Affirmed Gender Identities," in A. Reilly and B. Barry (eds.), *Crossing Boundaries: Fashion to Deconstruct and Reimagine Gender*, 47–59, London: Intellect Books.

The Center (2023), 'What Is LGBTQIA+'. Available online: https://gaycenter.org/community/lgbtq/ (accessed October 2, 2023).

Chauncey, G. (1994), *Gay New York: Gender, Urban Culture, and the Making of the Gay Male World, 1890–1940*, New York: Basic Books.

Chen, H.-L., and L. D. Burns (2006), "Environmental Analysis of Textile Products," *Clothing and Textiles Research Journal* 24 (3): 248–61. https://doi.org/10.1177/0887302X06293065.

Chidester, P. (2008), "May the Circle Stay Unbroken: Friends, the Presence of Absence, and the Rhetorical Reinforcement of Whiteness," *Critical Studies in Media Communication*, 25 (2): 157–74.

Clark, D. (1995), 'Commodity Lesbianism', in E. K. Creekmur and A. Doty (eds.), *Out in Culture*, 484–500, Durham: Duke University Press. https://doi.org/10.2307/j.ctv1220htt.35.

Clarke, V., C. Burgoyne, and M. Burns (2013), "Unscripted and Improvised: Public and Private Celebrations of Same-Sex Relationships," *Journal of GLBT Family Studies*, 9 (4): 393–418. https://doi.org/10.1080/1550428X.2013.808494.

Clarke, V., and K. Turner (2007), "Clothes Maketh the Queer? Dress, Appearance, and the Construction of Lesbian, Gay and Bisexual Identities," *Feminism & Psychology*, 17 (2): 267–76. https://doi.org/10.1177/0959353507076561.

Cobb, J. (2018), "Behind Nike's Decision to Stand by Colin Kaepernick," *New Yorker*, September 4. Available online: https://www.newyorker.com/news/daily-comment/behind-nikes-decision-to-stand-by-colin-kaepernick (accessed October 30, 2023).

Coke, H. (2020), "The Inspiring Life of Activist and Drag Queen Marsha P. Johnson," *Tatler*, June 25. Available online: https://www.tatler.com/article/who-is-marsha-p-johnson-drag-queen-gay-activist (accessed October 2, 2023).

Cole, S. (2000), *'Don We Now Our Gay Apparel:' Gay Men's Dress in the Twentieth Century*, London: Bloomsbury.

Cole, S. (2023), *Gay Men's Style: Fashion, Dress and Sexuality in the 21st Century*, London: Bloomsbury.

Cooley, C. H. (1902), *Human Nature and Social Order*, New York: Charles Scribner's Sons.

Connell, R. W., and J. Messerschmidt (2009), "Hegemonic Masculinity: Rethinking the Concept," *Gender & Society*, 19 (6): 829–59. https://doi.org/10.1177/0891243205278639.

Corrigall-Brown, C. (2012), 'The Power of Pictures: Images of Politics and Protest', *American Behavioral Scientist*, 56 (2): 131–4.

Crenshaw, K. (1989), "Demarginalizing the Intersection of Race and Sex: A Black Feminist Critique of Antidiscrimination Doctrine, Feminist Theory, and Antiracist Politics," *University of Chicago Legal Forum*, 1 (8): 139–67.

Crenshaw, K. (1991), "Mapping the Margins: Intersectionality, Identity Politics, and Violence Against Women of Color," *Stanford Law Review*, 43 (6): 1241–99.

Creswell, J. W. (2014), *Research Design: Qualitative, Quantitative, and Mixed Method Approaches*, Thousand Oaks, CA: Sage.

Cummings, S. (2016), "Lesbaru… I mean Subaru," *Medium*, October 21. Available online: https://medium.com/re-write/lesbaru-i-mean-subaru-c2291dfbe333 (accessed October 17, 2023).

Currie, D. H. (1993), "Here Comes the Bride: The Making of a 'Modern Traditional' Wedding in Western Culture," *Journal of Comparative Family Studies*, 24 (3): 403–21. Available online: https://www.jstor.org/stable/41602301.

Curtin, S. (2018), "Facebook Effect: How the Social Network Changed the World," *Yahoo Finance*, May 18. Available online: https://finance.yahoo.com/blogs/daily-ticker/facebook-effect-social-network-changed-world-122656206.html?guccounter=1&guce_referrer=aHR0cHM6Ly93d3cuZ29vZ2xlLmNvbS8&guce_referrer_sig=AQAAAENsFegbyrIUSx_qkamugEtxN74zkQ7JJTYsNbrusFAR1yvbg1jtP-XSfEEr2rEiT0xdWhNFz4PjLMfuHR19HFPFFS18OtGB_yM6PFW2G2tADKpz-5LpuuY5xQbhScq-jKLVyZXHhU1yZsZ-dKrEUo7XqiwEFlVHSTkGu8ZeCuxg (accessed October 2, 2023).

Daly, S. J., N. King, and T. Yeadon-Lee (2018), "'Femme It Up or Dress It Down': Appearance and Bisexual Women in Monogamous Relationships," *Journal of Bisexuality*, 18 (3): 257–77. https://doi.org/10.1080/15299716.2018.1485071.

DapperQ (2019), "About." Available online: https://www.dapperq.com/about/ (accessed February 14, 2024).

DapperQ Team (2016), "DapperQ 'iD' Wraps 3rd Annual Queer Fashion Tour at Brooklyn Museum and ICA/Boston," *DapperQ*, October 29. Available online: https://www.dapperq.com/2016/10/dapperq-id-wraps-3rd-annual-queer-fashion-tour-brooklyn-museum-icaboston/ (accessed December 16, 2023).

DapperQ Team (2022), "DapperQ's 7th Annual Queer New York Fashion Week Show Featured Star-Studded Lineup in 'Bloom,'" *DapperQ*, September 30. Available online: https://www.dapperq.com/2022/09/dapperqs-7th-annual-queer-new-york-fashion-week-show-featured-star-studded-lineup-in-bloom/ (accessed December 16, 2023).

Das, S., and R. Farber (2020), "User-Generated Online Queer Media and the Politics of Queer Visibility," *Sociology Compass*. https://doi.org/10.1111/soc4.12824.

D'Auklaire, N. (2020), "Rainbow Road: The Secret History of Advertising to LGBTQ+ Consumers," *sxm Media*, July 17. Available online: https://www.sxmmedia.com/insights/studio-resonate-showcase-rainbow-road-the-secret-history-of-advertising-to-lgbtq-consumers (accessed October 2, 2023).

Davis, F. (1992), *Fashion, Culture, and Identity*, Chicago: University of Chicago Press.

Day, F. (2018), "Between Butch/Femme: On the Performance of Race, Gender, and Sexuality in a YouTube Web Series," *Journal of Lesbian Studies*, 22 (3): 267–81. https://doi.org/10.1080/10894160.2018.1383800

DeHaan, S., L. E. Kuper, J. C. Magee, L. Bigelow, and B. S. Mustanski (2013), "The Interplay Between Online and Offline Explorations of Identity, Relationships, and Sex: A Mixed-Methods Study with LGBT Youth," *Journal of Sex Research*, 50 (5): 421–34. https://doi.org/10.1080/00224499.2012.661489.

Devin-Norelle, (2019), "DapperQ Celebrates 10 Years of Influencing Queer Culture and Fashion," *Out*, September 9. Available online: https://www.out.com/fashion/2019/9/09/dapperq-celebrates-10-years-influencing-queer-culture-and-fashion (accessed December 16, 2023).

Dinno, A. (2017), "Homicide Rates of Transgender Individuals in the United States," *American Journal of Public Health*, 107 (9): 1441–7. https://doi.org/10.2105/AJPH.2017.303878.

Dishman, L. (2020), "Meet the E-Commerce Company That Shifted from Menswear for 'Weirdos' to Clothes Real Women Are Snatching Up," *CO*, May 4. Available online: https://www.uschamber.com/co/good-company/the-leap/betabrand-work-from-home-fashion (accessed October 2, 2023).

Dolce Vita, A. (2012), "Gladiator Fashion Show," *DapperQ*, May 7. Available online: https://www.dapperq.com/2012/05/gladiator-fashion-show/ (accessed December 16, 2023).

Dolce Vita, A. (2013), "Store Guide: Out List of Best Places to Shop," *DapperQ*, October 30. Available online: https://www.dapperq.com/2013/10/store-guide-our-list-of-best-places-to-shop/ (accessed October 2, 2023).

Dolce Vita, A. (2014), "DapperQ Masculine Gender Queer Fashion Show at Brooklyn Museum," *DapperQ*, December 10. Available online: https://www.dapperq.com/2014/12/dapperq-masculine-gender-queer-fashion-show-brooklyn-museum-models-carried-blacklivesmatter-signs-ended-hundreds-handsup-protest/ (accessed December 16, 2023).

Dolce Vita, A. (2017), "DapperQ's 4th Annual New York Fashion Week Queer Runway Show," *DapperQ*, September 2. Available online: https://www.dapperq.com/2017/09/30387/ (accessed February 14, 2024).

Drew, D., and G. Yehounme (2017), "The Apparel Industry's Environmental Impact in 6 Graphics," *World Resources Institute*. Available online: https://www.wri.org/insights/apparel-industrys-environmental-impact-6-graphics?inline-read-more= (accessed December 16, 2023).

du Gay, P., S. Hall, L. Janes, A. K. Madsen, H. Mackay, and K. Negus (1997), *Doing Cultural Studies: The Story of the Sony Walkman*, London: Sage.

Duffy, E. N. (2017), "Benetton's Most Controversial Campaigns," *British Vogue*, December 8. Available online: https://www.vogue.co.uk/gallery/benettons-best-advertising-campaigns (accessed October 17, 2023).

Dye, L. (2009), "Consuming Constructions: A Critique of Dove's Campaign for Real Beauty," *Canadian Journal of Media Studies*, 5 (1): 114–28.

Elman, R. A. (1996), "Triangles and Tribulations: The Politics of Nazi Symbols," *Journal of Homosexuality*, 30 (3): 1–11. https://doi.org/10.1300/J082v30n03_01.

Entwistle, J. (2000) "Fashion and the Fleshy Body: Dress as Embodied Practice," *Fashion Theory*, 4 (3): 323–47.

Entwistle, J. (2023), *The Fashioned Body: Fashion, Dress, and Modern Social Theory*, Malden: Polity Press.

Erikson, E. H. (1968), *Identity, Youth and Crisis*, New York: W. W. Norton.

Erlick, E. (2018), "Trans Youth Activism on the Internet," *Frontiers*, 39 (1): 73–92.

EPA (2019), "Facts and Figures about Materials, Waste, and Recycling: Textiles: Material-Speficic Data." Available online: https://www.epa.gov/facts-and-figures-about-materials-waste-and-recycling/textiles-material-specific-data (accessed December 16, 2023).

Equality Fashion Week (2023), "NiK Kacy Presents Equality Fashion Week." Available online: https://www.equalityfashionweek.com/ (accessed January 22, 2024).

Eskridge, W. N. (2007), "Law and the Construction of the Closet: American Regulation of Same-Sex Intimacy, 1880–1946," *Iowa Law Review*, 82 (4): 1033–44.

Esterberg, K. G. (1996), "'A Certain Swagger When I Walk': Performing Lesbian Identity," in S. Seidman (ed.), *Queer Theory/Sociology*, 259–79, Oxford: Blackwell.

Factor, R., and E. Rothblum (2008), "Exploring Gender Identity and Community among Three Groups of Transgender Individuals in the United States: MTFs, FTMS, and Genderqueers," *Health Sociology Review*, 17: 235–53.

Faderman, L. (1991), *Odd Girls and Twilight Lovers: A History of Lesbian Life in the Twentieth Century*, London: Penguin.

Farrell-Beck, J., and J. Parsons (2007), *Twentieth Century Dress in the United States*, New York: Fairchild.

Feinberg, L. (1993), *Stone Butch Blues*, Ithaca: Firebrand.

Fetner, T., and M. Heath (2016), "Do Same-Sex and Straight Weddings Aspire to the Fairytale? Women's Conformity and Resistance to Traditional Weddings," *Sociological Perspectives*, 59 (4): 721–42. https://doi.org/10.1177/0731121415601269.

Folx (2022), "Trans Swimming Guide: Everything You Need to Know about Getting Wet This Summer," June 22. Available online: https://www.folxhealth.com/library/

trans-swimming-guide-everything-you-need-to-know-about-getting-wet-this-summer#:~:text=If%20your%20binder%20is%20made,laps%20or%20swimming%20for%20exercise (accessed January 22, 2024).

Freitas, A. J., S. B. Kaiser, J. Chandler, C. Hall, J. Kim, and T. Hammidi (1997), "Appearance Management as Border Construction: Least Favorite Clothing, Group Distancing, and Identity ... Not!" *Sociological Inquiry*, 67 (3): 323–35.

Freitas, A. J., S. B. Kaiser, and T. Hammidi (1996), "Communities, Commodities, Cultural Space, and Style," in D. L. Wardlow (ed.), *Gays, Lesbians, and Consumer Behavior: Theory, Practice, and Research Issues in Marketing*, 83–107, Binghamton: Haworth Press.

Garrison, S. (2018), "On the Limits of 'Trans Enough': Authenticating Trans Identity Narratives," *Gender & Society*, 32 (5): 613–37.

Gebhart, N., and K. L. Reddy-Best (2023), "Liberalism, Abolition, and Slogan T-Shirts: Commodity Activism in the Midwestern United States," *Critical Studies in Fashion and Beauty*, 13 (2): 255–80. https://doi.org/10.1386/csfb_00048_1.

Geczy, G., and V. Karaminas (2013), *Queer Style*, London: Bloomsbury.

Gerbner, G., L. Gross, and M. Morgan (2002), "Growing Up with Television: Cultivation Processes," in J. Bryant and D. Zillman (eds.), *Media Effects: Advances in Theory and Research*, 43–67, Mahwah: Erlbaum.

gc2b (2023a), "Black Half Binder." Available online: https://www.gc2b.co/collections/2-0-bfcm-2023/products/black-half-chest-binder-classic-2 (accessed December 9, 2023).

gc2b (2023b), "Our Binders." Available online: https://www.gc2b.co/pages/gc2b-binders (accessed December 9, 2023).

Gillis, J. R. (1985), *For Better, for Worse: British Marriages, 1600 to the Present*, New York: Oxford University Press.

Givhan, R. (1998), "Abercrombie & Fitch's New Gay Niche: A Catalog with Wholesome Appeal," *Los Angeles Times*, August 13. Available online: https://www.latimes.com/archives/la-xpm-1998-aug-13-ls-12539-story.html (accessed October 17, 2023).

Glass, R. (2014), "Critical Hope and Struggles for Justice," in V. Bozalek, B. Leibowitz, R. Carolissen, and M. Boler (eds.), *Discerning Critical Hope in Educational Practices*, 101–12, London: Routledge.

Gold, M. (2019), "New York Passes a Ban on 'Conversion Therapy' after Years-Long Efforts," *New York Times*, January 21. Available online: https://www.nytimes.com/2019/01/21/nyregion/conversion-therapy-ban.html (accessed October 30, 2023).

Gomez, I., R. Usha, A. Salganicoff, L. Dawson, C. Rosenzweig, R. Kellenberg, and K. Gifford (2022), "Update on Medicaid Coverage of Gender-Affirming Health Services," *KFF*, October 11. Available online: https://www.kff.org/womens-health-policy/issue-brief/update-on-medicaid-coverage-of-gender-affirming-health-services/ (accessed October 30, 2023).

Grabe, S., L. M. Ward, and J. S. Hyde (2008), "The Role of the Media in Body Image Concerns Among Women: A Meta-Analysis of Experimental and Correlational Studies," *Psychological Bulletin*, 134: 460–76.

Green, D. (2018), "Dykes in the City: An Interview with Founder, Nicky Cutler," *Cornell Fashion + Textile Collection* (blog), March 15. Available online: https://blogs.cornell.edu/cornellcostume/2018/03/15/dykes-in-the-city-an-interview-with-founder-nicky-cutler/ (accessed November 4 2023).

Green, D. (2023), "Dykes in the City: Archiving Fashion Media," *Cornell University Media Studies*. Available online: https://mediastudies.as.cornell.edu/dykes-city-archiving-fashion-media (accessed November 4, 2023).

Greenberg, J. (1992), "ACT UP Explained," *The ACT UP Historical Archive*. Available online: https://actupny.org/documents/greenbergAU.html (accessed October 2, 2023).

Greyscale Goods (2015), "Greyscale Goods: Beyond Labels, Just Goods," *Kickstarter*, July 1. Available online: https://www.kickstarter.com/projects/547476930/greyscale-goods-beyond-labels-just-goods (accessed December 9, 2023).

Guest Authors (2011), "Dapper Queer Boxers from Let's Be Brief," *DapperQ*, September 18. Available online: https://www.dapperq.com/2011/09/dapper-womens-boxers-from-lets-be-brief/ (accessed December 9, 2023).

Hall, A. V., E. V. Hall, and J. L. Perry (2016), "Black and Blue: Exploring Racial Bias and Law Enforcement in the Killings of Unarmed Black Male Civilians," *American Psychology*, 71 (3): 175–86. https://doi.org/10.1037/a0040109.

Hall, R. (1950), *The Well of Loneliness*, New York: Pocket Books.

Hammidi, T. N., and S. B. Kaiser (1999), "Doing Beauty: Negotiating Lesbian Looks in Everyday Life," *Journal of Lesbian Studies*, 3 (4): 55–63. https://doi.org/10.1300/J155v03n04_07.

Harmon, J., and K. L. Reddy-Best (2020), "Fashion Social Marketing: Analysing Reactions to Lane Bryant's #PlusIsEqual," *Fashion, Style & Popular Culture*, 7 (2–3): 333–50. https://doi.org/10.1386/fspc_00022_1.

Hartman, J. E. (2013), "Creating a Bisexual Display: Making Bisexuality Visible," *Journal of Bisexuality*, 13 (1): 39–62. https://doi.org/10.1080/15299716.2013.755727.

Hartman-Linck, J. E. (2014), "Keeping Bisexuality Alive: Maintaining Bisexual Visibility in Monogamous Relationships," *Journal of Bisexuality*, 14 (2): 177–93. https://doi.org/10.1080/15299716.2014.903220.

Harwood, J. (1997), "Viewing Age: Lifespan Identity and Television Viewing Choices," *Journal of Broadcasting and Electronic Media*, 41: 203–13.

Hayfield, N. J. (2011), "Bisexual Women's Visual Identities: A Feminist Mixed-Methods Exploration," PhD diss., University of the West of England, Bristol.

Hayfield, N. J., V. Clarke, E. Halliwell, and H. Malson (2013), "Visible Lesbians and Invisible Bisexuals: Appearance and Visual Identities Among Bisexual Women," *Women's Studies International Forum*, 40 (8): 172–82. https://doi.org/10.1016/j.wsif.2013.07.015.

Hemmings, C. (1999), "Out of Sight, Out of Mind? Theorizing Femme Narrative," *Sexualities*, 2 (4): 451–64. https://doi.org/10.1177/136346099002004005.

Holliday, R. (1999), "The Comfort of Identity," *Sexualities*, 2 (4): 475–91. https://doi.org/10.1177/136346099002004007.

Howard, V. J. (2000), "American Weddings: Gender, Consumption and the Business of Brides," PhD diss., University of Texas at Austin.

Hull, K. E. (2006), *Same-Sex Marriage: The Cultural Politics of Love and Law*, Cambridge: Cambridge University Press.

Huxley, C., V, Clarke, and E. Halliwell (2014), "Resisting and Conforming to the 'Lesbian Look': The Importance of Appearance Norms for Lesbian and Bisexual Women," *Journal of Community & Applied Social Psychology*, 24 (3): 205–19.

Indian Health Services (n.d.), "Two-Spirit." Available online: https://www.ihs.gov/lgbt/twospirit/ (accessed January 26, 2024).

Jackson, H., and C. Kube (2019), "Trump's Controversial Transgender Military Policy Goes into Effect," *NBC News*, April 12. Available online: https://www.nbcnews.com/feature/nbc-out/trump-s-controversial-transgender-military-policy-goes-effect-n993826 (accessed October 2, 2023).

James, W. (1890), *The Principles of Psychology*, New York: Henry Holt.

James, S. E., J. L. Herman, S. Rankin, M. Keisling, L. Mottet, and M. Anafi (2016), *The Report of the 2015 U.S. Transgender Survey*, Washington: National Center for Transgender Equality. Available online: https://transequality.org/sites/default/files/docs/usts/USTS-Full-Report-Dec17.pdf (accessed October 2, 2023).

Johnson, G. (2019), 'White Gay Privilege Exists All Year, But It Is Particularly Hurtful During Pride', *NBC News*, June 30. Available online: https://www.nbcnews.com/think/opinion/white-gay-privilege-exists-all-year-it-particularly-hurtful-during-ncna1024961 (accessed October 2, 2023).

Johnston, J., and J. Taylor (2008), "Feminist Consumerism and Fat Activists: A Comparative Study of Grassroots Activism and the Dove Real Beauty Campaign," *Signs: Journal of Women in Culture and Society*, 33 (4): 941–66.

Jones, J. M. (2017), "In U.S., 10.2% of LGBT Adults Now Married to a Same-Sex Spouse," *Gallup*, Available online: https://news.gallup.com/poll/212702/lgbt-adults-married-sex-spouse.aspx?g_source=Social+Issues&g_medium=newsf (accessed November 25, 2023).

Kacy, NiK (2023a), "Destiny Collection." Available online: https://www.nikkacy.com/collections/destiny (accessed December 4, 2023).

Kacy, NiK (2023b), "Fortune Collection." Available online: https://www.nikkacy.com/collections/fortune (accessed December, 4, 2023).

Kaiser, S. B. (1997). The Social Psychology of Clothing: Symbolic Appearances in Context. Fairchild.

Kaiser, S. B. (2012), *Fashion and Cultural Studies*, New York: Bloomsbury.

Kaiser, S. B. (2021), "1980s and Beyond: Queering Fashion," in L. Welters and A. Lillethun (eds.), *The Fashion Reader*, 193–6, New York: Bloomsbury.

Kaiser, S. B., and D. N. Green (2021), *Fashion and Cultural Studies*, New York: Bloomsbury.

Kaiser, S. B. and S. R. McCullough (2010), "Entangling the Fashion Subject through the African Diaspora," *Fashion Theory*, 14 (3): 361–86.

Kaiser, S. B., R. H. Nagasawa, and S. S. Hutton (1995), "Construction of an SI Theory of Fashion: Part 1. Ambivalence and Change," *Clothing & Textiles Research Journal*, 13 (3): 172–83.

Kätsyri, J., N. Ravaja, and M. Salminen (2012), "Aesthetic Images Modulate Emotional Responses to Reading News Messages on a Small Screen: A Psychophysiological Investigation," *International Journal of Human-Computer Studies*, 70 (1): 72–87.

Katz, J. (2013), "Queer Activist Fashion," in V. Steele (ed.), *A Queer History of Fashion: From the Closet to the Catwalk*, 167–92, New Haven: Yale University Press.

Kidwell, C. (1979) "*Cutting a Fashionable Fit: Dressmakers' Drafting Systems in the United States*." Washington: Smithsonian Institution Press.

Kimport, K. (2012), "Remaking the White Wedding? Same-Sex Wedding Photographs' Challenge to Symbolic Heteronormativity," *Gender and Society*, 26 (6): 874–99. https://doi.org/10.1177/0891243212449902.

King, M., J. Semlyen, S. S. Tai, H. Killaspy, D. Osborn, D. Popelyuk, and I. Nazareth (2008), "A Systematic Review of Mental Disorder, Suicide, and Deliberate Self Harm in Lesbian,

Gay and Bisexual People," *BMC Psychiatry*, 8 (70). https://doi.org/10.1186/1471-244X-8-70.

Kirrin Finch (2023), "Kirrin Finch x DapperQ." Available online: https://kirrinfinch.com/blogs/news/kirrin-finch-x-dapperq (accessed December 16, 2023).

Knauer, N. J. (2019), "LGBT Elders: Making the Case for Equity in Aging," in C. A. Ball (ed.), *After Marriage Equality: The Future of LGBT Rights*, 105–26, New York: New York University Press.

Kols, L., and J. Sobal. (2013), "Weight and Weddings: Engaged Men's Body Weight Ideals and Wedding Weight Management Behaviors," *Appetite*, 60: 133–39. https://doi.org/10.1016/j.appet.2012.09.031.

Kozlowski, A., C. Searcy, and M. Bardecki, M. (2018), "The ReDesign Canvas: Fashion Design as a Tool for Sustainability," *Journal of Cleaner Production*, 183: 197–207.

Kvidal-Røvik, T. (2018), "The Meaning of the Feminist T-Shirt: Social Media, Postmodern Aesthetics, and the Potential for Sociopolitical Change," *Media and Communication*, 6 (2): 210–19.

Lane-Steele, L. (2011), "Studs and Protest-Hypermasculinity: The Tomboyism within Black Lesbian Female Masculinity," *Journal of Lesbian Studies*, 15 (4): 480–92. https://doi.org/10.1080/10894160.2011.532033.

Lautmann, R. (1981), "The Pink Triangle," *Journal of Homosexuality*, 6 (1–2): 141–60, https://doi.org/10.1300/J082v06n01_13

Lennon, S. J., K. K. P. Johnson, and N. A. Rudd (2017), *Social Psychology of Dress*, New York: Fairchild Books.

Levitt, H. M., E. A. Gerrish, and K. R. Hiestand (2003), "The Misunderstood Gender: A Model of Modern Femme Identity," *Sex Roles*, 48 (3–4): 99–113. https://doi.org/10.1023/A:1022453304384.

Levitt, H. M., and K. R. Hiestand (2004), "A Quest for Authenticity: Contemporary Butch Gender," *Sex Roles*, 50 (9–10): 605–21. https://doi.org/10.1023/b:sers.0000027565.59109.80.

Levitt, H. M., and S. G. Horne (2002), "Explorations of Lesbian-Queer Genders," *Journal of Lesbian Studies*, 6 (2): 25–39. https://doi.org/10.1300/J155v06n02_05.

Lewin, E. (1998), *Recognizing Ourselves: Ceremonies of Lesbian and Gay Commitment*, New York: Oxford University Press.

LGBTQ+ Victory Fund (2023), "We Work to Build Long-Term LGBTQ+ Political Power by Helping Elect LGBTQ+ Leaders at Every Level of Government." Available online: https://victoryfund.org/our-candidates/?search=&candidate_category=winning-candidates (accessed October 30, 2023).

Linder, J. R., and E. A. Daniels (2018), "Sexy vs. Sporty: The Effects of Viewing Media Images of Athletes on Self Objectification in College Students," *Sex Roles*, 78: 27–39.

Lodewick, C. (2022), "Major Corporations are Going All in for Pride Month While Also Supporting Anti-LGBTQ+ Legislators," *Fortune*, June 1. Available online: https://fortune.com/2022/06/01/major-corporations-donate-anti-lgbtq-legislators-pride/ (accessed October 30, 2023).

Mallory, C., and Sears, B. (2020), "Economic Impact of Marriage Equality since Obergefell," *The Williams Institute UCLA School of Law*, May. Available online: https://williamsinstitute.law.ucla.edu/publications/econ-impact-obergefell-5-years/ (accessed November 25, 2023).

Maltry, M., and Tucker, K. (2002), "Female Fem(me)ininities," *Journal of Lesbian Studies*, 6 (2): 89–102. https://doi.org/10.1300/J155v06n02_12.

Mamp, M. (2021), "Fashioning a Male Actress: Charles Pierce," *Dress*, 47 (2): 121–37. https://doi.org/10.1080/03612112.2021.1932113.

Massoud, M. F. (2022), "The Price of Positionality: Assessing the Benefits and Burdens of Self-Identification in Research Methods," *Journal of Law and Society*, 49 (1): S64–S86. https://doi.org/10.1111/jols.12372.

Matthews, D. L., and K. L. Reddy-Best (2022), "Negotiations of Women's Black and Activist Identity through Dress on the College Campus, 2013–2019," *Clothing & Textiles Research Journal*, 40 (2): 91–106. https://doi.org/10.1177/0887302X20968809.

McGuire, J. K., and A. Chrisler (2016), "Body Art among Transgender Youth: Marking Social Support, Reclaiming the Body, and Creating a Narrative Identity," in Y. Kiuchi and F. A. Villarruel (eds.), *The Young Are Making Their World: Essays on the Power of Youth Culture*, 97–118, Jefferson: McFarland.

McGuire, J. K., J. L. Doty, J. M. Catalpa, and C. Ola (2016), "Body Image in Transgender Young People: Findings From a Qualitative, Community Based Study," *Body Image*, 18: 96–107. https://dx.doi.org/10.1016/j.bodyim.2016.06.004.

McGuire, J. K. and A. Reilly (2022), "Aesthetic Identity Development among Trans Adolescents and Young Adults," *Clothing and Textiles Research Journal*, 40 (3): 235–50. https://doi.org/10.1177/0887302X20975382.

McHugh, K. (2014), "Sodomy Laws," in Bruce A. Arrigo (ed.), *Encyclopedia of Criminal Justice Ethics*, 882–4, Los Angeles: SAGE.

McLean, K. (2008), "Silences and Stereotypes: The Impact of (Mis)constructions of Bisexuality on Australian Bisexual Men and Women," *Gay and Lesbian Issues and Psychology Review*, 4 (3): 158–65.

McManis, M. H., M. M. Bradley, W. K. Berg, B. N. Cuthbert, and P. J. Lang (2001), "Emotional Reactions in Children: Verbal, Physiological, and Behavioral Responses to Affective Pictures," *Psychophysiology*, 38 (2): 222–31.

Mears, P. (2008), "Exhibiting Asia: The Global Impact of Japanese Fashion in Museums and Galleries," *Fashion Theory*, 12 (1): 95–120. https://doi.org/10.2752/175174108X269586.

Miller, S. (2017), "Onslaught of Anti-LGBT Bills in 2017 Has Activists Playing Defense," in H. W. Wilson (ed.), *LGBTQ in the 21st Century*, 9–13, Amenia, NY: Grey House.

Mirola, W. A. (2007), "Gay Liberation Front," in G. Anderson and K. G. Herr (eds.), *Encyclopedia of Activism and Social Justice*, 606–7, Thousand Oaks: Sage.

Moon, L. (2018), "Torrid.com Shoes That Fit Trans Women," YouTube, November 27. Available online: https://www.youtube.com/watch?v=N4w2peMLKfw (accessed January 22, 2024).

Moore, J. G. (2020), *Patternmaking History and Theory*, New York: Bloomsbury.

Mullet, K. K., C. L. Moore, and M. B. Prevatt Young (2009), *Concepts of Pattern Grading: Techniques for Manual and Computer Grading*, New York: Fairchild.

Mukherjee, R., and S. Banet-Weiser (2012), *Commodity Activism Cultural Resistance in Neoliberal Times*, New York: New York University Press.

National Center for Transgender Equality (2023a), "Understanding Nonbinary People: How to Be Respectful and Supportive," January 12. Available online: https://transequality.org/issues/resources/understanding-nonbinary-people-how-to-be-respectful-and-supportive#:~:text=You%20don't%20have%20to,person%20asks%20you%20to%20use (accessed October 2, 2023).

National Center for Transgender Equality (2023b), "Understanding Transgender People: The Basics," January 27. Available online: https://transequality.org/issues/resources/understanding-transgender-people-the-basics (accessed October 2, 2023).

National Museum of African American History & Culture (n.d.), "Gladys Bentley (1907–1960)." Available online: https://nmaahc.si.edu/gladys-bentley (accessed May 12, 2024).

Navarrete, H. R. (2021), "The Queer Fashion Show Archives: Keeping History Alive," *City on a Hill*, June 10. Available online: https://cityonahillpress.com/2021/06/10/the-queer-fashion-show-archives-keeping-history-alive/ (accessed November 4, 2023).

Newton, E. (1979), *Mother Camp: Female Impersonators in America*, Chicago: University of Chicago Press.

Ogle, J. P., A. Johnson, K. L. Reddy-Best, J. Harmon, K. Morris, and P. Kittersong (2023), "Forming and Maintaining Positive Body Image among Nonbinary Individuals," *Body Image*, 47. https://www.sciencedirect.com/science/article/abs/pii/S1740144523001419#:~:text=Six%20themes%20were%20identified%20as,and%20self%2Dcare%2C%20and%20using.

Ogle, J., C. Morgan, and K. Hyllegard (2022), "Authentic Style-Fashion-Dress Negotiations of Lesbian Married Couples on their Wedding Day," *Journal of Consumer Culture*, 22 (3), 652–73. https://doi.org/10.1177/1469540521990858.

O'Neill, M. G. (2014), "Transgender Youth and YouTube Videos: Self-Representation and Five Identifiable Trans Youth Narratives," in C. Pullen (ed.), *Queer Youth and Media Cultures*, 34–45, London: Palgrave Macmillan.

Oram, S. (n.d.a), "Target Excludes Trans Women from 2022 Pride Collection," *Qwear*, May 10. Available online: https://www.qwearfashion.com/home/target-excludes-trans-women-from-pride-collection (accessed January 22, 2024).

Oram, S. (n.d.b), "Why I Founded Qwear: The Clothes That Made Me," *Qwear*, November 27. Available online: https://www.qwearfashion.com/home/why-i-founded-qwear-the-clothes-that-made-me (accessed December 16, 2023).

Otnes, C., and T. Lowrey (1993), "'Til Debt Do Us Part: The Selection and Meaning of Artifacts in the American Wedding," *Advances in Consumer Research*, 20: 325–9.

Otnes, C. C., and E. H. Pleck (2003), *Cinderella Dreams: The Allure of the Lavish Wedding*, Berkeley: University of California Press.

Pajer, N. (2019), "There Are New Options in Trans Underwear," *New York Times*, May 1. Available online: https://www.nytimes.com/2019/05/01/fashion/transgender-underwear.html (accessed January 22, 2024).

Palamutcu, S. (2015), "Energy Footprints in the Textile Industry," in S. S. Muthu (ed.), *Handbook of Life Cycle Assessment (LCA) of Textiles and Clothing*, 31–61, Cambridge: Woodhead Publishing. https://doi.org/10.1016/B978-0-08-100169-1.00002-2.

Paoletti, J. (2012), *Pink and Blue: Telling the Boys from the Girls in America*, Bloomington: Indiana University Press.

Paoletti, J. (2015), *Sex and Unisex: Fashion, Feminism, and the Sexual Revolution*, Bloomington: Indiana University Press.

Paris Is Burning (1990), [Film] Dir. Jennie Livingston, USA: Off White Productions.

Pepin, J., T. S. Zimmerman, C. A. Fruhauf, and J. H. Banning (2008), "An Analysis of Wedding Books for Grooms: A Feminist Perspective," *Journal of Feminist Family Therapy*, 20 (4): 328–55. https://doi.org/10.1080/08952830802382169.

Peralta, E. (2013), "Court Overturns DOMA, Sidesteps Broad Gay Marriage Ruling," *NPR*, June 26. Available online: https://www.npr.org/sections/thetwo-way/2013/06/26/195857796/supreme-court-strikes-down-defense-of-marriage-act (accessed October 2, 2023).

Piacentini, M., and Mailer, G. (2004), "Symbolic Consumption in Teenagers' Clothing Choices," *Journal of Consumer Behavior*, 3 (3): 251–62. https://doi.org/10.1002/cb.138.

Play Out Apparel (2023a), "Abby & Liz." Available online: https://www.playoutapparel.com/pages/abby-liz (accessed November 20, 2023; note, as per website, Play Out is now closed).

Play Out Apparel (2023b), "Our Mission." Available online: https://www.playoutapparel.com/pages/our-mission (accessed December 5, 2023; note, as per website, Play Out is now closed).

Play Out Apparel (2023c), "Pouch Bikinis." Available online: https://www.playoutapparel.com/collections/pouch-bikinis (accessed December 5, 2023; note as per website, Play Out is now closed).

Polhemus, T. (1994), *Streetstyle: From Sidewalk to Catwalk*, New York: Thames and Hudson.

Qwear (n.d.a), "About Qwear Fashion." Available online: https://www.qwearfashion.com/statement (December 16, 2023).

Qwear (n.d.b), "Deconstructing Fashion & Queer Performance." Available online: https://www.qwearfashion.com/fashion-shows/dismantle-me/2015 (accessed January 19, 2024).

Qwear (n.d.c), "Femme Desire, 2016." Available online: https://www.qwearfashion.com/fashion-shows/femme-desire-2016 (accessed January 19, 2024).

Qwear (n.d.d), "Home Page." Available online: https://www.qwearfashion.com/ (accessed December 16, 2023).

Qwear (n.d.e), "Qwear Pride 2020 Fashion Show." Available online: https://www.qwearfashion.com/fashion-shows/qwear-pride-2020-fashion-show (accessed January 19, 2024).

Radhakrishnan, S. (2020), "Sustainable Consumption and Production Patterns in Fashion," in M. A. Gardetti and S. S. Muthu (eds.), *The UN Sustainable Development Goals for the Textile and Fashion Industry*, Singapore: Springer. https://doi.org/10.1007/978-981-13-8787-6.

Rahilly, E. P. (2015), "The Gender Binary Meets the Gender-Variant Child: Parents' Negotiations with Childhood Gender Variance," *Gender & Society*, 29 (3): 338–61. https://doi.org/10.1177/0891243214563069.

Razinsky, H. (2016), *Ambivalence: A Philosophical Exploration*, Lanham: Rowman and Littlefield.

Reddy-Best, K. L. (2015), "The Politicization of Fashion in Virtual Queer Spaces: A Case Study of Saint Harridan and Tomboy Tailors," Proceedings of the 41st Annual Meeting and National Symposium of the Costume Society of America, San Antonio, Texas, May 28–30.

Reddy-Best, K. L. (2017), "Miki Vargas: Queer Fashion Photographer and *The Handsome Revolution*," *Clothing Cultures*, 4 (2): 153–70. https://doi.org/10.1386/cc.4.2.153_1.

Reddy-Best, K. L. (2018a), "'I Cut It [Her Hair] Real Short Right After I Got the Job': Queer Coding During the Interview for LGBTQ+ Women," *Fashion, Style & Popular Culture*, 5 (2): 221–34. https://doi.org/10.1386/fspc.5.2.221_1.

Reddy-Best, K. L. (2018b), "LGBTQ Women, Appearance Negotiations, and Workplace Dress Codes," *Journal of Homosexuality*, 65 (1): 615–39. https://doi.org/10.1080/00918369.2017.1328225.

Reddy-Best, K. L. (2020a), *Dress, Appearance, and Diversity in U.S. Society*, Ames: Iowa State University Digital Press. Available online: https://iastate.pressbooks.pub/dressappearancediversity/ (accessed January 22, 2024).

Reddy-Best, K. L. (2020b), "The Politicization of Fashion in Virtual Queer Spaces: A Case Study of Saint Harridan, One of the Pioneering Queer Fashion Brands in the Twenty-First Century," in A. Reilly and B. Barry (eds.), *Crossing Boundaries: Fashion to Deconstruct and Reimagine Gender*, 91–108, New York: Bloomsbury Publishing.

Reddy-Best, K. L., and K. Baker Jones (2020), "Is This What a Lesbian Looks Like? Lesbian Fashion and the Fashionable Lesbian in the United States Press, 1960s to 2010s," *Journal of Lesbian Studies*, 24 (2): 159–71. https://doi.org/10.1080/10894160.2019.1685816.

Reddy-Best, K. L., and L. D. Burns (2013), "Avant-Garde Fashion: A Case Study of Martin Margiela," *International Journal of Costume and Fashion*, 13 (1): 1–13.

Reddy-Best, K. L., and D. Goodin (2020), "Queer Fashion and Style: Stories from the Heartland—Authentic Midwestern Queer Voices through a Museum Exhibition," *Dress: The Journal of the Costume Society of America*, 46 (2): 115–40. https://doi.org/10.1080/03612112.2019.1686875.

Reddy-Best, K. L., and A. Howell (2014), "Negotiations in Masculine Identities in the Utilikilts Brand Community," *Critical Studies in Men's Fashion*, 1 (3): 223–40. https://doi.org/10.1386/csmf.1.3.223_1.

Reddy-Best, K. L., and E. Olson (2020), "Trans Traveling and Embodied Practices: Panopticism, Agency, Dress, and Gendered Surveillance," *Annals of Tourism Research*, 85: 1–11. https://doi.org/10.1016/j.annals.2020.103028.

Reddy-Best, K. L., and Pedersen, E. L. (2014), "The Relationship of Gender Expression, Sexual Identity, Distress, Appearance, and Clothing Choices for Queer Women," *International Journal of Fashion Design, Technology, and Education*, 8 (1): 54–65. https://doi.org/10.1080/17543266.2014.958576.

Reddy-Best, K. L. and E. L. Pedersen (2015), "Queer Women's Experiences Purchasing Clothing and Looking for Clothing Styles," *Clothing & Textile Research Journal*, 33 (4): 265–79. https://doi.org/10.1177/0887302X15585165.

Reddy-Best, K. L., D. Goodin, and K. Streck (2023a), *21st Century Queer Fashion Brands: Oral History Project*, Ames: Iowa State University Digital Press. Available online: https://iastate.pressbooks.pub/queerfashionbrands/ (accessed October 2, 2023).

Reddy-Best, K. L., A. Reilly, K. Morris, D. N. Green, K. Streck, and K. Doty. (2023b), "Chest-Binding Practices for Trans and Nonbinary Individuals within Different Spatiotemporalities: Redefining the Meaning of Space, Place, and Time," *Fashion Theory*, 27 (6): 833–60. https://doi.org/10.1080/1362704X.2023.2196761.

Reilly, A., and E. J. Saethre (2014), "The Hankie Code Revisited: From Function to Fashion," *Critical Studies in Men's Fashion*, 1 (1): 69–78. https://doi.org/10.1386/csmf.1.1.69_1.

Reilly, A., J. Catalpaand, and J. McGuire (2019), "Clothing Fit Issues of Trans People," *Fashion Studies*, 2 (1): n.p. https://doi.org/10.38055/FS010201.

Reilly, A., and E. J. Saethre (2014), "The Hankie Code Revisited: From Function to Fashion," *Critical Studies in Men's Fashion*, 1 (1): 69–78. https://doi.org/10.1386/csmf.1.1.69_1.

Reynolds, P. (2018), "In 'Forms & Alterations,' Artists Use Fashion to Unravel Gender Politics and Identity," *WBUR*, February 1. Available online: https://www.wbur.org/news/2018/02/01/forms-alterations-fashion (accessed January 22, 2024).

Riedel, S. (2022), "Target's 2022 Pride Collaboration Features Binders and Packing Briefs from TomboyX," *them*, May 9. Available online: https://www.them.us/story/targets-2022-pride-collaboration-features-binders-and-packing-briefs-from-tomboyx (accessed October 30, 2023).

Riedel, S. (2023), 'Target Will Remove Some Pride Merchandise After a Conservative Outrage Campaign', *them*, May 24. Available online: https://www.them.us/story/target-removing-pride-merchandise-matt-walsh-gays-against-groomers (accessed October 30, 2023).

Ring, T. (2024), Why the Boy Scouts of America is Changing its Name and Embracing Everyone," *Advocate*, May 8. Available online: https://www.advocate.com/news/how-boy-scouts-became-inclusive (accessed September 23, 2024).

Ritchie, D. (2003), *Doing Oral History: A Practical Guide*, Oxford: Oxford University Press.

Roach-Higgins, M. E., and J. B. Eicher (1992), "Dress and Identity," *Clothing and Textiles Research Journal*, 10 (4): 1–8.

Rolley, K. (1990), "Cutting a Dash: The Dress of Radclyffe Hall and Una Troubridge," *Feminist Review*, 35 (1): 54–66.

Romero, A. P. (2017), "1.1 Million LGBT Adults Are Married to Someone of the Same Sex at the Two-Year Anniversary of *Obergefell* v. *Hodges*," The Williams Institute UCLA School of Law. Available online: https://williamsinstitute.law.ucla.edu/wp-content/uploads/Obergefell-2-Year-Marriages.pdf (accessed November 25, 2023).

Rossiter, H. (2016), "She's Always a Woman: Butch Lesbian Trans Women in the Lesbian Community," *Journal of Lesbian Studies*, 20 (1): 87–96. https://doi.org/10.1080/10894160.2015.1076236.

Rothblum, E. (1994), "Lesbians and Physical Appearance: Which Model Applies?" in B. Greene and G. M. Herek (eds.), *Lesbian and Gay Psychology: Theory, Research and Clinical Applications*, 84–97, London: Sage.

Rothblum, E. (2010), "The Complexity of Butch and Femme among Sexual Minority Women in the 21st Century," *Psychology of Sexualities Review*, 1 (1): 29–42.

Rothman, L. (2022), "Read the 'Yep, I'm Gay' Ellen DeGeneres Interview From 1997," *Time Magazine*, April 14. Available online: https://time.com/4728994/ellen-degeneres-1997-coming-out-cover/ (accessed October 17, 2023).

Rotman, D., and J. Preece (2010), "The 'WeTube' in YouTube—Creating an Online Community through Video Sharing," *International Journal of Web-Based Communities*, 6 (3): 317–33. https://www.researchgate.net/deref/http%3A%2F%2Fdx.doi.org%2F10.1504%2FIJWBC.2010.033755.

Sadeghi, M. (2021), "Face Check: Posts Criticizing Biden Order on Gender Discrimination Lack Context," *USA Today*, February 2. Available online: https://www.usatoday.com/story/news/factcheck/2021/02/02/fact-check-biden-executive-order-discrimination-transgender-women-sports/6686171002/ (accessed October 2, 2023).

Salfino, C. (2021), "Why Made in the USA is Still Important to Consumers', *Sourcing Journal Online*, July 1. Available online: https://sourcingjournal.com/topics/lifestyle-monitor/made-in-usa-apparel-fashion-textile-manufacturing-mckinsey-softwear-coronavirus-288767/ (accessed January 22, 2024).

Salfino, C. (2022), "Consumers: It Matters Where Fashion Is Made," *Sourcing Journal Online*, June 30. Available online: https://sourcingjournal.com/topics/lifestyle-monitor/made-in-usa-fashion-grown-and-sewn-rob-magness-gitman-bros-353188/ (accessed January 22, 2024).

Sears, C. (2015), *Cross-Dressing, Law, and Fascination in Nineteenth-Century San Francisco*, Durham: Duke University Press.

Sender, K. (1999), "Selling Sexual Subjectivities: Audiences Respond to Gay Window Advertising," *Critical Studies in Media Communication*, 16 (2): 172–96. https://doi.org/10.1080/15295039909367085.

Schilt, K. (2009), "Jorgensen, Christine (1926–1989)," in J. O'Brien (ed.), *Encyclopedia of Gender and Society*, 474, London: Sage.

Schofield, N. A., and K. L. LaBat (2005), "Exploring the Relationship of Grading, Sizing, and Anthropometric Data," *Clothing and Textiles Research Journal*, 23 (1): 13–27. https://doi.org/10.1177/0887302X0502300102.

Schrock, D. P., E. M. Boyd, and M. Leaf (2009), "Emotion Work in the Public Performances of Male-to-Female Transsexuals," *Archives of Sexual Behavior*, 38 (5): 702–12. https://doi.org/10.1007/s10508-007-9280-2.

Schwartz, S. J., K. Luyckz, and V. L. Vignoles (2011), "Introduction: Toward an Integrative View of Identity," in S. J. Schwartz, K. Luyckz, and V. L. Vignoles (eds.), *Handbook of Identity Theory and Research*, 1–30, New York: Springer Science & Business Media.

Serano, J. (2007), *Whipping Girl: A Transsexual Woman on Sexism and the Scapegoating of Femininity*, New York: Seal Press.

Simmons, H., and F. White (2018), "Our Man Selves," in L. Erickson-Schroth (ed.), *Trans Bodies, Trans Selves: A Resource for the Transgender Community*, 1–23, Oxford: Oxford University Press.

Simon, J., and K. L. Reddy-Best (2024), "Cereal Box Chic, Ready-to-Wear, and Couture: Estévez's Unique Fashion Designer Evolution as a Cuban American in the 20th Century," *Dress: The Journal of the Costume Society of America*. https://doi.org/10.1080/03612112.2024.2298096.

Singh, A. (2019), *Changing Scenario of Business and E-Commerce: Trends and Issues*, Oakville: Society Publishing.

Smart, C. (2008), "'Can I Be Bridesmaid?' Combining the Personal and Political in Same-Sex Weddings," *Sexualities*, 11 (6): 761–76. https://doi.org/10.1177/1363460708096917.

Snorton, C. R. (2009), "'A New Hope': The Psychic Life of Passing," *Hypatia*, 24 (3): 77–92. https://www.jstor.org/stable/20618165.

Steele, F. (2013), *A Queer History of Fashion: From the Closet to the Catwalk*, New Haven: Yale University Press.

Stein, A. (1998), "All Dressed Up. But No Place to Go? The Style Wars and New Lesbianism," in C. K. Creekmur and A. Doty (eds.), *Out in Culture: Gay, Lesbian, and Queer Essays on Popular Culture*, 476–83, Durham: Duke University Press.

Stocchetti, M., and K. Kukkonen (2011), *Images in Use: Towards the Critical Analysis of Visual Communication*, Amsterdam: John Benjamins.

Stone, G. P. (1969), "Appearance and the Self," in M. E. Roach and J. B. Eicher (eds.), *Dress, Adornment, and the Social Order*, 216–45, New York: John Wiley and Sons.

Streck, K. G., and K. L. Reddy-Best (2023), "Trans YouTubers and DIY Undergarments: 'Queer-and-Trans-World-Making-and-Sharing' in the Fashion System's Informal Economies," *Critical Studies in Fashion & Beauty*, 14 (1): 57–86. https://doi.org/10.1386/csfb_00055_1.

Stryker, S. (1968), "Identity Salience and Role Performance," *Journal of Marriage and the Family*, 30 (4), 558–64.

Stuzo (2023), "Yup, Still Tank." Available online: https://www.stuzoclothing.com/collections/womens/products/yup-still-gay-tee-cut (accessed December 9, 2023).

Tarnoff, B. (2016), "How the Internet Was Invented," *Guardian*, July 15. https://www.theguardian.com/technology/2016/jul/15/how-the-internet-was-invented-1976-arpa-kahn-cerf (accessed October 17, 2023).

Tate, C. C., J. N. Ledbetter, and C. P. Youssef (2013), "A Two-Question Method for Assessing Gender Categories in Social and Medical Sciences," *Journal of Sex Research*, 50 (8): 767–76. https://doi.org/10.1080/00224499.2012.690110.

Taub, J. (2003), "What Should I Wear? A Qualitative Look at the Impact of Feminism and Women's Communities on Bisexual Women's Appearance," *Journal of Bisexuality*, 3 (1): 9–22. https://doi.org/10.1300/J159v03n01_02.

Tawfiq, W., and S. Marcketti, S. (2017), "Meaning and Symbolism in Bridal Costumes in Western Saudi Arabia," *Clothing and Textiles Research Journal*, 35 (3): 215–30. https://doi.org/10.1177/0887302X17704718.

The Williams Institute (2021a), "More Than 60% of Suicide Attempts among LGBQ People Happen Within Five Years of Realizing They Are LGBTQ," *UCLA School of Law*, July 1. Available online: https://williamsinstitute.law.ucla.edu/press/suicide-coming-out-press-release/ (accessed January 22, 2024).

The Williams Institute (2021b), "Transgender People Over Four Times More Likely Than Cisgender People to Be Victims of Violent Crime," *UCLA School of Law*, March 23. Available online: https://williamsinstitute.law.ucla.edu/press/ncvs-trans-press-release/ (accessed January 22, 2024).

The Williams Institute (2023), "More Than 40% of Transgender Adults in the US Have Attempted Suicide," *UCLA School of Law*, July 20. Available online: https://williamsinstitute.law.ucla.edu/press/transpop-suicide-press-release/ (accessed January 22, 2024).

@TomboyX (2020), "Our CEO sat down with Trinity this week and they agreed to work together to establish a protocol for ourselves & other agencies to ensure the trans community feels welcome, cared for, & respected on photoshoot sets. We are dedicated to learning & getting better every day," Twitter, March 12. https://twitter.com/tomboyx/status/1238254399186776069.

TomboyX (2023a), "4.5" Trunks—TENCEL™ Modal Black Rainbow." Available online: https://tomboyx.com/collections/4-5-trunks/products/4trunk-blackrb (accessed December 5, 2023).

TomboyX (2023b), "Bikini—TENCEL™ Modal Black." Available online: https://tomboyx.com/collections/bikini/products/bikini-black (accessed December 5, 2023).

TomboyX (2023c), "Our Story." Available online: https://tomboyx.com/pages/ourstory (accessed December 5, 2023).

Tortora, P. G., and S. B. Marcketti (2021), *Survey of Historic Costume*, New York: Bloomsbury.

Transguy Supply (2023a), "Cake Bandit—Neptune Absorbing Boxers." Available online: https://transguysupply.com/collections/packing-underwear/products/period-packing-boxers?variant=40842376282155 (accessed December 9, 2023).

Transguy Supply (2023b), "STP Freely Uncut." Available online: https://transguysupply.com/collections/ftm-stp/products/stp-freely-uncut?variant=39435183718443 (accessed December 9, 2023).

@Trinity (2020), "I'm very disappointed in Tomboy x. I just recently worked with them again, and within a minute of me arriving they informed me that they cast me to model their WOMEN'S CELEBRATION print and reactively I said, No I'm not," Twitter, March 5.. https://twitter.com/trinity_bree/status/1235806657537433600?lang=en.

Tulloch, C. (2010), "Style-Fashion-Dress: From Black to Post-Black," *Fashion Theory*, 14 (3): 361–86.

UC Davis LGBTQIA Resource Center (2023), "LGBTQIA Resource Center Glossary." Available online: https://lgbtqia.ucdavis.edu/educated/glossary#q (accessed October 2, 2023).

United Nations (2015), "Do You Know All 17 SDGs?" *Department of Economic and Social Affairs: Sustainable Development*. Available online: https://sdgs.un.org/ (accessed December 16, 2023).

Varangis, E., N. Lanzieri, T. Hildebrandt, and M. Feldman (2012), "Gay Male Attraction Toward Muscular Men: Does Mating Context Matter?" *Body Image*, 9 (2): 270–8. https://doi.org/10.1016/j.bodyim.2012.01.003.

Vartabedian, J. (2019), "Bodies and Desires on the Internet: An Approach to Sex Workers' Websites," *Sexualities*, 22 (1–2): 224–43. https://doi.org/10.1177/1363460717713381.

Walker, L. M. (1993), "How to Recognize a Lesbian: The Cultural Politics of Looking Like What You Are," *Signs*, 18 (4): 866–90. https://www.jstor.org/stable/3174910.

WE ARE MORTALS (n.d.), "Fluidity Dress." Available online: https://www.wearemortals.com/shop/fluidity-dress (December 9, 2023).

Williamson, C. (2011), "Tania Hammidi on LA's Queer Fashion Scene," *DapperQ*, December 6. Available online: https://www.dapperq.com/2011/12/la-queer-fashion/ (accessed November 4, 2023).

Wilson, E. (2013), "What Does a Lesbian Look Like?" in V. Steele (ed.), *A Queer History of Fashion: From the Closet to the Catwalk*, 167–92, New Haven: Yale University Press.

Winch, A., and A. Webster (2012), "Here Comes the Brand: Wedding Media and the Management of Transformation," *Continuum Journal of Media & Cultural Studies*, 26 (1): 51–9. https://doi.org/10.1080/10304312.2012.630143.

Winkielman, P., and J. T. Cacioppo (2001), "Mind at Ease Puts a Smile on the Face: Psychophysiological Evidence that Processing Facilitation Elicits Positive Affects," *Journal of Personality and Social Psychology*, 81: 989–1000.

Wolff, T. B. (1997), "Compelled Affirmations, Free Speech, and the U.S. Military's Don't Ask, Don't Tell Policy," *Brooklyn Law Review*, 63 (4): 1141–212.

Wolitski, R. (2018), "HIV in the African American Community: Progress, But Our Work Is Far from Over," *HIV.gov* (blog), February 7. Available online: https://www.hiv.gov/blog/hiv-african-american-community-progress-our-work-far-over (accessed October 2, 2023).

Worsley, H. (2011), *100 Ideas That Changed Fashion*, London: Laurence King.

Yates, J. (2022), "Target Teams Up with LGBT+ Artists for Its Pride Month Collection Featuring Binders, T-shirts and More," *Pink News*, May 4. Available online: https://www.thepinknews.com/2022/05/04/target-pride-month-collection-lgbt-owned/ (accessed May 30, 2023).

Zaffalon, V. (2010), "Climate Change, Carbon Mitigation and Textiles," *Textile World*, 16 (4): 34–5. http://www.ccpittex.com/eng/texInfo/42652.html.

Zagorsky, J. L. (2016), "Why Are Fewer People Getting Married?" *Conversation*, June 1. Available online: https://theconversation.com/why-are-fewer-people-getting-married-60301 (accessed November 25, 2023).

Zukin, S. and J. S. Maguire (2004), "Consumers and Consumption," *Annual Review of Sociology* 30: 173–97. https://doi.org/10.1146/annurev.soc.30.012703.110553.

Index

2008 global financial crisis 37–8

Abercrombie & Fitch 33, 35–6
absent groom(s) 44, 45
ACT UP (AIDS Coalition to Unleash Power) 26, 28
activewear 104
activism 25–6, 29–30, 40–1, 43, 45–6, 56–8
    Black Lives Matter/Dapper Q 158–9
    commodity activism 36–42, 56
    femme masc shoes 99–100
    gay window advertising 35
    internet 142
    Pride Movement 36–42, 119–23, 162
    revolution and political landscape 27–30
    t-shirt activism 38, 122–3
Adams, Barbara 159
advertising 35–42
"aesthetic identity" frameworks 25
African American LGBTQ+ 149
    see also Black identity; Black spaces
AIDS crisis 26, 28, 30, 33
All Is Fair in Love and Wear (AFLW) 59–60, 112
ambivalence and ambiguity 17–19, 126
American fashion designers 31–2
The Androgynous Model reality show 141
androgyny 24
asexual 14
assigned female at birth (AFAB) 95–7, 156
attitude 24
Audio Helkuik 80, 117–9
authenticity 40, 41, 43–7
auto industry 35–6

Baker, Alyah 134
    see also Show and Tell Concept Shop
Balenciaga, Cristóbal 32
bathroom bill 29
Becker, Anji 159
    see also WE ARE MORTALS

Beefcake Swimwear 67–8, 104–105
behavior and mutual reinforcement 11–12
being and becoming 12
    see also identity
Belgian designers 33
Bentley, Gladys 21
Berg, Erin 139, 163
    see also Kipper Clothiers
Betabrand 33–4
Between Women 141–2
Biden, Joe 28
bi-erasure 24
bikinis 32, 67, 106–10
binary see heteronormativity; nonbinary
binders 110–12, 116–17, 145
biological identity 11
bisexual identity 14, 24, 32
Black identity 20–2, 29–30, 142
    Anita Dolce Vita 156–7
    Crystal Hudson 159
Black Lives Matter 156–7
Black spaces 14, 15
BlaQueer Style 20–1
"Bloom" fashion show 158
Bluestockings Boutique 64, 124–5
The Borga high heels 104
Boston University Art Galleries 153
boutiques 32
    see also Bluestockings Boutique
boxer briefs 106–10
boycotts 41
brands 12, 33, 45–6, 51–89
    case studies
        All Is Fair in Love and Wear 59–61
        Beefcake Swimwear 67–8
        Bluestockings Boutique 64
        Dapper Boi 72–3
        FLAVNT Streetwear 62–3
        FtM Essentials 65–7
        gc2b 60–1
        Greyscale Goods 88–9

Kipper Clothiers 78
　　　Kirrin Finch 73–4
　　　NiK Kacy Footwear 72, 74–6
　　　Outplay Swimwear 66–9
　　　Play Out Apparel 70–1
　　　Queer Supply 62, 63
　　　Rebirth Garments 81–2
　　　Show and Tell Concept Shop 83–5
　　　Strapping Sacramento 72, 76–7
　　　Stuzo 83, 85–6
　　　THÚY Custom Clothier 78–79
　　　TomboyX 70–1
　　　Transguy Supply 64, 66
　　　WE ARE MORTALS 83, 86
　　entrepreneurship 53–8
　　marketplace influences 43–9
　　timeline of brand founding 55
　　see also individual brands …
Brooklyn Museum 117, 156–60
Bryant, Lane 39–40
Butch Voices LA conference 148
butchness 19–23
Butler, Eleanor 19–20
button-up shirts 95–100, 106

Cake Bandit underwear line 116
California University 148, 151
Calvin Klein 35–6
capitalism 26, 45–6
　　2008 global financial crisis 37–8
　　community in the twenty-first century 54
　　neoliberalism 26, 36–42
　　pricing tensions 138–40
　　queer fashion socks 128
chain mail packers 114, 116
Chelsea boots 100, 103
chest, swimwear 103–6
cisgender identity 56
　　see also heteronormativity
Civil War 31
Clinton, Bill 28
coin pockets 101
collars 96
coming out 35, 58, 123, 166
commodity activism 36–42, 56
communities, community-making 54–8, 160
　　violence against LGBTQ+ 29–30, 143–4, 159–60
　　see also activism

compressing the chest 103–6
consumerism 36–42
　　same-sex marriage, authenticity 43–7
　　see also capitalism; vehicles for queer/trans sensibilities
contemporary queer fashion shows 148–60
contexts see situating the context
continua/spectra of sexuality 14–15
conversion therapy 29
Cornell's Fashion + Textile Collection's blog 53–4
corporate pride 36–42
criminalization of homosexuality 27
crowdfunding 47–9
Cruz-Herr, Sterling 156
　　see also DapperQ
Cubacub, Sky 115, 118, 120, 137, 139, 164
　　see also Rebirth Garments
Curve magazine 53
custom suit experience 93–5
customer-centric approaches 139
Cutler, Nicky 53

DADT ("Don't Ask, Don't Tell") 28, 35, 53–4
Dapper Boi 72–3, 97–8, 100–2, 121–3
DapperQ 117, 148–60
　　and community-making 160
decolonization philosophies 133
Defense of Marriage Act (DOMA) 29, 35
DeGeneres, Ellen 35
department stores 31–3
　　see also individual department stores …
deregulation in the financial sector 37–8
Deysach, Searah 145, 163–5
　　see also FtM Essentials
Dior, Christian 32
discrimination 135–6
　　bathroom bill 29
　　bi-erasure 24
　　Dykes in the City 53
　　HIV/AIDS crisis 28, 33
　　inclusivity laws 29
　　Joe Biden's executive order, 2021 28
　　school anti-bullying programs 29
　　social media and crowdfunding campaigns 47–9
　　sodomy laws 27
transphobia 151–2

198　Index

upside-down triangle as symbol 53
violence against LGBTQ+ 29–30, 143–4, 159–60
see also stigma/stereotypes
"Dismantle Me" fashion show 151, 154
DITC (Dykes in the City) 53–4, 148
DIY gender categories 142
"Do Ask, Do Tell" collection 53–4
Dolce Vita, Anita 156–58
DOMA (Defense of Marriage Act) 29, 35
dominant culture *see* heteronormativity
Dominique, Christian 56–7
see also All Is Fair in Love and Wear
"Don't Ask, Don't Tell" (DADT) 28, 35, 53–4
"Don't Say Gay" legislation 158
Dove Campaign for Real Beauty 39
drag balls 149
"Dress Code" fashion show 158
dressed bodies 11–26
Duds, Dyke *see* Oram, Sonny
Dunaway, Fran 139, 144, 161
see also TomboyX
Dyke Suds *see* Qwear
Dykes in the City (DITC) 53–4, 148

ecommerce *see* online fashion
education 37–8
ego identity 11–12
entrepreneurship 53–8
Entwistle, Joanne 16
environmental racism 133
Equality Fashion Week, Los Angeles 160
erasure 24
escorts 142
Estévez, Luis 32
e-tailing 33
ethical balancing 133–9
Euphues: The Anatomy of Wit (Lyly) 59

Facebook 33, 47, 123
factory conditions 135
fashion shows 158–60
fatphobia 118, 144
femininity
butchness 19–23, 26
femme masc shoes 102
marriage stereotypes 44
representation 141
unbifurcated queerness 98–9
"Femme Desire" 153, 156

femmes 20, 22–3
Anita Dolce Vita 156–7
boxer briefs/underwear 106–10
masc shoes 99–104
First Amendment 28
FLAVNT Streetwear 110, 119–20
"flawless wedding" concepts 43–4
fleshy body-shifting fashions 110–17
floating gusset designs 107, 116–17
Fluidity Dress 99, 102
footwear
Borga high heels 104
femme and masc shoes 99–104
gender-neutral shoes 48
NiK Kacy Footwear 48, 72, 74–6, 99–104, 119–20, 124
queer fashion socks 126–8
For Everyone Co. 38
"Forms & Alterations" exhibit 153
Fortune collection 100–1
Friedan, Betty 28
FtM Essentials 65–6, 113–14, 117, 146
FTM identity 13, 57

The Gap 32
Garcia, Marialexandra 135, 136, 164
see also Outplay Swimwear
gay identity
Crystal Hudson 159
Nazi Holocaust 53
revolution and political landscapes 27–8
window advertising 35–42
Gay Liberation Front (GLF) 27–8
gay sexuality 14
gc2b 60–1, 110–11, 125, 134
gender nonconforming 14
see also nonbinary
gender-affirming procedures 29
gender-equal 101–3, 108, 126
genderfuck styles 117–19
gender-neutral 48, 101–2, 106–7
genderqueer 12–13
Georgios 101–2
Gernreich, Rudi 32
"Gladiator: The Etymology of Female Muscle" 156
GLF (Gay Liberation Front) 27–8
Gonzalez, Naomi 139
see also TomboyX

Great Depression of the 1930s 31
Green, Denise 53–4
Greenwich Village, New York City 27–8
Greyscale Goods 88–9, 124
grooms 44, 45

Hall, Radclyffe 20
Hammidi, Tania 148
Haring, Keith 35
Harlem Renaissance 149
healthcare 29, 37–8
Helkuik, Audio 136–7, 159, 161
    see also Audio Helkuik
heteronormativity 12, 22–6
    marriage stereotypes 43–5
    and the media 141
    political landscapes 27–34
    queer fashion socks 128
    selective history 30–4
high heeled shoes 104
Hikes, Amber 159
HIV/AIDS crisis 26, 28, 30, 33
Holocaust and the Nazi Party 26, 53
home-shopping 33
homoeroticism 35–6
Honig, Peregrine 56–7, 161
    see also All Is Fair in Love and Wear
Hot Topic 33
Hudson, Crystal 159

"iD: a queer New York Fashion Week" 157, 159
identity 11–26
    biological/social identity 11
    and branding 54–8
    coming out 35, 58, 123, 166
    custom suit experience 93–5
    ego identity 11–12
    knot metaphors 16–17, 128
    in Western context 19–26
    see also activism; brands; *individual identities* …
"I'm not a boy" t-shirt design 121–3
inclusivity laws 29
Indigenous communities 12
inequality 37
Instagram 47
Institute of Contemporary Art, Boston 153, 155
interconnectedness 15

internalized role expectations and social roles 11–12
internet/social media 33, 39–40, 47–9, 80, 123, 142, 147
intersectional subject positions 11–15
"INVINCIBLE: Back from the Ruins" 148
in-your-face Pride 119–23

James, Charles 32
jeans 97–8, 101
Jorgensen, Christine 27
"Just Do It" 40–1

Kacy, NiK 135–6, 144, 160, 164–5
    see also NiK Kacy Footwear
Kadlec, Jeanna 145, 162
    see also Bluestockings Boutique
Kaepernick, Colin 40–1
kathoeys/köcoeks 12–13
Kawakubo, Rei 33
Kickstarter 47–9
Kipper Clothiers 45, 47, 78, 95
Kirrin Finch 45, 47, 73–5, 95–6
Kit and Sade of Queer Supply 143, 164
    see also Queer Supply
Kmart 35–6
(k)not metaphors 16–17, 128
Krakauer, Lindsay 136
    see also Let's Be Brief

The L Word 53
LAB, downtown Brooklyn 156
labor exploitation 37
Latina identity 29–30
lavender graduation ceremonies 26
"lavender menace" 28
"Legendary Children" fashion show 153
legislation
    bathroom bill 29
    DADT 28, 35, 53–4
    "Don't Say Gay" legislation 158
    inclusivity laws 29
    Obergefell v. *Hodges* 29, 43
    sodomy laws 27
lesbian identity 35–6
    brands, entrepreneurial beginnings 53
    butchness 19–23
    gay window advertising 35–6
    Nazi Holocaust 53
    revolution and political landscapes 27

same-sex marriage, consumerism, and authenticity 45
    television 53–4
    see also femmes
lesbian sexuality 14
"Lesbians Invented Hipsters" (*New York Times*) 24
Let's Be Brief 106–10, 123
LGBTQ+ messaging 35–6
    t-shirt activism 38, 121–3
    see also brands
LGBTQ+ rights movement see activism
Los Angeles queer fashion scene 148, 160
Love, Stoney Michelli 143–4, 164
    see also Stuzo
Low Rise Front Boxer Brief design 108
Lyly, John 59

McCardell, Claire 32
Macy's 31
magazines 53, 151, 152
Margiela, Martin 33
marginalized 12, 26
    see also discrimination
marketplace influences 43–9
marriage 29, 43–7
Marshall Field's 31
masculinity 45–7, 106–7, 117–18, 141
    butchness 19–23
    button-up shirts 95–7
    fashion shows 156, 159
    masc shoes 99–104
Matriarch 48
Mattachine Society 32
Medd, Sara 163
    see also Greyscale Goods
media & outlets 133, 140–3
    advertising 35–42
    "flawless wedding" concepts 43–4
    magazines/newspapers 44, 53, 151–2
    social media 33, 39–40, 47–9, 80, 94, 123, 145
    television 33, 35–6, 141
Medicaid 29
    see also healthcare
military service and DADT 28, 35, 53–4
"mirror epiphany" 25
mixing and matching gender details 97–8

modifications 16
Moffat, Laura & Kelly 95–7, 137, 163
    see also Kirrin Finch
monokini 32
MTF identity 13
mutual reinforcement 11–12

National Football League (NFL) 40–1
Nazi Party 26, 53
neoliberalism 26, 36–42
new Right politics 26
    see also Nazi Party
New York Fashion Week 157–60
newspapers 24
Nguyen, Thúy 93–5, 135–6, 139, 165
    see also THÚY Custom Clothier
niche fashion brands 33
NiK Kacy Footwear 48, 72, 74–6, 99–104, 119–21, 124
Nike 40–1
nineteenth century nuance 19–26
nonbinary 12–13, 14
    see also trans and nonbinary
Norell, Norman 32
not (knot) concepts 16–17, 128
nuance 19–26, 98–9

Obergefell v. *Hodges* 29, 43
objective *me*/subjective *I* 11
O'Donnell, Rosie 35–6
online fashion 26, 32–3
Oram, Sonny 150–1, 160
    see also Qwear
Outplay Swimwear 68–9, 104, 123

packing underwear/packers 112–17, 145–7
pan-Indian terms 12
pansexual 14
Pasche, Vicky 95–7, 121–2, 134, 138, 144, 2
    see also Dapper Boi
patriarchy see heteronormativity
The Peculiar Kind 141–2
period underwear 106–7, 116–17
Philly pride flag 159
Play Out Apparel 47–9, 71, 108–12
#PlusIsEqual campaign 39–40
politics
    fashion shows 160

political landscapes, heteronormativity 27–34
right-wing politics 26, 53
and technology, marketplace influences 43–9
see also legislation
Ponsonby, Sarah 19–20
Porter College 148–9
positioning consumer products 91–128
Pouch Front Bikini design 109
pricing 133–9
    tensions 138–9
Pride Movement 36–42, 119–23, 158
privatization 37–8
privilege 12
    see also heteronormativity
production
    location 134–8
    pricing 133–9
"protest masculinity" 20, 22
P-Town (Provincetown) 35–6
"Pursuit" fashion show 158

Queer Fashion Show (QFS) 158–9
Queer Fashion Week, Oakland 151
queer identity 15, 24, 29–30, 41–2
    BlaQueer Style 20–1
    brands, entrepreneurial beginnings 53–8
    contemporary queer fashion shows 148–60
    fashion shows 148–60
    media 140–7
    neoliberalism 36–7
    revolution and political landscape 27–30
    unbifurcated queerness 98–9
    vehicles for 93–128
        queer fashion socks 126–8
        queer makers/queering product copy 124–6
        styling services 126
queer platonic relationships 14
Queer Scouts collection 117–19
queer sexuality 14
Queer Supply 62–3, 119–21
queer-coded imagery 35–6
Queerture Fashion Show 148
questioning 14
Qwear 148–55, 160

"R/Evolution" fashion show 157–8
racial discrimination 135–6
    environmental racism 133
Radical Fashion magazine 152
"Radical Visibility" manifesto 118
rashguards 104
Raygun 38
reality television 141
Rebirth Garments 48–9, 81–2, 114, 117–18
reluctant groom *see* absent groom
representation
    in the media 140–2
    success and failures of 142–7
    see also visibility
retail chains 32
    see also individual retail chains …
revolution
    and political landscape 27–30
    see also activism
Rhodes, Chris & Courtney 136, 143, 162
    see also FLAVNT Streetwear
right-wing politics 26, 53
Rio de Janeiro Summit, 1992 133
Roberts, John 27
Rose, Scout 143, 159, 165
    see also Transguy Supply
Ru, co-owner of Qwear 149–50, 153–4

Sade see Kit and Sade of Queer Supply
Saint Harridan 1–3, 156–7
same-gender loving 14
same-sex marriage 29, 43–7
scar creams 117
school anti-bullying programs 29
SDGs (sustainable development goals) 133
Sears, Roebuck & Co. 31
self-discovery *see* identity
sexuality 14–15
Sharpe Suiting 124
shoes *see* footwear
Show and Tell Concept Shop 83–5, 124–6
situated bodily practices 16–17
situating the context 9–49
    gay window advertising 35–42
    identities, style-fashion-dress, and dressed bodies 11–26
    marketplace influences, politics and technology 43, 43–9
    political landscapes, heteronormativity 27–34

slender bodies in the media 141
slit features (button-up shirts) 99, 100
Sloane & Tate 124
snaps feature (button-up shirts) 97–8
social identity 11
social media 33, 39–40, 47–9, 80, 123, 142, 145
social welfare 37
socioeconomic status and capitalism 138–9
socks 126–8
sodomy laws 27
space
    ambivalence and ambiguity 17–19, 126
    for authenticity 43–7
    Black spaces 14, 15
specialty clothing stores 31–2
    see also individual specialty brands and stores …
standardization *see* heteronormativity
stand-to-pee devices (STPs) 110, 114, 116
Stewart, Susan 95–7, 134, 165
    see also Strapping Sacramento
stigma/stereotypes 7, 19, 22–4, 30, 40
    fashion shows 160
    femme and masc shoes 99
    representation 140–2
    subtle/in-your-face pride 123
    unbifurcated queerness 98–9
Stitch Fix, 2011 123
Stone, Gregory 18
Stonewall Riots 27–8
Strapping Sacramento 73, 76–7, 95
streetwear/streetstyle 32
    see also FLAVNT Streetwear
structured collars 96
studs 20, 22
Stuzo 85, 121–2, 158
style-fashion-dress 11–26
style(s)
    BlaQueer Style 20–1
    genderfuck styles 119–21
    narratives 16
    streetstyle 32
    unisex swimwear styles 103–6
styling services 123
subject positions 11–15
subtle Pride 119–23
Sugar, Abby 134, 136
    see also Play Out Apparel

suicide rates 29–30
supplements 16
supporting/compressing the chest 103–6
sustainable development goals (SDGs) 133
swimwear 32, 103–6, 145–6
    Beefcake Swimwear 67–8, 103, 105
    Outplay Swimwear 68–9, 104, 123
symbols and slogans 38–9, 40–1, 53
    t-shirt activism 38, 119–22

Target 32, 41
tattoos 20
technology 4, 32–3
    internet/social media 33, 39–40, 47–9, 80, 123, 145, 147
    marketplace influences 43–9
television 33, 35–6, 141
THÚY Custom Clothier 45–7, 78–79, 93–5
'Toaster Heaven' design 123
Tomboy Tailors 1–3
TomboyX 41, 71–2, 106–7, 116–17, 119–20, 123, 147
trans and nonbinary (TNB) 12–13, 24–6
trans/transgender identity 12–13, 15, 28
    brands, entrepreneurial beginnings 53–8
    commodity activism, corporate pride, and neoliberalism 41–2
    escort services 142
    FTM identity 13, 57
    media 142–9
    MTF identity 13
    revolution and political landscape 27–30
    scar creams 117
    see also vehicles for queer/trans sensibilities
transexual/tranny/transvestite 12–13
transfeminine 12–13, 29–30
Transguy Supply 64, 66, 113–17
transmasculine 12–13, 66, 143
transphobia 151
trans-supportive gear 110–17
    binders 110–12, 116–17, 145
    chest support/compression 103–4
    floating gusset designs 107, 117
    packing underwear/packers 110–16, 145–6
    period underwear 106–7, 116–17
    STPs 112, 116, 118
    tucking undergarments 110, 116–17
@Trinity (trans-man model) 145, 147

Trump, Donald 28
t-shirt activism 38, 119–22
tucking undergarments 110, 116–17
Tulloh, Carl 16
Turtle Island 12
Twitter (now X) 39–40, 47, 145, 147
two-spirit 12, 14

UCLA 148
unbifurcated queerness 98–9
underwear 106–10
    brands 41–2
        Bluestockings Boutique 64, 124–5
        Let's Be Brief 106–10, 123
        Play Out Apparel 47–9, 70–1, 106–10
        TomboyX 41, 71–2, 106–7, 116–17, 119, 123, 145, 147
    packing underwear/packers 110–16, 145–6
Underworks 145
"(un)Heeled: A Fashion Show for the Unconventionally Masculine" 158, 159
unisex swimwear 103
    see also Beefcake Swimwear
United Colors of Benetton 35, 36
United Kingdom, same-sex marriage 43–5
United Nations General Assembly 133
United States
    Department of Agriculture 31
    heteronormativity, selective history 30–4
    military and DADT 28, 35, 53–4
    production location 134–5
    revolution and political landscape 27–30
    same-sex marriage 29, 43–5
    Supreme Court, *Obergefell* v. *Hodges* 29, 43
university populations 158–9, 153
Upper Case Chase 117
upside-down triangle as symbol 53
Utilikilts brand 99
utilities, privatization 37–8

vehicles for queer/trans sensibilities 93–128
    boxer briefs/underwear for femmes 106–10
    button-up shirts 95–100
    chest support/compression 103–6
    custom suit experience 93–5
    femme and masc shoes 99–103
    genderfuck styles 117–19
    in-your-face Pride 119–23
    jeans, mixing/matching gender details 97–8
    queer fashion socks 126–8
    queer makers/queering product copy 124–6
    queer styling services 124
    subtle Pride 119–23
    trans-supportive gear 110–17
    unbifurcated queerness 98–9
    unisex swimwear styles 103–6
Velvetpark magazine 53
"VERGE" fashion event 154, 157
Vince Man's Shop, lower Manhattan 32
violence against LGBTQ+ 29–30, 141–2, 158–9
visibility 4–7
    bi-erasure 24
    DADT 28
    DITC 53–4
    fashion shows 148–60
    marketplace influences 43
    Pride Movement 36–42, 119–23, 159
    queer fashion socks 126
    "Radical Visibility" manifesto 118
    TNB 24–5
    see also activism; brands; identity
vodka industry 35–6
voluntary behavioral change 39–40

Walmart 32
Washington, Marli 134–8
    see also gc2b
WE ARE MORTALS 83, 86, 99, 102
websites see internet
weddings see same-sex marriage
The Well of Loneliness (Hall) 20
Wells, Brittner Mel 103–4, 144–5, 161
    see also Beefcake Swimwear
Western fashion 19–26, 30–4
    see also heteronormativity
workers' rights 37
    women working in factories 135

Xena: Warrior Princess 35–6

Yamamoto, Yohji 33
YouTube 85, 117, 142
"Yup, Still Gay" by Stuzo 122